The American University
in a Postsecular Age

The American University in a Postsecular Age

EDITED BY

DOUGLAS JACOBSEN

RHONDA HUSTEDT JACOBSEN

UNIVERSITY PRESS

2008

OXFORD
UNIVERSITY PRESS

Oxford University Press, Inc., publishes works that further
Oxford University's objective of excellence
in research, scholarship, and education.

Oxford   New York
Auckland   Cape Town   Dar es Salaam   Hong Kong   Karachi
Kuala Lumpur   Madrid   Melbourne   Mexico City   Nairobi
New Delhi   Shanghai   Taipei   Toronto

With offices in
Argentina   Austria   Brazil   Chile   Czech Republic   France   Greece
Guatemala   Hungary   Italy   Japan   Poland   Portugal   Singapore
South Korea   Switzerland   Thailand   Turkey   Ukraine   Vietnam

Published by Oxford University Press, Inc.
198 Madison Avenue, New York, New York 10016

www.oup.com

Oxford is a registered trademark of Oxford University Press

Library of Congress Cataloging-in-Publication Data
The American university in a postsecular age / edited by Douglas Jacobsen,
Rhonda Hustedt Jacobsen.
    p. cm.
Includes bibliographical references and index.
ISBN 978-0-19-532344-3
1. Universities and colleges—Religion. 2. Church and education.
I. Jacobsen, Douglas G. (Douglas Gordon), 1951– II. Jacobsen, Rhonda
Hustedt.
BV1610.A44 2008
379.2'80973—dc22   2007025707

9 8 7 6 5 4 3 2 1

Printed in the United States of America
on acid-free paper

Acknowledgments

Our first and most important word of thanks goes to our contributors. It has been a pleasure as well as an honor to work with each of them. We deeply appreciate the thought they have given to this topic and the time and energy they poured into their essays. Several contributors also provided guidance and critique as we wrote our own essays and we are especially indebted to them.

Our thinking about religion and higher education has been shaped over the past two decades by untold numbers of conversations with our fellow faculty members at Messiah College and with friends and colleagues at conferences and gatherings associated with, among others, the American Academy of Religion, the Association of American Colleges and Universities, the Council for Christian Colleges and Universities, the Council of Independent Colleges, and the Lilly Fellows Program. Those interactions have enlarged our understanding of education and enriched our lives in general, and this book would not have been possible without them.

We are grateful to the Lilly Endowment for supporting this project through the Program for the Theological Exploration of Vocation, and to Kim S. Phipps, president of Messiah College, for her ongoing support of our work related to this book. Rebekah Burch Basinger and Richard T. Hughes provided helpful feedback for our own essays, and Kathryn Hustedt Jacobsen offered careful and good-humored suggestions regarding the content and organization of various incarnations of the manuscript. Finally, we would like to thank all those at Oxford University Press who shepherded this book through the editorial and production process and especially Cynthia Read who saw merit in our original proposal.

Contents

Part II Religion, the Curriculum, and Student Learning

Part III A Framework for Academic Conversation

Introduction

For most of the twentieth century, and especially since the Second
World War, higher education has been largely a secular enterprise.
The goal of a college or university education has been to provide
students with scholarly ways of understanding both themselves and
the world around them that required little or no appeal to God, religion, or the sacred. The underlying assumption seemed to be that as
research and rational reflection explained more and more of the world,
religion would become an increasingly unnecessary part of human
life. Higher education prepares students for the future, and religion
was not particularly relevant for the future as it was envisioned at most
universities.

Few scholars, and even fewer ordinary citizens, would make the
same assumption today. Far from fading into oblivion, religion
seems to be increasing its visibility and influence; secularization is
no longer the default assumption. So, if religion is here to stay, at least
for the foreseeable future, how should the university respond? What
kind of attention does religion deserve in our newly postsecular age
and what role or roles might religion play within the teaching and
learning process?

This book explores those questions, especially as they relate to the
academic side of college and university life: how faculty teach, how
students learn, and how religion intersects with the scholarly en-
deavor in general. No one argues in this book that religion ought to be
part of every classroom, or even of most, and there is no presumption

that the inclusion of religion in the educational process is always good or beneficial. Instead, the contributors to this book—who are all well known educators representing a wide variety of disciplines and institutional settings— wrestle with the many different ways in which religion might or might not be positively included in the work of higher education. There are no easy answers here, but the essays in this volume set the table for a rich conversation about religion's interaction with the core goals and purposes of higher education: critical thinking, self-awareness, the search for truth, cultural literacy, dealing with diversity, and commitment to the common good.

This book is not a jeremiad against the university. Unlike a variety of recent books, it does not bemoan the decline or the intellectual corruption of American higher education. The American university is not at the point of collapse and getting religion is not its salvation. But religion is a significant and enduring fact of life that American universities must engage. How can the university better prepare students for a future in which religion will continue to exercise significant influence in the world and in individual lives? In a world where religion continues to matter, can colleges and universities foster intelligent discourse about the positive and negative aspects of religion? What are the connections between faith and learning, rationality and religion, spirituality and the search for truth?

No single individual is able to address all of those questions, so this is an edited book by necessity. It seeks to season and advance a lively discussion that is already underway—a lively discussion that is also to some degree fragmented. In those fragmented conversations, participants sometimes seem unaware that they are using the same vocabulary to express quite contradictory meanings; sometimes different groups seem to be talking past one another rather than to each other. For example, some individuals and groups emphasize spirituality as opposed to religion, and they consider authentic meaning-making and "being centered" (i.e., spirituality) to be dissimilar in every way from the imposed dogmas and dictates of "organized religion." Other participants in the conversation stress the social dimensions of religion, seeing faith and civic responsibility as intertwined virtues that make it possible to live peaceably with others in a religiously pluralistic world. Still other groups and individuals think it is crucial to help students maintain and deepen their religious connections to the historic communities of faith in which they have been reared.

This volume intentionally brings these divergent discussions into contact with each other, hoping to foster a more comprehensive and connected conversation that deals with religion in its entirety—including its personal and social dimensions, values and ideas, subjective and objective characteristics, and potential for good and ill.

In terms of the layout of this book, the first chapter sets the stage for this grand conversation by reflecting on the new "postsecular" turn in American culture and how that shift is creating new challenges and opportunities for higher education as a whole. The concluding chapter proposes a modest framework for talking about religion that hopefully will make it easier for educators both to locate themselves in the broader conversation and to see how their concerns relate to the concerns of others.

The twelve chapters that form the core of this volume are organized into two sections. The first group of essays focus on the institutional context of religion in higher education and on faculty attitudes and roles. Neil Gross and Solon Simmons describe the results of a survey of religiosity within the professoriate. Robert Wuthnow then analyzes the broader dynamics of faith in the contemporary academy. The next two chapters discuss the role of religion in two very different settings. John J. DiIulio Jr. examines religion in an elite non-sectarian university (the University of Pennsylvania) and the editors discuss the history and ideals of church-related higher education. The two concluding essays in this section, one by Mark U. Edwards Jr. and the other by R. Eugene Rice, focus on the pressures faculty feel, on the one hand, to avoid any conversation about religion and, on the other hand, to respond to student concerns about faith and the making of meaning.

The second group of essays focus on the place of religion in the curriculum and in student learning. Larry A. Braskamp's lead piece is a data-driven description of the religious hopes and experiences of college students from matriculation to graduation. The next two chapters, one by Robert J. Nash and DeMethra LaSha Bradley and the other by Elizabeth J. Tisdell, discuss different ways that student spirituality can enter into the educational process. Essays by Warren A. Nord and by Amanda Porterfield address the curricular and classroom implications of religion as a subject of study. Finally, Lee S. Shulman reflects on the ways that religious dispositions can broadly shape styles of pedagogy.

The essays in this book represent the wide variety of opinion that exists within the academy concerning the place of religion within the life and work of higher education, but this book does not include any essays that explicitly reject the notion that religion might play some role in college and university education. Certainly there are many who would contest the wisdom of allowing religion into the American university, and it is important to listen to those critical voices. Sometimes, however, those critics are reacting to caricatures of religion rather than to religion as it actually exists on college and university campuses today. The essays in this book undercut these stereotypes and are intended to stimulate constructive conversation among all who are seeking to discern the appropriate place of religion in the American university in our postsecular age.

The American University
in a Postsecular Age

I

Postsecular America: A New Context for Higher Education

Douglas Jacobsen and Rhonda Hustedt Jacobsen

The last two centuries have been a time of unprecedented change in human history, marked by an explosion in accumulated knowledge about the way the world is put together. Religion has been on the defensive as new intellectual insights cut deep and wide into realms that religion once dominated.

Consider human health. In the early 1800s the "germ theory" of disease had not yet been formulated, let alone accepted as a medical fact. When and why someone got sick was a mystery, and herbal remedies combined with procedures like bloodletting were the only treatments available. Modern medical science was not developed until well into the twentieth century. Penicillin was not discovered until 1928, and the use of antibiotics did not become commonplace until the 1940s. Before that, most diseases had to run their course, and medicine consisted largely of dealing with symptoms. Who lived and who died seemed to be a matter of either chance or God's choosing, and given those options most people hoped God was involved in some way. They asked God to keep them healthy and they prayed for healing when sick, often confessing their moral failures in case an illness was God's punishment for sin and promising new levels of religious devotion if cured. Health and religion seemed naturally connected.

That is no longer the case. We now understand disease differently, and most people would say we understand disease better. The existence of germs is no longer a conjecture, but a fact, and we know that germs come in different forms like bacteria, viruses, fungi, and parasites. We know how to effectively treat many of the diseases caused by these infectious agents, and every day we are learning how to do that better. Modern medicine has not defeated every sickness—a cure for AIDS has not yet been developed, many cancers remain deadly, some flesh-eating bacteria are presently immune to treatment, the common cold continues to irritate us, and new viruses like bird flu alarm us—but we assume that medical science has the potential to help us manage all these ills eventually. People still pray for healing when they are sick, some extremists refuse medical treatment as a sign of their trust in God, and a few researchers are investigating whether faith might have any measurable impact on sickness and health. But for most of us, a visit to the doctor is our first (and often only) response to disease. The operating theaters for medicine and for religion have been separated, and in the process the role of religion has shrunk.

Our understanding of how the world came to be—the origins of life and the universe—is another arena where the significance of religion has declined notably during the last two hundred years. In 1800, what we now call "young earth creationism" would have been the standard view of how the world began. God spoke and things appeared: first the earth; then the sun, moon, and stars; then plants and animals of various sorts; and finally humankind. Calculating the age of the earth based on the biblical narrative, Archbishop James Ussher (who was head of the Protestant Church of Ireland from 1625 to 1656) determined that the world had sprung into existence at God's command on a fine September morning 4,004 years before the birth of Christ. Two centuries ago, a majority of Europeans and Americans still thought Ussher had gotten things pretty much right. Then along came Darwin (and a host of other nineteenth-century geologists and biologists) and suddenly the world looked a whole lot older. Rather than being formed a few thousand years ago, the world appeared to be millions or even billions of years old; and rather than everything having been created by God all at once, life on earth seemed to have evolved slowly over time with "the survival of the fittest" serving as the stimulus for change and development. Here, too, religion seemed to be diminished as science grew in its influence and explanatory power.

But it wasn't just modern science that challenged religion. Society itself was changing in ways that often pushed religion farther and farther toward the fringes of life. While once church and state had ruled together, the new reality, at least in America, was separation of church and state. This did not mean that religion was automatically removed from the political domain. In the nineteenth century, for example, religious revivalism played a significant role in shaping politics. Preachers and politicians told the converted to vote in ways attuned to

God's will. But democracy cannot provide religion with a guarantee of influence, and through most of the twentieth century, religion seemed to be losing its grip on the political process.

Beyond politics, the daily routines of life became more complex. The invention of the electric light bulb allowed people to work all night as well as all day, and the natural rhythm of life changed. Automobiles and paved roads—both of which were extremely rare until after 1900—slowly turned ordinary people into commuters who spent more time in their cars than they ever spent in church. New forms of entertainment (radio, the movies, television, and video games) filled additional hours, time previously available for personal devotions and religious services. The religious calendar that had once determined the flow of the year as well as the structure of each week slowly gave way to new national holidays, the calendar of the public school system, living for the weekend, and taking kids to endless rounds of soccer or band practice. With the modern time squeeze, people felt they had less and less time to devote to formal religious activities.

Taken together, these trends, which seem to catalog the lessening of religion's influence in society and individual lives, eventually came to be called secularization. The founders of the discipline of sociology (most notably Émile Durkheim and Max Weber) define secularization as the slow erosion of religion's power and influence as modernity grows and flourishes. In particular, they deem the supernaturalist claims and premodern practices of religion to be contrary to the rationality of modern society and its ways of thought. For the most part, these early scholars of secularization had no antireligious axes to grind. Their goal was neither to support nor to undercut religious faith and life, but merely to describe what they saw happening around them. But what both they and many other ordinary folks thought they were observing (at least in western Europe, the source of almost all their data) was religion's slow but inevitable demise. Whether one liked what was happening or not, secularization seemed to be a simple fact of life. Religion was no longer as important as it had once been, and it seemed generally on the wane. Some people thought that it might eventually disappear altogether.

Responses to Secularization

People responded in different ways to the ostensibly empirical analysis that predicted religion's decline. Some religious groups were troubled, and they tried to resist or reverse the process of secularization. During the early years of the twentieth century, some of these resisters came to be called fundamentalists.

And the name stuck. These early fundamentalists were not religious radicals, but were instead old-fashioned believers who mourned religion's decline and who sorrowed because the modern world undercut the teachings and values of traditional faith. They were especially opposed to the new science of evolution because, in their eyes, it did away with both the idea of God as creator and the moral values of the Golden Rule (since the ethical implications of "survival of the fittest" contradicted Christ's injunction to love others in the same way we love ourselves). From the fundamentalist perspective, secularization was not an inevitable social process, but a temporary religious recession that needed to be reversed.

Not all religious people became fundamentalists, however. At the opposite end of the spectrum, some liberal religious leaders contended that the rise of modern science would help people understand that religion was never intended to be about facts. Science, not religion, was the domain of facts, and scientific explanations like the new evolutionary account of the origins of life ought to be accepted as true. What, then, was the role of religion? Religious modernists generally asserted that the stories of the Bible and other religious texts were about meaning and values, but not about truth in the sense of empirically testable hypotheses and propositions. Modernists hoped that the process of secularization would guide religions to give up their outworn and unnecessary metaphysical claims and to focus on what they really could contribute: moral guidance for life in an ever more complex world.

The views of many believers, probably most, fell somewhere in the continuum between religious fundamentalism and modernism. These moderates saw secularization, at least in small doses, as a welcome antidote to the magical thinking of individuals who pictured God as a powerful wonder-worker in the sky who was there to miraculously do their bidding. Moderates did not want religion to be restricted solely to the realm of meaning and values, as modernists argued, but they also thought that fundamentalism's stand-and-fight mentality did a disservice to religion. Their views of both faith and the world were more nuanced than either extreme, and moderates tried to accommodate modern developments while reaffirming the central tenets of faith.

Secularism

A fourth group of people had a different response to secularization and its prediction of religion's demise. They were skeptics who had no interest whatsoever in trying to salvage religion. Quite the contrary, they welcomed secularization as the fulfillment of their dreams. They wanted religion to disappear.

Skeptics of varying kinds had been actively working for the eradication of religion since at least the time of the Enlightenment in the eighteenth century, well before any significant diminution of religion's role in society was apparent. Some of these individuals were brilliant, including the famous French thinker Voltaire, who signed many of his letters "Ecrasez l'infame!" Eradicate the infamous thing. He was incensed by the two centuries of European warring that had followed the Reformation and by the religious zealots of his own day who were defending the corrupt regime of a reactionary monarch. Voltaire thought ill of most forms of Christianity, particularly loathing the Catholic Church while managing a smidgen of grudging respect for pacifists like the Anabaptists and for "the religion of the learned in China."[1]

Voltaire and other like-minded antireligious skeptics lodged three major complaints against religion. First, religion promotes fanaticism, and fanaticism inevitably gives rise to violence. Second, religion justifies injustice, especially injustices perpetrated by the state. Third, religion perpetuates superstition and magical beliefs, which inhibit the rational, scientific examination of the world. And, to be honest, the skeptics had a point: religion has at times done all of these things. Religion has also played a number of much more positive roles in human life and history, but it is easy to see how someone who focused only on these three concerns could wish that all religion would simply go away.

What is important to note, however, is that the attitude described—Voltaire-style antireligious skepticism—is a different entity than *secularization*. Secularization is a neutral notion, a description of empirically verifiable events. Voltaire's position—positive embrace of religion's decline and desire to hasten that decline—is something else. That something else is generally called *secularism*, and its proponents are known as *secularists*. Rather than being a mere description of the world, secularism is an ideology promoted by devotees who encourage free-thinking people everywhere to work for religion's demise.[2] It is a worldview that actively opposes religion, rather than a neutral description of the world as a place where the influence of religion happens to have lessened.

Secularism as a worldview has a very old lineage and comes in many different forms. The ancient Greek thinkers Euhemerus and Lucretius, who might be considered the founders of religious skepticism and secularism, both believed religion was nothing more than humanity's projection of its own hopes and values onto the beyond.[3] In more recent times, Andrew Dickson White, the first president of Cornell University, offered a different metaphor, likening the relationship between science and theology to a state of war in which one side or the other has to win and there is no possibility of compromise or adjudicated truce.[4] Marx and Engels—and Lenin and Stalin and Mao—were secularists of a different kind who saw religion as a disease that had infected humanity and that needed to be eliminated as rapidly as possible, even if doing so required massive violence. The modern history of Russia, China, and various other Communist states gives ample evidence that secularism in its most extreme forms can be as disastrous as the most fanatical forms of religion.

In the same way that all religion should not be judged by the excesses of a few extreme groups, secularism as a whole should not be judged by the behavior of its relatively few violent proponents. Far from the right-wing stereotype that portrays secularists as uniformly bent on destroying the moral and religious underpinnings of society, most secularists have been genuinely moral individuals motivated to oppose religion largely because they see religion as exercising a deeply immoral influence within the world. According to them, religion judges and divides people where no division is necessary, it heightens already existing tensions in the world by making relative differences absolute, and it draws people's attention away from many of the fixable problems of society by redirecting their energy toward personal salvation and future life in heaven. This last point is especially noteworthy. In its original Latin meaning, the word *secular* simply denotes the flow of time and events in this world, the here and now, and to be secular means to pay attention to ordinary life in the present. Secularism, in other words, need not be negatively antireligious. It can also take the form (and often does) of being a positive moral position that asks everyone to join together to make this world—the world in which all of us presently live alongside one another—a better place for everyone regardless of gender, ethnicity, nationality, or especially religion.

Secularization and Secularism in Higher Education

In the big scheme of things, universities have almost always located themselves on the secular, skeptical, and speculative side of society. Even in the Middle Ages, the Catholic universities of Europe were often viewed as seedbeds of radical ideas, heresy, and possible sedition, and both church and state kept a careful eye on what was sprouting in these schools. The same dynamic is observable today. The histories of many church-affiliated schools, in particular, are replete with stories of individuals who from the very moment of the institution's founding were able to detect secularizing tendencies that needed to be kept in check. Still, most religious leaders know that colleges and universities have an important role to play in society—exploring new ideas, discovering new truths about the world, educating new generations of leaders, and critiquing the old orthodoxies of the past, whether those orthodoxies are academic or religious in nature—and they have no qualms about that. Most religious leaders would also agree that the focus of higher education should generally be on the "secular" world (i.e., the present world in which we all live), pondering questions raised by the sciences, the arts and humanities, and various fields of professional study. Even among the most devout, few if any would expect or desire higher education to make religion its central or primary concern. Colleges and universities are not seminaries.

But careful and critical investigation of the ordinary "secular" world is not the same as secularist education. In the twentieth century, the forces of secularization and secularism intertwined, and as a result higher education was reshaped in new and dramatic ways. The story has been told numerous times[5] with a basic narrative describing the way that many colleges and universities that had formerly been either supportive of religious faith or neutral with regard to matters of religion became more secularist in attitude and orientation (i.e., actively antireligious), eventually relegating religion to the edges of the academic domain.

At first, the process of higher education's secularization moved relatively slowly. As late as the mid-twentieth century, religion was still part and parcel of the educational experience at many of the nation's leading colleges and universities. In 1951, when the young Catholic graduate William F. Buckley wrote *God and Man at Yale*,[6] a blistering critique of how religion was marginalized and mocked at his Ivy League alma mater, the Yale leadership defended the school, at least in part, with public affirmations of the school's enduringly Christian and religious character. No one was suggesting that Yale was a bastion of old-time religion—religion at Yale was clearly on the progressive side of the continuum—but it is equally evident that as late as the early 1950s the administration did not feel comfortable describing Yale as a secular institution.[7]

But in the 1960s the lay of the land changed at most mainstream colleges and universities in the United States. These institutions shifted from being quietly secular institutions like Buckley's Yale to being more visibly secular*ist* institutions where religion was intentionally pushed to the side. This increasingly secular character of American higher education seemed perfectly sensible to most people. If the world was becoming secularized, why be concerned about religion? If religion really was wielding less and less influence in society and might soon effectively disappear, why study religion at all? The best counterarguments were based on the fact that religion was not yet entirely dead and that religion had played a significant part in human history for millennia. Those arguments were convincing enough to allow a number of religious studies departments to survive and for religion to continue to be a subject for analysis in some history, anthropology, and sociology departments. Religion as a source of inspiration or insight concerning human life and thought was rejected, however, and when religion was studied it was typically treated as a natural phenomenon that was best explained reductionistically in terms of something else. Thus religion could be discussed as wish fulfillment or as a masked form of power or as a coping mechanism for the oppressed, but it was not to be discussed as an encounter with God or a source of transcendent values.

By the late 1970s, religion as a matter of living faith and practice had essentially been bleached from the goals and purposes of higher education at the nation's major universities. Higher education was about public knowledge, and public knowledge was defined in purely secular terms. Given that the goal of the university is to educate students for the future and given the assumption that religion was making its last curtain call, there seemed to be no reason for university education to take either God or religion seriously as an aspect of higher learning. Students, if they were so inclined, could hold onto their religious beliefs in private, but those personal religious beliefs and practices were considered to have scant connection with the public knowledge that was being developed and disseminated in the classroom.

The Emergence of the Postsecular Age

A generation later, the religious landscape in America has changed once again. Rather than disappearing, the power and influence of religion seems to be growing. Sociologists are still sorting through the data and they do not all agree,[8] but a cultural consensus has emerged: religion will likely exercise a significant role in human affairs for a long time to come. If secularization means that the world is getting a little less religious every day, then we live in a postsecular world.

Putting a "post-" in front of any word often signals a complex redefinition of the subject under discussion, but that is not what we have in mind. What we mean by the term *postsecular* is the simple fact that secularization as a theory about the future of human society seems increasingly out of touch with realities on the ground. To speak, as we do, about the emergence of a postsecular age is not a veiled attempt to foster and encourage religion's resurgence. Nor is it a claim that more religion is better for the world than less. *Postsecular* is used merely as a descriptive term.

Religion is not disappearing. We have entered an era when secularization is not in the ascendancy and when secularists are feeling challenged. It is no wonder that people like Richard Dawkins, Daniel C. Dennett, Sam Harris, and

Christopher Hitchens have recently published hyperbolically critical accounts of religion and its dangers. They sense that the tide has changed, so they are working feverishly to hold back the influence of religion and to reinvigorate the secularist cause.[9] As those writers attest, acknowledging that our age is post-secular has powerful implications for how we see the world and comport ourselves in it. While it may have made sense to ignore religion when everyone thought it was fading away, that stance is no longer viable. Whether one likes religion or not, it is time to take it seriously and address issues of religion head-on.

Much of the world's renewed awareness of and interest in religion is motivated by fear. The rise of violent religious extremism—most visibly present within Islam, but also evident in other religious traditions—has galvanized world consciousness, leading scholars like Samuel P. Huntington to postulate that the future of the world will be driven by conflicts of culture that are largely religious in character. His book *The Clash of Civilizations and the Remaking of the World Order* argues that the most significant conflicts around the globe in the years ahead will no longer be battles between nation-states, but skirmishes between various geographic culture blocs that embody different values and very different ways of understanding the world. All nine of the groups he mentions—Western, Latin American, African, Islamic, Sinic [Chinese], Hindu, Orthodox, Buddhist, and Japanese—are defined by the religious traditions that have shaped their histories and that continue to inform their cultural habits of thought and life.[10]

When Huntington first published his views, many politicians and policy wonks opined that Huntington was mistaken. In their modern, secular world, international politics pertained to economics and the power positioning of nations. If and when religion mattered, its significance was at best slight, mere froth on top of, or code words for, the more important issues of diplomacy, military planning, and trade negotiations. But many have since changed their minds—even if they continue to take issue with Huntington's specific scenario of future events—and they are now willing to consider religion as an independent variable in their analyses of foreign affairs.

Madeleine Albright, secretary of state during the Clinton administration, reflects this sea change when she describes in her book *The Mighty and the Almighty* how she had to adjust her views to take religion into account after the terrorist attacks on New York and Washington:

> The 1990s had been a decade of globalization and spectacular technological gains; the information revolution altered our lifestyle, transformed the workplace, and fostered the development of a whole

new vocabulary. There was, however, another force at work. Almost everywhere, religious movements are thriving.... What does one make of this phenomenon? For those who design and implement U.S. foreign policy, what does it mean? How can we best manage events in a world in which there are many religions, with belief systems that flatly contradict one another at key points? How do we deal with the threat posed by extremists who, acting in the name of God, try to impose their will on others?[11]

Albright's posture with regard to religion is shaped by worries about international relations and national security—how do we keep the irrational forces of faith in check?—but the resurgence of religion in our postsecular world is not only about terrorism and fear, it is also about humanity's ongoing search for meaning, purpose, and comfort in a world where life is not always easy. Take, for example, the well documented revival of religion in Russia that has occurred during the last twenty-five years. During the heyday of Communism only about 25 percent of the Russian population said they believed in God. By 1991 that figure had risen to 45 percent, and by 1998 it was 60 percent. This is a remarkable pattern of growth, and it has virtually nothing to do with violence, terrorism, or political posturing. Russians are looking for a God who is concerned about their personal lives and for a religion that can serve as both "a binding force to hold their marriages together and a heritage to pass on to their children."[12] After years of being forced to swallow the thin gruel of Communism, they are hoping religion will provide sustenance for their souls.

Similar trends in religious growth and vitality are evident around the world. In Latin America, Pentecostal churches are multiplying at a phenomenal rate. In Africa, a dramatic Christian expansion is occurring in the south, simultaneous with revitalization of Islam in the north. In Asia, Hinduism and Buddhism, each taking myriad different forms, are flourishing and sometimes flexing their political muscles. Around the world the Catholic Church has risen in stature, partly because of the rock star power of the late Pope John Paul II. In the United States, too, religion is more visible. While the so-called mainline religious groups have been losing members for several decades (a trend that contributed to the predictions of secularization theory), many conservative religious movements and organizations have been growing, not just in number but also in simple visibility. Religious subject matter is now standard fare on television, in the movies, on the radio, and on the Internet. Religion is no longer a subject to be avoided in coffee shops or at cocktail parties. Quite the contrary, questions about religion or spirituality can now be broached in polite conversation without embarrassment.

A Rearview Look at Secularization

The new postsecular vantage point makes it easier to look back at the 1960s, 1970s, and 1980s and discover that religion was more robust in those decades than was previously assumed. Yes, this was the time when a host of theologians were talking about the "death of God" and reflecting on what religion might look like in a thoroughly "secular city,"[13] but these were also the years when Billy Graham was first gaining popularity and when the evangelical movement (which now claims 20–25 percent of the American population) was starting to coalesce. Hippies and others were exploring a wide new range of non-Christian religious options, many imported from Asia, with Zen Buddhism and Hare Krishna leading the way. And New Age spirituality was just beginning to dawn.

There is no question that religion was being squeezed out of some parts of the culture during those decades, but elsewhere it was flourishing. Classic secularization theory said religion's loss of significance would be most keen in the political realm, yet the civil rights movement of the 1960s—one of the most important social movements in American history—was deeply grounded in Christian faith. The more radical black nationalist movement, led by people like Malcolm X, had religious roots in the Islamic tradition. Many of those who were opposed to the war in Vietnam were motivated by religious faith, including individuals like the Berrigan brothers and Thomas Merton, all of them Roman Catholic priests. One of the era's most articulate economic analyses also was Catholic in origin: the American bishops' pastoral letter *Economic Justice for All: Catholic Social Teaching and the United States Economy* (1986), which presciently warned of growing disparity between the wealthy and the poor in the nation. And it was in the 1970s, that the Christian Right first began to formally organize as a religiously motivated conservative opposition force in American politics.

If religion was playing this kind of pivotal role in American culture even in the heyday of secularization, then surely it is a force that deserves attention today. To say our age is postsecular is, in some sense, simply to point out that America remains the religion-soaked nation that it has always been.

Implications for Higher Education

Today religion is everywhere, and it may be more visible at colleges and universities than anywhere else. The religious diversity of literally the whole world is on display on many campuses, including various forms of Hinduism,

Buddhism, and Islam, every imaginable variety of Christianity and Judaism, and religions so new that they were not in existence a century ago. Recent survey data indicate that roughly four out of every five college students describe themselves as "spiritual" and that more than half of all professors say they believe in God (with that number jumping to almost three-quarters if belief in "a Higher Power of some kind" is included).[14]

Religion's increased visibility on campuses mirrors the resurgence of visible religion in the culture at large. *Newsweek* and *Time* regularly feature cover stories on subjects like the Bible, Islam, and Jesus; musical performers and sports professionals thank God publicly for their successes; and "values voters" have become a potent political force within the nation. The best-selling nonfiction book of the last decade was *The Purpose Driven Life*, written by the evangelical pastor Rick Warren, and the fiction blockbuster was Dan Brown's novel *The Da Vinci Code*, with its central plot premised on an ancient Gnostic version of Christianity in which Jesus marries Mary Magdalene. Religion has made a comeback both in the culture at large and on college and university campuses in particular.

In many ways it was easier for universities back in the heyday of secularization when religion was unobtrusive. A university could presume that studying religion was a bit like paying attention to monarchical theories of government made irrelevant by democracy, to pre-Linnean classifications of animal life made obsolete by Darwin, or to the "science" of phrenology debunked by advances in psychology and physiology. Religion could be considered a bit anachronistic, yet still maintain a place in the curriculum. Scholars have never disputed its immense historical influence, nor have they questioned that ancient and contemporary religious texts and practices contribute to the social, economic, and political structures of a given culture. But treating religion as a subject that might appeal to someone's historical or social scientific curiosity is far different from seeing religion as a valid source of human meaning, as a driving force in scholarly research, or as a core concern for higher education.

It's not easy to navigate this new terrain. For example, a faculty committee at Harvard University recently drafted a report recommending that all undergraduate students complete one or another course in a category called "reason and faith." That proposal set off a storm on campus and beyond, and in the end the task force substituted a "culture and belief" requirement, clarifying that "religious beliefs and practices are topics that some courses in this category should address." The course requirement was ratcheted down, but the Harvard report still strongly defends the inclusion of religion in the curriculum. It declares, "Religion has historically been, and continues to be, a force shaping identity and behavior throughout the world. Harvard is a secular institution, but religion is an important part of our students' lives. When they get to college, students often struggle to sort out the relationship between their own beliefs and practices and those of fellow students, and the relationship of religious belief to the resolutely secular world of the academy."[15]

The university is indeed "resolutely secular"—it studies the world as it really exists. But it is not a place dedicated to secularism, to the removal of religion from the hallowed halls of learning or from the world at large. The university studies the world as it is. And we now live in a postsecular world, or, perhaps more accurately, a postsecular*ist* world. Religion—religion in all its grand and gracious as well as its vain and violent incarnations—is part of that reality. This postsecular perspective is new, and it presents higher education with significant challenges as well as opportunities.

PART I

Religion, Institutions, and Faculty Roles

2

The Religious Convictions of College and University Professors

Neil Gross and Solon Simmons

A common account of the history of American higher education runs as follows. In their early years, America's colleges and universities served religious ends. Harvard, founded in 1636, had been started to train ministers, and although by the early nineteenth century some college and university professors could be found advancing the cause of science, their primary mandate remained that of instructing students in the classics and teaching them lessons in theology and moral philosophy that would prepare them for the business of citizenship and life. In the closing decades of the nineteenth century, however, an "academic revolution" occurred.[1] Especially at elite institutions, professors began thinking of themselves as scientists and scholars whose major task was to seek out truth, not to propagate religious dogma. Under pressure from industry and the state to produce scientific breakthroughs that would result in technological progress and social reform, professors reconfigured themselves as researchers who specialized in their subject areas, published their findings, trained graduate students, established their own criteria for evaluating academic work, and demanded the freedom to pursue truth even when it offended religious or political authorities. Academic freedom was institutionalized, many schools severed ties to religious denominations, and reforms that started at the top of the academic hierarchy soon trickled down.

In the mid-twentieth century, additional changes took place as enrollments skyrocketed and as students and faculty members from a variety of ethnic, religious, and class backgrounds entered the system. Seeking legitimacy, these new entrants to the academic arena shielded themselves from prejudice and attack by further embracing universalistic ideals of science and eschewing religious value commitments.[2] The secularization of American higher education was completed in the 1970s and 1980s with the mass hiring of new faculty who, shaped by the social movements of the 1960s, were deeply suspicious of religion in general and of Christianity in particular. As a result of this process, or so the story goes, academe finally became, in the words of historian George Marsden, "a haven largely freed from religious perspectives."[3]

In broad brushstroke this story is not wrong, but it leads too readily to the conclusion that, as a result of secularization, most college and university professors today are irreligious. At a moment when sociologists of religion are busy reassessing secularization theory in general—the thesis, subscribed to by such founders of modern social theory as Karl Marx, Émile Durkheim, and Max Weber, that one of the defining characteristics of modernity is a decline in religious belief and in the authority of religious institutions—it is worth reconsidering as well the secularization of American higher education. In this essay, we take a small step in that direction by answering a straightforward question: How religious, if at all, are America's college and university professors today?

Our conclusions are based on data collected in 2006 in a nationally representative survey of professors in nearly all fields and types of higher education institutions. Although the main focus of the survey was professors' political attitudes, we included a number of standard measures of religiosity as well. We found that while college and university professors on the whole are indeed less religious than other Americans, it is hardly the case that the professorial landscape is characterized by an absence of religion. We also found substantial variation in religiosity from discipline to discipline and across different types of institutions.

This essay begins with an overview of our methodology, moves on to summarize key findings, and concludes by considering implications for future research. Although there exists a substantial research literature on religion and the university, empirical knowledge of the religiosity of professors is thin. In light of this—and the importance of the topic to all sides in the debate over how integrated with religion higher education should be—we concentrate here on adding to the base of public knowledge some interesting and relevant factual descriptions, leaving for other venues the task of integrating our findings into ongoing streams of sociological and historical scholarship.

Methodology

Our survey of professors was designed in response to a number of recent studies, many with explicitly ideological aims, purporting to show that the contemporary American professoriate is not only dominated by liberals but is also a site of discrimination against conservative professors, students, and ideas. These studies, ranging from audits of voter registration records to surveys, often suffer from a number of methodological problems. Perhaps the most important such study was carried out by Stanley Rothman, S. Robert Lichter, and Neil Nevitte, who in 1999 surveyed professors at 183 U.S. colleges and universities.[4] Rothman, Lichter, and Nevitte, who have not publicly released the data from their survey, asked a variety of social and political attitudes questions and reported a response rate of 72 percent, yielding a sample of 1,643 cases. In a much publicized paper, they claimed, on the basis of an analysis of these data, that 72 percent of U.S. professors identify themselves as "left of center" politically. Our view was that Rothman, Lichter, and Nevitte skewed their sample by failing to include any professors teaching in community colleges, where 40.3 percent of American undergraduates at four-year colleges or universities have at some point been enrolled.[5] More problematic is that many of the questions they asked—including those dealing with key measures of political attitudes—were, in our opinion, poorly phrased.

We sought to remedy those problems in our own research. To do so, we constructed a new questionnaire with more than 100 items measuring professors' political and social attitudes, along with a wide range of social background questions. The vast majority of our questions were taken verbatim from well-established surveys of the U.S. population such as the General Social Survey (GSS), the National Election Study (NES), and the Pew Values Survey. This approach enhances the reliability of our data and allows us to more accurately compare faculty attitudes to those of the general population.

Our survey, called the "Politics of the American Professoriate" study, was administered by the Center for Survey Research at Indiana University.[6] Precontact and invitation letters were sent to 2,958 professors in the spring of 2006. Professors were selected for inclusion through a stratified random sampling procedure. The sample was split: two thirds of professors were drawn from the twenty most popular fields of study as measured by the number of bachelor's degrees awarded in 2004 (the last year for which data were then available), and the remaining third were drawn from all other fields in which bachelor's degrees were awarded that year. To locate professors, we

used the National Center for Education Statistics' dataset on degree comple-
tions to randomly select colleges and universities where either bachelor's or
associate's degrees in the relevant field were awarded. We then obtained,
through an examination of departmental Web sites, or phone calls if necessary,
a list of full-time faculty teaching in that school and department, and then
randomly selected one faculty member to include in the study. We also stratified our sample to ensure adequate representation of faculty members
teaching at community colleges, four-year colleges and universities, nonelite
PhD-granting institutions, and elite doctoral universities (defined as those
listed in the top fifty in the latest *U.S. News and World Report* ranking). The
survey achieved a response rate of 51 percent, yielding 1,471 valid cases. We
were not able to detect any significant response bias.

Once compiled, the data were weighted to even out the effects of over-
sampling certain fields and institutions. They also received a weighting to
correct for the effects of having slightly undersampled women and African
Americans. We believe our sample to be generalizable to the more than
630,000 professors who teach full-time in colleges and universities in the
United States. It is important to note that professors were only eligible to be
included in our study if they taught in departments offering undergraduate
degrees. Thus, professors of law and medicine and those teaching in a variety
of other professional fields were not surveyed, although professors of business
were, since many business schools offer undergraduate instruction.

Are Most Professors Atheists?

A common perception of the college or university professor is that she or he is
an atheist who rejects religion in favor of science or critical inquiry, although
results from our survey offer a more nuanced picture. When asked to select the
statement that comes closest to expressing their views about God—a question
taken from the GSS—only 10 percent of our respondents chose the statement
"I don't believe in God," while an additional 13.4 percent chose the statement
"I don't know whether there is a God, and I don't believe there is any way to
find out." Less than a quarter of the professors we surveyed, in other words,
would be classified as atheists or agnostics.

This level of nonbelief—while less than stereotypes about atheist professors would suggest—is much higher than in the U.S. population as a whole.
When the same question was asked on the GSS in 2000 only 2.8 percent of the
general American population said they did not believe in God, with an addi-

tional 4.1 percent saying they did not know if God existed and that there was no way to find out. The figures for the college-educated population—a more reasonable comparison group for professors—show greater religious skepticism, with about 11.1 percent of those with four or more years of college falling into the ranks of atheists and agnostics. Even in comparison with this more educated group, professors display a greater attraction to atheistic and agnostic views.

Nevertheless, atheists and agnostics still constitute only a minority of American professors. Nearly 20 percent (19.6 percent) of respondents to our survey agree with the statement "I don't believe in a personal God, but I do believe in a Higher Power of some kind," while another 4.4 percent agree with the statement "I find myself believing in God some of the time, but not at others." More surprising, 16.9 percent are of the view that "while I have my doubts, I feel that I do believe in God," and 35.7 percent of respondents say "I know God really exists and I have no doubts about it." In other words, well over half the surveyed professors can be described as believers in God.

The percentage of professors expressing religious belief is not uniform: it varies across types of institution. One commonsensical finding is that professors teaching at religiously affiliated colleges and universities are more likely to be believers. Whereas about 50 percent of professors at nonreligiously affiliated schools say either that they believe in God despite their doubts or that they have no doubts about God's existence, this is true of 68.9 percent of professors at religiously affiliated schools (who compose 13.9 percent of all those surveyed in our study).

A second significant finding—one consistent with prior research—is that professors at elite doctoral-granting universities are less religious than professors teaching at other kinds of institutions. More than a third (36.6 percent) of respondents with appointments in elite doctoral schools are either atheists or agnostics, as compared to 15.2 percent of respondents teaching in community colleges, 22.7 percent of those teaching at institutions granting bachelor's degrees, and 23.5 percent of those teaching in nonelite doctoral-granting universities. And whereas about 40 percent of professors at community colleges and four-year schools say they have no doubt God exists, this is true for only 20.4 percent of professors at elite doctoral institutions. Belief in God—including both those who believe despite occasional doubts and those who have no doubts—is actually highest at four-year, bachelor's degree–granting colleges and universities, which may be a function of the fact that so many religiously affiliated institutions fall into this category. But the basic point remains: Contrary to popular opinion, atheists and agnostics constitute a minority of professors at American colleges and universities, and this is true even at elite schools where skepticism toward religion is most pronounced. (Figure 2.1 summarizes the survey results according to institutional type.)

Atheists and agnostics are also more likely to be found in some disciplines than in others. Psychology and biology have the highest proportion of atheists and agnostics, at about 61 percent. Not far behind is mechanical engineering, where 50 percent of professors are atheists or agnostics. Next in line come economics, political science, and computer science, where about 40 percent of the professors fall into the category of nonbelief. At the other end of the spectrum are the professors who say they have no doubt that God exists: 63 percent of accounting professors, 56.8 percent of elementary education professors, 48.6 percent of professors of finance, 46.5 percent of marketing professors, 46.2 percent of art professors and professors of criminal justice, and 44.4 percent of nursing professors. It remains to be determined whether there is something in the nature of these fields that causes them to be associated with higher levels of professorial religiosity, such as distance from the traditional liberal arts core, or whether observed differences reflect something else, such as the way fields of study vary in popularity at different types of institutions.

Setting aside institutional and disciplinary affiliation, who are those professors who express confidence in God's existence? A majority (58.7 percent) of

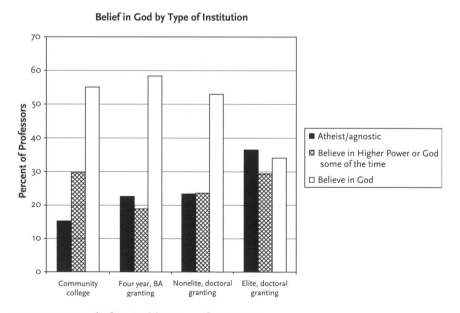

FIGURE 2.1. Belief in God by Type of Institution

believers—those who say they believe in God despite occasional doubts or who say they have no doubts—are affiliated with a variety of Protestant denominations, but the largest single group of faculty believers are Roman Catholics, who account for 27.3 percent of all respondents in this category. Jews, Muslims, Buddhists, and Hindus together compose less than 6 percent of believers.

A significant percentage of respondents to our survey—18.8 percent—say the term *born-again Christian* describes them at least slightly well, and about a third of the professors who believe in God consider themselves to be born-again Christians. Professors who are born-again are extremely rare at elite doctoral institutions, composing only about 1 percent of professors at such institutions, but they are not uncommon among community college professors and professors teaching at baccalaureate schools. As might be expected, born-again Christians are much more likely to be found at religiously affiliated institutions: almost 30 percent (29.6 percent) of those who teach at religious colleges and universities describe themselves as born-again, in contrast to 17 percent of those teaching at colleges or universities with no religious affiliation.

What Is Their Religious Orientation?

One of the most important sociological lessons that has been learned from American religious pluralism is that *how* one believes in God matters as much as *whether* one believes. Attendance at religious services represents one expression of belief, and we found that a sizeable number of professors report frequent attendance at religious services. The numbers for faculty are slightly lower than the figures for the American population as a whole, but they are still relatively high. The latest figures from the GSS suggest that about 48.6 percent of Americans attend religious services once a month or more. The corresponding figure for faculty respondents to our survey is 39.9 percent. Professors at baccalaureate institutions attend religious services most frequently, with 45.5 percent saying they do so once a month or more. In contrast, only 27 percent of professors at elite doctoral institutions attend religious services that often.

We also queried respondents about their views of the Bible. Based on a question from the GSS, they were given the following options and were asked to select the statement that came closest to describing their own feelings about the Bible: "The Bible is the actual word of God and is to be taken literally, word for word"; "The Bible is the inspired word of God but not everything in it should be taken literally, word for word"; or "The Bible is an ancient book of fables, legends, history, and moral precepts recorded by men." On the 2000 version of the GSS, 30 percent of all respondents (and 13 percent of the college-educated respondents) chose "actual word of God"; 49.2 percent (56.8 percent of the college-educated) said "inspired word"; and 17.5 percent (25.9 percent of the college-educated) selected "ancient book of fables." On this matter, divergences between professors and the general population are stark, as one might expect given that the culture of academe encourages professors to take a historical and critical view of texts. Only 6.1 percent of faculty respondents to our survey say the Bible is the "actual word of God," while 51.6 percent describe it as "an ancient book of fables, legends, history, and moral precepts." In the middle, about 42 percent of our respondents hold the view that the Bible is "the inspired word of God." Here again differences are evident by type of institution, with community college professors three times as likely to subscribe to the "actual word of God" position, and a strong majority of professors at elite doctoral universities (72.9 percent) taking the "ancient book of fables" view.

In seeking to learn more about faculty self-perceptions, we also asked a question we wrote ourselves: "In religious matters, do you generally consider yourself a progressive, a moderate, a traditionalist, or not religious?" Consistent with our finding on atheists and agnostics, about a third of our respondents describe themselves as not religious. More than a quarter (28 percent) consider themselves religious moderates, another quarter (25.5 percent) describe themselves as progressives, and one in eight (12.6 percent) are self-described traditionalists. Looking at orientations across types of institutions, it is interesting to note that community colleges are more likely to have a polarized population functioning at the extremes of the distribution: 40 percent of the faculty members at these schools describe themselves as religious progressives and 25.3 percent as traditionalists. At other types of institutions, religious moderates are more common. While believers can indeed be found in the upper echelons of academe, those campuses appear to be places where there is either less interest in or less space for more fervent forms of religiosity.

Views of Religion, Politics, and Science

So far, we have examined faculty members' religious beliefs. But what are their views on the intersection of religion, education, and science? In general, we found that even though many professors are religious themselves, most faculty members are secularists in terms of political philosophy. That is, they generally believe in the separation of church and state and are also generally opposed to any efforts that would blur the boundaries between religion and science.

One question we included in our survey that speaks to this issue—an item drawn from the NES—deals with prayer in the public schools. Overall, 75.1 percent of the professors in our study say that public schools should not be allowed to start each day with a prayer. On this question, the difference between professors teaching at elite doctoral schools and at community colleges is dramatic. An overwhelming majority (92.1 percent) of professors at elite schools express a secular view, while only 45.2 percent of professors at community colleges do so. Differences from discipline to discipline are also significant, with a majority of the professors in several popular fields—elementary education, nursing, accounting, and information management—expressing support for prayer in public schools. While it is clear that many faculty members endorse a strict notion of church-state separation, a significant minority do not.

We also asked respondents to weigh in on the controversy over the notion of "intelligent design." Our question asked respondents how much they agreed or disagreed with the following statement: "The theory of intelligent design *is* a serious scientific alternative to the Darwinian theory of evolution." Overall, 84.1 percent of professors surveyed disagreed with the statement, with 75.3 percent registering strong disagreement. Agreement was strongest at community colleges, where 30.6 percent of professors see intelligent design as a serious scientific alternative, and it was weakest at elite doctoral universities, where just 5.6 percent of professors hold that view.

Professors' general insistence on keeping religion and science apart, however, does not, in the eyes of most professors, mean that colleges and universities are hostile to religious believers. In a previous survey we conducted examining the general public's attitudes toward professors, we found that 80.8 percent of the individuals we surveyed agreed with the statement "American colleges and universities welcome students of faith." We included this same question in the "Politics of the American Professoriate" survey, and found that about the same percentage of professors agree with the statement (83.9 percent). While faculty may want to keep prayer out of the classroom and to keep religion and science apart, they do not believe that colleges and universities are poisonous climates for faith.

In seeking to better understand potential tensions on campus related to faith and politics, we looked more closely at one specific flash point: how religious identity corresponded with political orientation. We noted above that about 20 percent of the professors surveyed identify themselves as born-again Christians. Where do these born-again faculty fall along the political spectrum? A preliminary answer is provided by examining the relationship between being a born-again Christian professor and political party affiliation, which we measured by using a series of items from the NES to construct a seven-point party affiliation scale ranging from strong Democrat to strong Republican. Whereas 36.5 percent of professors who do not self-identify as born-again Christians can be classified as strong Democrats, this is true of only 13.2 percent of born-again faculty. Similarly, while only 13.3 percent of the non-born-again Christians in the professoriate are Republicans of any stripe, 57.6 percent of the born-again faculty place themselves in the Republican camp. There are some born-again Christians in the professoriate who are political liberals, but the vast majority of born-again faculty appear to be conservative as measured by party affiliation. Looking at religious belief more generally, we found that 90.1 percent of Republican professors say they believe in God, as compared to 42.6 percent of non-Republicans. This suggests that, within the professoriate, conservative political views are often linked with religious views. While this is not surprising, it does mean that it is difficult to separate faith from politics when discussing the religious views and values of college and university faculty today.

Implications for Future Research

The findings presented above are preliminary, but we believe they raise a number of significant questions for further study.

First, the fact that a higher proportion of professors are religious than the usual story of academic secularization would lead us to believe suggests that more research is needed both on the ways in which professors' religious values and commitments may influence their thinking and, conversely, on how their intellectual development may affect their religiosity. There is a good deal of anecdotal evidence, both historical and contemporary, that religious or spiritual value commitments can push a thinker's ideas in one direction rather than another, and it is easy to imagine how academic inquiry might shape and change religious belief. Under the influence of the narrative of academic secularization, however, intellectual historians and sociologists of knowledge have often failed to pay attention to these dynamics within academe. This is a tendency that should be corrected.

Second, our findings indicate that, when it comes to religion, professors at elite research universities and professors at local community colleges inhabit different worlds, embracing what the sociologist of science Karin Knorr Cetina would call different "epistemic cultures,"[7] or cultures of knowledge making. More research is needed if we are to understand the different dynamics of scholarship, teaching, and student learning that predominate in these different worlds, especially as these relate to religion. For example, to what extent does personal talk about religion and spirituality undercut one's credibility in the upper echelons of the academic universe, and what strategies do professors who are religious employ to deal with the situation? On the other hand, what assumptions might be built into community college culture about the expression of religious values in the classroom? If we had answers to those questions we could begin to ask how, if at all, these differing cultures of higher education affect student learning, self-understanding, and value formation.

Finally, although our research suggests that professorial religiosity has been previously underestimated, it is clear that on the whole, and measured various ways, professors are less religious than the general U.S. population. Because this is so, and in the context of growing pressures on young people to go to college and the ongoing political mobilization of conservative Christians, we should expect more calls in the coming years for higher education to open itself up to religious perspectives, and more battles to be fought over the religious content of the college curriculum (though we do not mean to suggest that only conservative Christians will issue such calls). Understanding how movements to change the academy in this and other ways grow and develop— and how their advances may be met by countermovements with differing aims—is an important new frontier in the sociology of higher education.

Neil Gross is Assistant Professor of Sociology at Harvard University. **Solon Simmons** is Assistant Professor of Conflict Analysis and Sociology at the Institute for Conflict Analysis and Resolution at George Mason University.

3

Can Faith Be More Than a Sideshow in the Contemporary Academy?

Robert Wuthnow

I am a sociologist by training and a dyed-in-the-wool empiricist by temperament, but the role of religion in the academy is not one that can be addressed from a firm empirical base. From time to time, one hears arguments that students are much more interested in religion or more comfortable expressing their faith on campus now than they were, say, before the tragedy of September 11, 2001, or that faculty on secular campuses are more accepting of religious believers than they were a generation ago. We are tantalized in these speculations by the occasional result from national surveys of college freshmen or by reports of enrollments in religious studies courses.[1] There are also the valuable historical studies that George Marsden, James Burtchaell, and others have done, or the more contemporary studies of Conrad Cherry, Richard Hughes, or John Schmalzbauer.[2]

Yet, whenever I approach this topic wearing my empiricist hat, I feel much less confident than I do about almost any other aspect of American religion. Generalizations about church attendance in the wider population or about the effects of religious convictions on voting are hard enough to maintain; those about what is happening on campuses are even more difficult. In the absence of good empirical evidence, I nevertheless want to present a *possible* scenario of how the role of faith in the academy may have changed over the past four or five decades.[3]

The Marginalization of Religion

According to the historian Diane Winston, the study of religion has, until fairly recently, been on the sidelines or marginalized and probably remains so on most campuses.[4] There may be opportunities to study religion, but these are in seminaries that have no formal connections to colleges or universities, in the occasional divinity school (such as at Yale or Harvard) that *is* part of a university but is viewed by the university's central administrators as a relic that might just as well cease to exist, or perhaps in a religious studies department or program that attracts few students and is poorly funded. The study of religion may also be marginalized by virtue of flourishing more at small church-related colleges than at large public universities.

This view of how the study of religion is marginalized is similar to what other scholars have suggested about the role of faith or the possibilities for expressing sincere religious convictions in the academy. These possibilities are also marginalized, again at seminaries or on church-related campuses, or through campus ministries or in private late-night dorm room discussions that have little relation to what goes on in the classroom. The challenge, then, according to Winston and others is to *mainstream* the study of religion or the expression of faith by initiating centers, funneling foundation money into curricular initiatives and research, promoting new campus ministries, hosting conferences that bring together interested scholars, and seeking innovative ways to change the thinking of faculty and students and thus the climate on college and university campuses. I want to elaborate on this imagery of side-show and center stage, perhaps redefining it slightly, and then in that context examine its implications.

The marginalization of religion in the academy took place, if we follow George Marsden, over a fairly long period. We need not trace that history here, other than to note, as Marsden suggests and as Christian Smith has recently examined sociologically, that the secular trend came about partly through strategic compromises and power plays;[5] it was not just a gradual epistemo-logical shift. At the same time, the change was indeed epistemological as much as it was political. Clergy and church boards lost control over the purse strings and administration of major colleges; Christianity also ceased to be regarded as having a particular corner on the truth.

It will probably be helpful to jump from the longer-term history to a more recent decade, the 1960s, since that period is within the personal memory of those of us who were students or faculty at the time. As an image with which to think about the marginalization of faith in the academy, the 1960s can be taken as a kind of extreme case. In the society at large, the presidency of John F. Kennedy helps to bring this image into focus. Under Kennedy's leadership, the nation's elites eagerly imagined that we would pioneer space travel and conquer the moon by applying the principles we were learning from science and engineering. We also imagined that we could conquer Communism by applying scientific principles to warfare, to our military campaigns, and to foreign policy, and our military involvement in Indochina became the test case for that vision. Although Kennedy is sometimes remembered as the president who gained political respectability for American Catholics, it is just as accurate to recall that Kennedy presented himself as someone who happened to have been reared Catholic, much in the same way someone might have been reared Irish, and promised that whatever personal religious convictions may have come from that upbringing would never influence his conduct in public office. This is not to suggest any criticism of Kennedy; it is only to recall something of the cultural climate of the era. The official mood was in many ways continuous with that of the 1950s, but also different. For instance, if we remember Eisenhower as the president who, as Will Herberg reminded us, argued that any old faith would do, we also need to recall that Eisenhower publicly supported the so-called Freedom Declaration advanced by the National Association of Evangelicals—a declaration that American freedom depended on our faith in God—and carried on the tradition of declaring an annual national day of penance and prayer.[6]

In American higher education, the shift in mood from the 1950s to the 1960s was also evident. The GI Bill brought veterans to campuses in the 1950s who were older than the typical college student, who had experienced the rigors of war, and who were often supporting families of their own. Polls conducted in the late 1950s and early 1960s showed that Americans with college educations were *more likely* to attend church or express orthodox religious views, whereas surveys a decade later showed those with college educations were now *less likely* to exhibit these kinds of religious commitment.[7] Just as in Washington, the mood on campuses emphasized the virtues of science and technology. Money was being lavished on physics and chemistry departments and on engineering schools. Majoring in science or engineering was a sure way to obtain employment at General Electric, DuPont, or a similar company. In the social sciences, modernization was the reigning orthodoxy. It suggested that societies would gradually modernize as a result of technological innovation and economic development and in the process politics would become more rational; religion, along with other superstitions, would cease to matter. Students studied classical philosophy and Shakespeare for wisdom that preceded or transcended the teachings of particular religious traditions, and through anthropology or philosophy learned that there were universals in ethics and in social behavior that could be understood rationally and apart from particular ethnic or religious traditions.

All of this was reinforced by the fact that the United States was indeed making progress in developing atomic energy, launching satellites, inventing new consumer products, and keeping the Soviet Union at bay. Having weathered the Great Depression and World War II, it was easy to believe that science, positivist social science, and rational thought were the wave of the future. Even if there were doubters and critics who raised questions about the uses of atomic weapons or other technological innovations, we knew we had inherited a brave new world and that if religion had a place in it, it was more as a way of sustaining ourselves emotionally than as a source of truth or public policy. By the end of the 1960s, as college campuses mushroomed with the influx of baby boomers, church attendance in the nation at large was down dramatically from its 1958 high and most studies showed that the longer that students were in college and the more elite the institutions they attended, the less religious they were.

The Emergence of Postmodernism

Also by the end of the 1960s, though, a new mood was emerging that would become more prominent during the 1970s and 1980s. Some have referred to this new orientation as *postmodernism*, a term that if too sweeping in generality and significance did at least capture the sense in some quarters that the universals sought and claimed in modernization theory would never be found.[8] At a more popular level, the protests against the Vietnam War that began in earnest at the end of the 1960s were accompanied by questioning the very applications of science and technology on which presidents Kennedy, Johnson, and Nixon had pinned their hopes for American victory. Some broader questioning of epistemological assumptions also came about with the drug culture and with campus experiments with new religious movements.

More significant for the longer term, however, was the emergence of what has subsequently been called *identity politics*. The civil rights movement evolved between the late 1950s and the early 1970s from a quest for inclusion to a struggle for racial identity. The quest for gender equality followed a similar trajectory, as did the subsequent move toward greater equality for gays and lesbians. These movements deeply affected American campuses. Colleges that had been the exclusive or nearly exclusive preserve of white males became more inclusive along lines of race and gender. Opportunities expanded for people of color to gain advanced degrees and for women to pursue a wider variety of careers. New institutional arrangements also appeared: African American studies programs, women's studies departments, Third World centers, Asian American student organizations, and so on. The underlying epistemological shift was that more legitimate claims could be made for the role of cultural traditions in shaping knowledge and for multiple approaches to knowledge. The ensuing debate about ways of knowing was evident in a variety of fields: in social philosophy in the famous debate between Habermas and Gadamer, in which the former argued for the ascendancy of rational speech acts and the latter emphasized the embeddedness of values in cultural traditions; in philosophy of science in the shift from a Popperian vision of positive knowledge to Feyerabend's anarchic vision, Latour's social constructivism, or even Kuhn's emphasis on paradigms and puzzle solving; in education in the shift from Stanford-Binet measurements of IQ to Howard Gardner's arguments about multiple intelligences; and in literature in the new popularity of Derrida and Jamison and the reactions of more traditional defenders of the literary canon such as Alan Bloom. It is in this context that we must understand the changing role of religious studies and expressions of faith.

It is probably overstated to suggest, as some have, that the advent of postmodernism, if it can be called that, was the first step toward a new appreciation of the truth of Christianity, Judaism, or other religious traditions. That was probably so only for those who reacted against the seemingly radical relativism of postmodernism. But the epistemological uncertainty, not to mention the dynamic campus politics that accompanied it, did create opportunities for rethinking the place of faith in the academy. If it was now legitimate to be African American or gay, and to argue that there were special ways of knowing that might come from emphasizing one's racial tradition or approaching literature through the lens of queer theory, it also became more legitimate to be Catholic or Jewish or Presbyterian. Exactly *how* it was legitimate was of course unclear and for that reason became a matter of debate and was worked out differently in different settings. But at least the opportunity for discussion and for new arguments and programs became possible. It became possible, for example, to argue that:

- Having a religious studies program at a state university might be just as legitimate as having one in gender studies;
- Having a campus religious group that was recognized by the administration might be as acceptable as a group for gays and lesbians;
- Including a course on the Protestant Reformation in the history department curriculum might be just as valuable as one on the French Revolution;

- Encouraging students to talk about their religious backgrounds in a seminar could be just as useful as prompting them to discuss their ethnic heritage or where they grew up;
- And sending one's son or daughter to, or deciding to teach at, a church-related college where Christian values could be openly discussed could be just as beneficial as being at some larger institution dominated by "secular humanism."

In short, the academy started to acknowledge the value of diversity and in so doing opened up opportunities for expressions of faith to be part of that diversity.

The Current State of Religion on Campus

There is a problem, however, with describing all of this as a linear shift from one campus culture or epistemological paradigm to another. A more accurate description would have to acknowledge that American higher education is currently a mixture of *both* of the scenarios I have just described. Moreover, these different understandings of scholarship are institutionalized in different parts of the typical campus, and this pattern of institutionalization deeply affects how faith can be expressed and religion understood.

The view that knowledge is best achieved through science and reason remains firmly institutionalized in the natural sciences, in engineering schools, and in more recent additions to the curriculum such as computer science, artificial intelligence, neuroscience, evolutionary psychology, and genomics. These are the components of the typical campus that require the greatest financial investment and that benefit most from government grants and corporate partnerships. They are also the most attractive programs for wealthy alumni—especially those trained during the governing ethos of the early 1960s—who wish to be associated with cutting-edge breakthroughs in scientific research. The same emphasis on scientific methods and rational thought is usually evident in economics departments and increasingly in political science departments and public policy programs dominated by rational choice theories of human behavior. The same emphasis is often evident as well in philosophy departments that feature analytic philosophy and in ethics courses that look for rational, context-free principles of ethical argumentation.

The more pluralistic orientations to knowledge that are associated with postmodernity are typically institutionalized in the humanities. History and literature departments, not the physics or material science departments, include courses on the distinctive contributions of ethnic traditions or gendered perspectives. Specialized programs in African American studies, Latino studies, Asian American studies, or gender studies are taught by faculty in the humanities and located in those administrative divisions. The same is true of religious studies departments or interdisciplinary programs or centers for the study of religion. The social sciences, for their part, remain the most likely to be epistemologically divided. Whereas economics and political science may be governed by rational choice approaches, anthropology is more likely to incorporate the cultural perspectives of the humanities, and sociology is more likely to be divided between positivists and ethnographers who are only united in their respect for empiricism.

There are at least two important implications of this institutional patterning for the expression of faith and the study of religion. The first pertains more to secular universities than to church-related colleges, although it probably applies to some of the latter as well. It has to do with the power dynamics of the typical campus. Power is ultimately vested in those parts of the university that emphasize science and rational argumentation. The big money is there, the cutting-edge discoveries are there, the claims to be advancing knowledge into new frontiers are there, and so are the needs for new facilities, the requirements for funding, and the opportunity to invest in students who will pursue remunerative careers. Although these parts of the university may be burdensome in terms of money and administrative time, and are by no means without their own problems, it is easy for administrators to make the case that this is the kind of knowledge that universities should be producing.

The other part of the university—the part that deals with history and tradition and ethnic identity and religion—is a necessity, and is recognized as such by most administrators of liberal arts institutions. But it is often a political necessity more than anything else. It involves starting a new program to meet the demands of some newly organized student constituency, or maintaining an old department even though one wonders if there is any possibility of learning anything new in that discipline. These are the departments and programs that are maintained because they offer service courses for the cultural enrichment of undergraduates and because they may train a very small number of graduate students and an even smaller number who actually get jobs in that discipline. Being associated with this part of the university means that religious studies programs or campus ministries are likely to be supported, but often more because of campus politics than because of genuine enthusiasm.

The second implication is that religion and faith commitments have largely become matters of cultural tradition and have ceased being about truth. The trivially obvious meaning of this implication is that no self-respecting physicist would argue that there is anything special to be gained by framing a theorem in physics from a Christian or Jewish perspective rather than from any other perspective. Less trivially obvious perhaps is the fact that an economist who happened to be a Christian could still value the insights of rational choice theory and a sociologist who happened to be Buddhist could examine census figures the same way any other sociologist could. More interesting is the likelihood that religion will be studied as a cultural *object*, as it were, from the outside, rather than as a valuable perspective that one might try to understand from the inside. Thus, a class on Christianity would be more likely to examine its historical development than to challenge students to consider whether they actually found Christianity believable. Or a course in sociology of religion might include a film about Wiccans, but certainly stop short of encouraging students to consider becoming Wiccan. These are simply academic conventions that we take for granted. So is the idea that there should be a rather impenetrable fire wall between the way faith may be discussed in the classroom and the way it may be practiced in one's personal life. In the classroom, the acceptable mode is to teach *about* religion, leaving the teaching *of* religion and the practice *of* faith to be promoted by chaplains, campus clergy, or student ministries.

I should note here that if religious studies has become more acceptable within humanities and social science programs, if only as a nod to cultural diversity, this is a significant change from at least one perspective. That perspective comes from comparisons of religious commitment among faculty in various disciplines from some surveys conducted in the late 1960s and 1970s. Those studies showed that faculty in the humanities and social sciences were much less likely than faculty in the sciences, engineering, and applied fields (such as business and education) to be religiously involved or religiously oriented. The reason, as I have argued elsewhere, may have been that the sciences, engineering, and applied fields were more clearly codified, either as scientific pursuits or as professional roles, and thus could be compartmentalized more easily from one's private life, whereas the humanities and social sciences were less codified and thus spilled more readily into scholars' personal lives (some, for instance, claimed they were "intellectuals" and thus could not separate their academic from their personal lives).[9] Whatever the interpretation, the humanities and social sciences seemed least "musical" with respect to religion, to borrow Max Weber's famous image. If religious studies are now more acceptable among those fields, that is worthy of note.

Yet, another small piece of evidence is also relevant. This is from a national survey of the general U.S. public that I conducted in 2003. This survey focused on attitudes toward religious diversity. It showed that college graduates, and especially those who had majored in the humanities or social sciences, were especially likely to regard all religions as being equally true, rather than considering any one of them to be uniquely true. In short, religions were viewed as interchangeable cultural traditions.[10]

Returning momentarily to the image of movement from sideshow to mainstream, then, we see, if what I have outlined here is correct, that faith and religion in the academy may have more opportunities to overcome marginalization now than a generation ago. But this change can also be viewed as a kind of devil's bargain, for the process in no way suggests that faith and religion will again become center stage in American higher education. Instead they become articles of personal biography, aspects of some community or group's cultural history, rather than anything resembling truth.

There are, of course, exceptions that must immediately be acknowledged. At some church-related colleges it is possible to believe that the truth taught at secular universities is so biased as to not be truth at all. In that sad state of affairs, the search for truth in what remains of the Christian community becomes a heroic struggle. There are also more widely accepted ways of accommodating to the current situation by redefining what we mean by truth, about which I will say more in a moment. My point here is only that we should not exaggerate the opportunities presently available for somehow moving religion and faith once again into the academic mainstream. Both the politics and the epistemology of higher education suggest that the study of religion and personal expressions of faith will remain on the margins.

Accommodation, Resistance, or Intentional Reframing

What, then, are the possible strategies by which faculty and students who remain committed to the idea that faith should matter can put that commitment into practice? One possibility is to accept as valid the situation in which we find ourselves and try to be responsible members of the academic community within that framework. We might call this a strategy of accommodation. A second possibility is to deliberately question the given situation and indeed put ourselves in a kind of countercultural position in relation to it. We might term this a strategy of resistance. There may also be a third alternative, a strategy of intentional reframing.[11]

The strategy of accommodation is, I have to acknowledge, sufficiently attractive that I find myself consciously or unconsciously following it much of the time. On this view, the truth that we know from science and from reason is accepted as that which the academy ought to be concerned. As people of faith, we may regard it as partial and yet consider it the most that is humanly possible at any point in human history. Reality is thus seamless enough that people can have some common understanding of it whether they follow one particular faith tradition, a different faith tradition, or none. If the ways of God, so to speak, are ultimately beyond human knowing, then they are not fully disclosed to any particular faith tradition, any more than they are to science or philosophy. There are, however, aspects of truth that may be better preserved and communicated in religious language and through communities of religious narrative than through such other media as science and philosophy.

By broadening the meaning of truth in this way, we come, then, to an appreciation of the place of religion and faith in the academy. Just as music or literature should be part of the academy, so should religion. In likening religion to music and literature, though, we largely accept the institutional realities that characterize the present-day academy. Music appreciation and literary criticism may be usefully taught in the classroom, but musical performance and the production and consumption of literature may require additional venues, such as conservatories, recording studios, book stores, and book discussion groups. So it is with religion. Classroom instruction may enhance the life of faith by conveying knowledge, examining the conditions under which people seek faith, and criticizing expressions of faith in relation to some normative standard. But the actual practice of faith occurs elsewhere. Discussions *about* religion, therefore, are appropriately included in the academy, but do not take the place of private devotion, campus ministries, and houses of worship in the wider community.

The strategy of resistance takes the realities of human evil and the limitations of given social arrangements more seriously. If accommodation is a kind of priestly acceptance of the academy, resistance adopts a more prophetic orientation to it. This orientation has recently been advocated by Derek Alan Woodard-Lehman, who argues that mainstream higher education serves the liberal nation-state, which is antithetical to Christendom, and thus requires Christian scholars to adopt a stance of prophetic pilgrims speaking in a pagan wilderness.[12] The prophet is always more confident than many of his or her fellow travelers that he or she knows the ways of God. In the prophetic view, certain formulations of truth are more true than others, and some may have been granted by special dispensation to particular individuals or communities. The prophet usually takes an oppositional stance toward some particular aspect of business as usual (such as the tenure and promotion system or the prevalence of quantitative methods in his or her discipline).

The prophet also seeks an alternative institutional base in order to separate himself or herself, so to speak, from the corrupting influences of the world. The church-related college may be one such institutional base. Another may be a formally organized network of like-minded scholars, such as a society of Christian sociologists or an association of Muslim political scientists. Yet another may be an informal group, such as a gathering of faculty or students that meets periodically for discussion and support, much in the same way that a women's consciousness group or a dissertation writers group does. An oppositional group of this kind probably questions or feels aggrieved by the prevailing status system within its discipline or on its campus. It thus seeks reform and possibly redress. It finds value in writing and lecturing for venues outside the mainstream. It probably does not hope to overthrow the prevailing worldviews it encounters in the academy, but it may hope to bring in perspectives that would otherwise be overlooked.

The third alternative, which I refer to as intentional reframing, represents a kind of middle way between accommodation and resistance. It is for this reason harder to describe. Like the accommodationist approach, it accepts much of what goes on in the academy. It accepts, for example, most of the methods of inquiry that have developed over the years. At the same time, it recognizes that the pursuit of knowledge is always flawed by self-interest, academic politics, and other human limitations. It therefore adopts an intentional stance of questioning or even skepticism in its consumption and pursuit of higher learning. To employ the other meaning of the phrase "faith in the academy," this approach does have faith in the academy in the sense that it trusts the academy, up to a point, to be an institution that has proven over the years to be effective in generating and transmitting knowledge. It trusts the laws under which colleges and universities are chartered and accredited, for example, and anticipates that these laws will work reasonably well under most circumstances to guard against fraud and deception. It has faith that such conventions as academic freedom or the processes by which tenure and promotion decisions are made will in most cases be fair and conducive to good scholarship. But, just as faith in the democratic system of government always requires citizens to reserve granting absolute faith to their representatives, so faith in the academy is similarly tempered. One is reminded that intellectual integrity always includes a critical element. In a word, one *questions* as well as accepts. And the stance from which one questions is, for a person of faith, grounded in the convictions associated with that faith. These are convictions that generally precede a person's involvement in the academy or at least transcend it. They are normative convictions about what is important in life and about how to conduct one's life with the utmost integrity.

For persons reared in the Christian tradition, the paradoxical nature of so many of the biblical teachings may, as Richard Hughes has suggested, be especially conducive to an intellectual style that acknowledges complexity.[13]

Paradoxical thinking is capable of both accepting and rejecting, of saying "yes and no" rather than "yes or no," and thus may be especially conducive to grappling with complex issues and with keeping the discussion of those issues going. But the question of whether one's questions or instincts are *better*, as a result of being grounded in faith, than someone else's is a red herring. The more important question is whether a person who wishes to live according to his or her faith is seriously striving to live up to those desires. For some, it may require intense participation in a faith community, especially one outside the academy, to gain the support needed for a commitment of this kind. For others, introspective withdrawal may be more effective, and for still others it may be that becoming absorbed with a particular author or following the inspiration of a mentor in one's field provides the support required.

To end on a more personal note, the relation of religious faith and the life of scholarship and teaching has, for me, not been one that I could formulate in any concise statement about faith and learning or that I could equate with any particular revelatory experience. It has been, rather, one of periodic troubling or unsettling. There have been times, for instance, when I have been guided mostly by puzzlement over the tensions seemingly inherent in the human condition. How can such self-interested people as we clearly are also find it within ourselves to care deeply, even sacrificially, for others? How does a society that has so much inertia built into it manage to reinvent itself enough to face new challenges? How do we render the drudgery of the usual workaday world meaningful enough to believe we are also pursuing our higher values? I have tried to keep my eye on some of the enduring questions that have been raised by previous generations of social theorists, reading their work less for lasting answers than for validation that these are indeed enduring questions that must be addressed anew by each generation.

If faith is in these ways a kind of goad that pushes me to ask difficult questions, it is also a source of reassurance. The danger in being puzzled by large questions or being troubled by the problems one witnesses on such a devastating scale is believing that one's own small efforts should make a considerable impact toward answering those questions or resolving those problems. The reality is rather that what any of us does matters very little. And yet this is where the idea of faith being embedded in community becomes reassuring. The idea is not so much that one feels better by virtue of constantly having other people around to stroke one's ego or salve one's wounds. That touchy-feeling idea of community is, I fear, one that religious leaders sometimes promote in hopes of encouraging involvement in their particular congregations, and, if so, it is one that will sooner or later prove disappointing, even to them. The better view of community is one that acknowledges the inevitable interdependence in which we are all engaged and the necessary limits that imposes on any of us. Accepting those limitations requires humility and that, in turn, is probably the most important reason for faith.

Robert Wuthnow is Andlinger Professor of Sociology, Chair of the Department of Sociology, and Director of the Center for the Study of Religion at Princeton University.

4

A Level Playing Field for Religion in Higher Education

John J. DiIulio Jr.

Unlike other Ivy League universities, the University of Pennsylvania was not founded as a sectarian school. Penn, as it is commonly known, was founded in Philadelphia in 1749 by Benjamin Franklin. During much of the twentieth century, Penn, like many other Ivy League schools, was not always fair or friendly toward religion. Today, however, Penn is becoming a national lamplight for how so-called secular elite or mainstream colleges and universities should define religion's role in higher education. Since the mid-1990s, Penn has increasingly given religion its due both on campus in the curriculum and off campus in the community. Although there is still some way to go, Penn now generally respects religion's intellectual and civic importance.

And Penn is not alone. Despite the secularization of the academy that began in the 1940s and 1950s, today ever more colleges and universities all across the country seem increasingly inclined to welcome student interest in religion as an ally to liberal arts learning, a springboard to community service, and a suitable subject for scholarly studies of many different types.

This slow but steady reversal has been a long time in coming. In *God and Man at Yale*, first published in 1951, William F. Buckley Jr. famously fretted that the country's top schools were not only retreating from their historic religious identities, but marching toward secular ideologies.[1] The ensuing half-century proved that young Buckley was more right than he knew. Over that period, religion was generally kicked to the intellectual and civic curb in higher education. Academic leaders, many religious believers among them, began by severing schools' sectarian roots but ended by institutionalizing radically secular visions. It became legitimate, even fashionable, to tolerate virtually any secularism while exiling religion.

Today, however, religion is increasingly seen, heard, and tolerated, if not always respected or sincerely embraced, throughout higher education. Guarded optimism is in order. There is reason to hope that, over the next decade or two, religion in higher education will find itself on a mostly level playing field in terms of undergraduate liberal arts course offerings, support for student groups and service projects, and graduate programs and professional research. Certain nonsectarian principles can help us get there.

Ben Franklin and Religion at Penn

Contemporary biographers disagree somewhat about Benjamin Franklin's religious beliefs. We know that old Ben frequented Philly taverns on Saturday nights more than he fancied Philly churches on Sunday mornings. It is doubtful that Franklin believed, even provisionally, in any spiritual concept or ultimate reality, or that he was even so much as a deist.[2] Certainly, unlike George Washington, he was no devout, Bible-believing Christian.[3] And, unlike James Madison, he was not influenced by religious thinkers like Reverend John Witherspoon, president of New Side Presbyterian College of New Jersey at Princeton and the only clergyman to sign both the Declaration of Independence and the United States Constitution.[4] Before Ben Franklin's thirtieth birthday, his brash, youthful energies had irreverently exploded misconceptions on every topic his genius touched. Even in his last two years, he was arguably more a man of the European Enlightenment than of the Great Awakening.

Still, Franklin was never the least bit antireligious or irreligious. He never argued that modern science or philosophy should relegate religion to a limbo of lesser intellectual or civic significance. Much to the contrary, Penn's founder consistently maintained that religion tends to "serve as a powerful regulator of our actions, give us peace and tranquility in our minds, and render us benevolent, useful and beneficial to others."[5] His best-selling biographer, Walter Isaacson, rightly depicts him as an "apostle of tolerance" who personally "contributed to the building funds of each and every sect in Philadelphia" (churches, synagogues, and mosques), and "opposed religious oaths and tests in both the Pennsylvania and the federal constitutions."[6]

Communiter bona profundere deum est. That is the Latin for "To pour forth benefits for the common good is divine." It is the motto that Franklin gave to the Library Company of Philadelphia, which he founded in 1731, nearly two decades before he founded Penn. But it could as fittingly have been Franklin's motto for the little "Academy," later "College of Philadelphia" and then "University of the State of Pennsylvania," that became the University of Pennsylvania.

In essence, Franklin wanted Penn's faculty, staff, and students to approach religion much as he himself did, namely, as a profoundly interesting and largely positive intellectual and civic force in human affairs. He wanted Penn to become a proudly nonsectarian, but not radically secular, institution of higher learning. He wanted Penn to be self-consciously nondenominational—accommodating and friendly to all faiths without being captive to any particular faith or unfriendly to doubters or nonbelievers.

Academic politics, however, were present at Penn's creation. As Penn undergraduate Jennifer Reiss has brilliantly documented, some of the most heated battles concerned Franklin's insistence on Penn's nonsectarian and nondenominational character.[7] Nobody pushed for a radically secular Penn. It is unlikely that anyone at that time could have so much as imagined an institution of higher learning bereft of all regard for religion, let alone one organizationally bound and determined to define higher learning in opposition to belief in a higher being.

Something like that radically secular day would eventually dawn at many otherwise excellent schools including Penn; but, in the mid-eighteenth century, Franklin's higher education vision was attacked not from the (nonexistent) secular left but by the era's religious right. Cosmopolitan Franklin was not popular with all Christian leaders. Like the man himself, Penn's nonsectarian character troubled orthodox Christian educators and observers who had nothing to do with the school but who nonetheless had many concerns about its founder. It appears, however, that the serious disagreements over religion that most directly affected the institution's early development were internal. Franklin's chief antagonist regarding the role of religion at Penn was Reverend William Smith, an Anglican minister.

Reverend Smith arrived at the college in 1754, a handpicked Franklin faculty protégé, but he soon alienated his patron over many issues. Smith became Penn's first provost in 1755 and immediately proceeded to take charge of all aspects of the school's curriculum and student life.

In 1756, Franklin, serving as a trustee, formally accused the minister of trying to indoctrinate students. Smith strongly denied the charge, and the trustees voted to exonerate him. But Franklin was right. Smith was eager to turn Penn into an Anglican outpost of sorts. For instance, in 1756, Smith wrote to his superiors in the Church of England, boasting that "the Church, by soft and easy Means daily gains ground.... Of Twenty-Four Trustees fifteen or sixteen are regular Churchmen.... We have Prayers twice a days, the Children learn the Church-Catecism."[8] During the two decades after 1756, tensions between Franklin and Smith grew more personal. In 1758, Smith even tried to discredit Franklin's reputation for being "the Chief Inventor of the Electrical apparatus"—a charge that was quickly rebuffed.[9] For his part, Franklin never missed a chance to volley with Smith. Their final exchanges came as the war for independence loomed. Franklin sided with the patriots while Smith semi-sided with the loyalists.

After the break with England, Franklin wasted no time in getting the patriot-dominated Pennsylvania Assembly to investigate Smith's control over the school, which by then was known as the College of Philadelphia. The Franklin-friendly Assembly issued a scathing critique. It charged that Smith and the other trustees had opposed the "present Government" and had displayed "Enmity to the common Cause."[10] It also charged that the school's finances were a wreck, and intimated that Penn's fiscal management had been both wholly incompetent and slightly corrupt. The Assembly also dredged up and found Smith guilty of the Franklin-minted religious indoctrination charge that the Trustees had cleared the minister of two decades earlier: "that the fair and original Plan of equal Privileges to all denominations hath not been fully adhered to."[11]

In 1777, the Assembly fired Smith and through the next decade the minister maneuvered to get his old job back. When Franklin died in 1790, Smith eulogized him before a philosophical society gathering, but even this attempt to curry favor with the dead did not help his cause. In 1791, the Assembly assumed full administrative control of the school and renamed it the University of Pennsylvania. Thereafter, Smith sued Penn for back salary, eventually settling with the institution in 1795. He died in Philadelphia in 1803.

Today "Provost Smith" is remembered only in an obscure carving above a single doorway in one of the Penn Quadrangle's student housing subdivisions. My informal poll of a few dozen Penn trustees, faculty, staff, and students turned up none who could so much as name Smith as first provost or cite a single fact about him. In stark contrast, Founding Father Franklin's grand, larger-than-life statue (one of several Franklin sculptures on campus) rises majestically before the entrance to Penn's center-campus College Hall. Franklin is ubiquitous in Penn architecture, art, and lore. If Penn were a Catholic university, Franklin would be its patron saint.

Religion at Penn Two Centuries Later

In the 1970s, I became an undergraduate at "Saint Ben's." Then, as now, Penn introduced its history to students as if that history had nothing whatsoever to do with religion. The school's founding myth, so to speak, is that Penn, begat by patriot-scientist Franklin, was a secular virgin birth. Actually, as we have witnessed, the school's founding was more like a political C-section performed by Franklin with help from others who shared his nonsectarian, not secular, vision for Penn.

In the 1970s, however, Penn's all-secular founding myth was translated into an institutional environment that was too often unwelcoming toward religion. As a commuting Catholic student from a nearby neighborhood, I did not need to attend Sunday mass at the Catholic church that flanked Penn's campus. But I recall that other practicing Catholic students who lived on campus felt like they were expected to hide their religious identities. Among other reasons for this feeling, it was not uncommon for faculty in certain classes to take gratuitous swipes at religious believers. "If you still believe in God," my behavioral psychology professor bellowed in his introductory lecture, "you will feel very uncomfortable in this course. This is science!"

One Ash Wednesday I walked down the main campus thoroughfare (Locust Walk) with an orthodox Jewish classmate. Earlier that day the priest had given my forehead a conspicuous dab of ashes. My walking partner pulled an extra yarmulke from his pocket and offered to let me wear it. "Here," he joked, "let them stare at this, too." On another occasion, I volunteered to help connect a university child tutoring project to local black churches that I had gotten to know during my stint as a campaign operative for the city's first major black mayoral candidate. But the responsible university administrator reacted as if I had proposed a new Inquisition: "We're not going to force people to go to church!"

Force people to go to church? Still believe in God? During my undergraduate days, Penn generally reflected the radically secular view that religious identities were best left at the university gates, expressed only in private places and spaces, or shed well before graduation.

But when I returned to Penn in 1998, things had clearly changed for the better. At the time, I was on Princeton's public policy faculty. Penn's School of Arts and Sciences had invited me to deliver its annual Steinberg Symposium lectures. With encouragement from the symposium's multidisciplinary Penn faculty committee, I agreed to focus the three days of speeches and panels on religion in the public square. Specifically, the symposium focused on how local "sacred places" that served "civic purposes" could assist in revitalizing low-income urban communities.

The response from the entire Penn community, as well as from people in the surrounding West Philly neighborhoods, exceeded all expectations. Naturally, people in the religious studies department and the university chaplain's office could be counted on to show interest. But faculty, staff, and students from all across the campus participated. To accommodate the overflow crowds, several scheduled events were moved to the school's largest auditorium (Irvine). In between the speeches and panels, I was booked solid, but I still could not meet with all the faculty members and student groups that wanted to hear more about public-private community-serving partnerships involving religion.

During the 1990s, Princeton, too, had developed a more robust identity as a place where noted faculty took religion seriously, and where student interest in religion as an academic subject was far more welcome than not. My own particular empirical research interest, however, was at the action-oriented intersection of religion and urban civil society.

In the mid-1990s, Penn's School of Social Work had launched a local research project aimed at estimating the extent to which the city's religious congregations (mostly churches, synagogues, and mosques) delivered social services to the poor. I had already had a hand in that project from my perch as senior advisor to a Philadelphia-based nonprofit research organization (Public/ Private Ventures). And, during the three-day symposium, I met Penn faculty from multiple fields who shared my particular interest in religion. I also met several Penn administrators who were running community service projects tied to local religious groups, plus many undergraduate student leaders who were active in religious associations and who, all together, represented many different faiths.

So, in 1999, after thirteen great years at Princeton, I left to begin a new religion program at Penn. After various twists and turns (a few occasioned in 2001 when I took an academic leave to serve in the White House as the nation's first "faith czar"), that initiative lives on today within Penn's School of Arts and Sciences as the Program for Research on Religion and Urban Civil Society (PRRUCS). The program, of which I serve as faculty director, has been supported financially mainly by the Pew Charitable Trusts as part of its religion research "centers of excellence" project. Many other nonsectarian universities have also participated in this multiyear, multimillion-dollar Pew project, and each one, like Penn, was required to make assorted matching commitments in order to qualify for the support.

The PRRUCS program has helped to level the playing field for religion at Penn with respect to both teaching and research. A steering committee, consisting of senior faculty and staff, and chaired by the dean of the College of Arts and Sciences, guides the curricular portion of the program. This steering committee oversees the selection processes by which faculty members receive course development grants, and undergraduate students are awarded research grants.

In addition, PRRUCS supports the development of new courses dealing with religion as well as modifications of existing courses that did not previously include a focus on religion. Preference is given to courses that explore different areas of the relationship between religion and society, but the courses may be global in scope, may focus on either contemporary or historical issues, and may include academically based community service components. In addition to providing summer salary or other direct support to participating faculty members, program funds may be used for site visits, course materials, and other course-related expenses. During its first few years, PRRUCS supported several dozen courses variously led by faculty in the humanities, the social sciences, and the natural sciences.

In addition, PRRUCS has an advanced research component that has supported PhD candidates in social work, city and regional planning, and arts and sciences; postdoctoral fellows from various academic fields; public events and speakers; and both resident and nonresident senior fellows. At present, the main PRRUCS research venture is a collaborative effort with Harvard University focused on mapping the urban "civic assets" of Catholic nonprofit organizations engaged in community-serving work.[12]

But PRRUCS is hardly the only expression of how Penn is increasingly living up to Franklin's nonsectarian, not secular, vision of religion's role in higher education. Within the last decade, the Penn Office of the Chaplain was relocated to an attractive building at one of the most desirable and visible spots on the main campus. In welcoming the Class of 2010, the office's Web site offered the following description: "Religious life at Penn is dynamic, varied and central to the lives of large numbers of undergraduates and graduate students." Amen. Penn's campus now bustles with student religious associations.

One program started by the Penn chaplain's office is known as Programs in Religion, Interfaith and Spirituality Matters, or P.R.I.S.M. Founded in 2002, P.R.I.S.M. is a student interfaith group. Its mission statement aptly describes it as "dedicated to advancing knowledge about religious life and promoting interactions among the various religious groups on campus. . . . It is an organization whose sole purpose is to help students balance their academic and spiritual lives at Penn. Through innovative interfaith programming we have been able to show the entire student body that. . . . religion and spirituality are extremely important."

The P.R.I.S.M. network includes student-leaders from the Baha'i, Hindu, evangelical Christian, Muslim, Catholic, Jewish, and other student religious associations. In terms of religious self-identification, the two biggest student subgroups at Penn are Catholics and Jews. Much of Catholic student life revolves around the Newman Center that is co-located with the church that is closest to campus (Saint Agatha-Saint James). At a typical Sunday evening mass, the church is packed with over 500 students. Much of Jewish student life revolves around the Hillel Center that is located adjacent to the Penn president's residence. On weekdays, both the Newman Center and the Hillel Center are beehives of student-initiated community service projects, study groups, recreational activities, outside speakers, and more.

In fact, many Catholic, Jewish, and other Penn students increasingly find one another and work together in ways that go beyond interfaith dialogue or occasional joint events. For example, during Penn's spring break week in 2006, students from Newman, Hillel, Campus Crusade for Christ, a group sponsored by the chaplain's office, and Civic House (Penn's undergraduate student service "hub") did a joint community service project in hurricane-devastated New Orleans and the Gulf Coast. In September 2005, the former two-term mayor of New Orleans and class of 1980 Penn alumnus, Marc H. Morial, had come to campus in his role as cochairman of the university's Robert A. Fox Leadership Program. Morial had challenged students to "do something for real" and, with the full support of the Fox Program and in partnership with Civic House, the student religious associations rose to the challenge. About one hundred students headed to the Gulf Coast and performed much-needed volunteer work (mainly housing rehabilitation), often in partnership with local religious organizations.

When it comes to Penn's willingness to partner with faith-based organizations that serve civic purposes, this spring break experience is now the rule, not the exception. For example, over the last decade or so, the university's renowned Center for Community Partnerships (CCP) has involved both local and national religious leaders in a wide range of curricular and service initiatives. Among its myriad programs, for example, the CCP sponsors the Program in Universities, Communities of Faith, Schools, and Neighborhood Organizations (PUCFSN). The program in West Philadelphia provides a wide range of social services to local residents (after school, computer learning, arts, mentoring, health care), and works in collaboration with the pastoral care department at the Hospital of the University of Pennsylvania and with pastors of several local churches.

In sum, for over a decade now, Penn has been resurrecting Franklin's original vision of religion's intellectual and civic place in higher education.

Penn today is more nonsectarian than secular, more dedicated to promoting religious pluralism than to exorcising religion from classroom and campus life. The university is by policy and practice, in both letter and in spirit, more accommodating than not to faculty, staff, and students of all faiths and of no faith. With respect to both curricular and extracurricular institutional recognition, respect, and support, religion at Penn is on an increasingly level playing field when it comes to teaching, research, and service. Faculty, staff, and student religious identities, interests, and motivations are treated much the same by Penn as all other identities, interests, and motivations.

Not surprisingly, however, not all issues have been resolved. For instance, even though they are based on campus and sponsor many events and activities that are open to the entire university community and primarily benefit non-members, Penn does not recognize donations to student religious associations as donations to the university. Also, student-leaders of certain religious associations at Penn feel that, for all the goodwill and progress that has been made, they are still sometimes victims of double standards that uniquely disfavor religion. For example, during the academic year 2005–6, the undergraduate student activities council funded the production of a student publication containing sexually graphic photographs of students and "erotic" writing. Evangelical Christian students, several of them members of Campus Crusade for Christ, politely debated their peers and thoughtfully complained to university officials. Essentially, they were told that the university, via the council, takes no cognizance of, and neither approves nor disapproves, the content of any student-initiated publications that it funds. Did this mean, they asked, that the council would also "take no cognizance" of and fund the production of an "orthodox" rather than "erotic" student publication containing sectarian religious art and biblical verses? As of this writing, they have yet to get a straight answer. The de facto answer, given without reasons, is no.

God and Man at Yale

In 1790, Yale University's president, Reverend Ezra Stiles, wrote to a sick and dying Franklin imploring him to accept Jesus as Lord and Savior. In reply, Franklin refused to "dogmatize" on the subject of Christ's divinity, and playfully added that, anyway, he would know the truth of the subject soon enough.[13] Unlike Franklin's Penn, Stiles's Yale began as a sectarian school.

In 1951, however, young William F. Buckley Jr., a twenty-five-year-old Roman Catholic graduate of Yale, charged that Yale had slid past nonsectarianism to radical secularism. *God and Man at Yale* was Buckley's first book—he would later write many more and would eventually become known as the intellectual godfather of the country's post-1950 conservative movement—and it sparked a huge controversy. Most of the text is devoted to detailing how Yale at mid-century was straying, not from the Holy Gospels, but from the gospel according to Adam Smith. In economics and other courses, claimed Buckley, Yale faculty were criticizing capitalism, courting big-government biases, and selling socialism. But it was the forty pages of the book's opening chapter that triggered the strongest reactions. Therein he told how Yale was supposedly trashing its own religious traditions and adopting a new antireligious bias.

Buckley's book was not, however, a born-again brief for re-Christianizing Yale. His goals were rather more nonsectarian. Thus he wrote: "In evaluating the role of Christianity and religion at Yale, I have *not* in mind the ideal that the University should be composed of a company of scholars exclusively or even primarily concerned with spreading the Word of the Lord. I do *not* feel that Yale should treat her students as potential candidates for divinity school. . . . I think of Yale, then, as a *nondenominational* educational institution *not* exclusively interested in the propagation of Christianity."[14] What young Buckley questioned, however, was whether "academic activity at Yale tends to reinforce or to subvert Christianity," and he criticized "the orientation and direction given to students" in religion courses and "other courses that deal or could deal with religious values."[15]

In retrospect, the fascinating thing is how indignant Yale's defenders were at the mere suggestion that Yale and her sister elite universities were no longer true to their historically Christian heritage. For example, Yale insider McGeorge Bundy, then associate professor of government at Harvard, wrote what functioned as the university's official reply to the book. In *The Atlantic Monthly*, under the heading "The Attack on Yale," Bundy fumed that what young Buckley

> has done is to take the flimsiest of evidence or no evidence at all, and ignore whatever goes against his thesis. . . . He condemns as antireligious a teacher whose profoundly religious influence I myself know from classroom experience and personal friendship. . . . and quite without proof—he asserts the ineffectiveness of the saintly man who is Yale's chaplain. He makes no mention of the fact that not one of the ministers or chaplains at Yale, of any faith, agrees with his analysis; he never considers the generally agreed opinion of these and other observers that Yale is more religious than the rest of Protestant America and more religious than it was a generation ago.[16]

Several such Yale-endorsed rebuttals to Buckley were explicitly tinged with contempt for the fact that Buckley was a Roman Catholic. After making his claim that Yale was becoming "more religious," Bundy goes on to scold Buckley: "Most remarkable of all, Mr. Buckley, who urges a return to what he considers to be Yale's true religious tradition, at no point says one word of the fact that he himself is an ardent Roman Catholic. In view of the pronounced and well-recognized difference between Protestant and Catholic views on education in America, and in view of Yale's Protestant history, it seems strange for any Roman Catholic to undertake to define the Yale religious tradition. . . . It is stranger still for Mr. Buckley to venture his prescription with no word or hint of his special allegiance."[17]

In his critique of Buckley, Bundy had rich company. The then-prominent Reverend William Sloane Coffin, a Yale trustee, dismissed Buckley's book as "really a misrepresentation," a publication "distorted by his Roman Catholic point of view. Yale is a Puritan and Protestant institution by its heritage and he should have attended Fordham or some similar institution."[18]

These hyper-defensive responses by Yale's Protestant leading lights were elicited by a Catholic boy-author's first book arguing (or perhaps Bundy and company would say "pontificating") in favor of four level-the-playing-field points regarding religious pluralism in higher education:

1. Diverse religious viewpoints, including, but by no means exclusively, ones derived from the sectarian traditions of Yale and other schools, should be respected, not reviled, on campus.
2. Assorted evidence that Yale and other schools were on the way to losing their respective historic faith identities, and starting to promote antireligious biases in their stead, should be duly acknowledged.
3. Alumni who supported these schools on the assumption that they were intellectually balanced and fair toward religion should be prepared, if persuaded to the contrary, to let the administration and faculty know their displeasure.
4. Yale and other schools might before long become bastions of an orthodox secularism off limits to orthodox religious believers and expressly antithetical to traditional Judeo-Christian viewpoints and values.

In fact, virtually every major empirical work on the subject published since mid-century has done more to validate than to falsify Buckley's frets and predictions. From the early 1950s through the mid-1990s, many sectarian-born colleges and universities did, in fact, reduce or eliminate their respective ties to the particular denominations that founded them. By the late 1960s and early 1970s, many had, in fact, become strictly or radically secular.

Buckley had argued that every society "is confronted with value alternatives, as with atheism versus faith, collectivism versus individualism."[19] Most "universities," he observed, "have espoused . . . one value as opposed to another. Democracy as opposed to totalitarianism is an example. Democracy may not be truth, but so far as at least Yale University is concerned, it is the nearest thing to truth that we possess, so that while a faculty member is perfectly free to point out the limitations, defects, and weaknesses of democracy, as is right and proper, he is not privileged, at the margin, to advocate the abolition of democracy in favor of totalitarianism."[20]

But the leading colleges and universities, warned Buckley, were on the way to affording such rights in the name of "academic freedom," echoing the "absolute that there are no absolutes, no intrinsic rights, no ultimate truths," and denying outright "any intelligent conception of an omnipotent, purposeful, and benign Supreme Being who has laid down immutable laws, endowed his creatures with inalienable rights, and posited unchangeable rules of human conduct."[21] Buckley was equally perspicacious in predicting that, despite reports at the time that the country as whole was undergoing "a 'revival' of religion," neither ostensibly faith-friendly postwar trends in mass opinion, nor such of these trends as had supposedly "centered about the college campus," would reverse the trend at Yale or her sister schools.[22]

Buckley was right. Radical secularism, not nonsectarianism or nondenominationalism, ruled the higher education roost for much of the late twentieth century. But, over the last decade or so, Yale, Penn, and even, of late, fair Harvard have been developing more even-handed, pluralistic postures toward religion.

Faith and Reason at Harvard

In October 2006, a Harvard University curriculum committee recommended that every Harvard undergraduate be required to take at least one course in an area that the committee called "Reason and Faith." In a public comment on the Harvard proposal, Notre Dame University president John I. Jenkins and provost Thomas Burish noted that "Harvard is the drum major of higher education: Where it leads, others follow."[23]

The Harvard committee itself recognized that the university's students were part of an academy that had become, in the committee's own words, "profoundly secular."[24] As Jenkins and Burish explained: "For centuries scholars, scientists and artists agreed that convictions of faith were wholly compatible with the highest levels of reasoning, inquiry and creativity. But in recent centuries this assumption has been challenged and assertions of faith marginalized in, and even banished from, academic departments and university curricula."[25]

With respect to defining religion's role in higher education, a trinity of faith-friendly intellectual and civic trends—greater student interest, increased academic legitimacy, and enhanced legal protections—all bode well for leveling the academic playing field with regard to religion in ways similar to those being discussed at Harvard.

Most college and university students are interested in religion and spirituality. They live in a world where religion remains a vital force in domestic and international affairs. Moreover, most young Americans believe in God and consider religion indispensable to everyday life. For instance, in June 2006, Harvard University's Institute of Politics (IOP) reported on an IOP-sponsored survey of 1,200 college students, drawn randomly from a national database of nearly 5.1 million students. The survey found that 70 percent of college students say "religion is important or very important in their lives," a quarter say "they have become more spiritual since entering college," and only 7 percent say "they have become less spiritual" in college.[26]

Given how even the most competitive schools must now compete for students, it is likely that if students want more God talk, more religion courses, more opportunities to research religion, more on-campus outlets for religious instruction and worship, and more opportunities to volunteer in conjunction with community-serving religious organizations, national and local, then the schools will respond.

Various demographic and democratizing changes are driving this pro-religion churn on many campuses. Since young Buckley's days, Yale, Penn, Harvard, and other elite schools have democratized themselves to the point where class differences and distinctions have only quite limited (legacy-loving) salience. The same process has also racially diversified the campuses, bringing to them unprecedented numbers of low-income and working-class African American, Latino, and Asian American students, among other groups.

These low-income, working-class, and minority students are not, for the most part, eager to leave their racial, ethnic, or religious identities at the campus gates. For instance, the famous community-serving ministry of Boston's Reverend Eugene F. Rivers III was organized in the mid-1980s among Black Pentecostal Harvard undergraduate students. Today, the most active student religious groups at many top-tier schools are led by religiously committed minority students. In fact, the head of the Penn student activities council during the aforementioned row over its funding of a pornographic publication was an evangelical Christian.

Here are the makings of a multicultural and pluralistic ethos in higher education that empowers all religious believers—Methodists, Muslims, and Mormons, Jews and Jehovah's Witnesses—a new "political correctness" that will neither warmly empower nor wantonly exile religious beliefs, motivations, and lifestyles. There can be an on-campus religious identity politics that frees orthodox believers, among them young Black Baptists, Latino Pentecostals, and Korean Evangelicals, to live out their respective faith traditions as they choose, not keep them in the closet. As one intensive four-campus study suggested, the ethos of America's "de-centered, diverse, religiously tolerant institutions of higher learning is a breeding ground for vital religious practice and teaching."[27] This ethos fosters religious choice that is, in turn, a powerful force stimulating religious interest and enthusiasm on many college campuses today.

Reinforcing student religious identities and interest in religion is the growing academic respectability of religion and religious believers within the academy at large and particularly in the natural and social sciences. The radical secular conceit that "religion" is the enemy of "science" has become almost too tired and too silly to require rebuttal. The head of the international human genome project is a self-described orthodox religious believer in the Protestant tradition who rejects pseudo-scientific theories like "intelligent design," but embraces recent advances in physics, chemistry, and other fields while also defending so-called "theistic evolution."[28] Several dozen leading medical schools, including Harvard's and Penn's, have programs in spirituality and health. The programs are predicated largely on hundreds of scientific, peer-reviewed studies, some by religious believers (notably the late Dr. David B. Larson, an evangelical Christian), others not, that link various "faith factors" to a variety of physical and mental health outcomes, including prevention, recovery, and coping with chronic and serious illness.[29]

The social sciences are now teeming with statistical analyses, some by religious believers (including yours truly), some not, finding one or more of three different types of religious influences to be associated with significant increases in multiple pro-social behaviors.[30] For instance, in 2006, a National Academy of Sciences panel judged the empirical evidence on religion and crime sufficiently weighty to merit commissioning a Princeton-trained economist who previously taught at Harvard to do a special report on the subject in relation to prisoner reentry programs. "The opportunities for adding to our knowledge base," the report concluded, "are enormous."[31]

More generally, while there has been no beeline from the Vienna Circle to the Vatican, logical positivism and related epistemological creeds have fallen from intellectual grace, while assorted philosophies of science positing that "faith" and "reason" are not so plainly at odds (and may even, as in the Catholic intellectual tradition, be complementary), have gained ground. Simultaneously, scholars like Princeton's Robert George, a Catholic public law intellectual and moral philosopher, have revived interest in natural law doctrine and challenged "orthodox secularists" with arguments claiming that the doctrine's truth can be demonstrated with or without any reference to religious precepts or first principles.[32]

Or, rather than follow the ideas, one can follow the money to the conclusion that religion's academic respectability is on the rise. Fifteen years ago, few major foundations funded teaching or research related to religion. Today, many major foundations, not to mention numerous small to medium-sized ones, are pouring millions of dollars each year into religion-relevant activities in higher education. The John M. Templeton Foundation, the Pew Charitable Trusts, the Ford Foundation, and many others, both liberal and conservative, have begun to pump more money into campuses for faculty to research and teach, not preach, a wide range of topics related to religion.

In addition to strong student interest and growing academic respectability, public laws and policies are changing in ways that should encourage colleges and universities to refrain from religiously based discrimination against individuals and groups. Since 1996, various so-called charitable choice laws have been put on the federal government's books. Basically, these laws and related ones prohibit government and its administrative agents, including nonprofit organizations, from discriminating against religious individuals and groups. There are also various old and new religious freedom laws on the federal books, plus a host of recent executive orders forbidding government and its administrative agents to engage in religiously based discrimination in personnel, procurement, and other decision-making domains. Since 2001, there has been bipartisan talk in Congress of targeting such laws and regulations more strongly toward higher educational institutions.

Even financially mighty private schools like those in the Ivy League take money from Uncle Sam. By every indication, therefore, it will become increasingly incumbent upon all colleges and universities to play fair on religion. If they do not, then they will risk losing some of their federal and other public funding; lagging behind in "faith factor" and related professional research, teaching, and service ventures for which private funding is increasingly available; and, most sadly of all, needlessly alienating religious faculty, staff, and students who only want the same respect and support that most higher education institutions now reflexively afford to people of whatever other worldview or lifestyle.

Level Principles: "Good Will" toward "All Sects"

There are many faculty at Harvard and other Ivy League schools, including me, who would not be hired by a school like Calvin College or any number of other outstanding religious schools. I could not sign these schools' respective "faith statements" because I am a practicing Roman Catholic. Others on Penn's faculty could not sign the same statements because they are Jewish, Muslim, agnostic, or atheist. It is, however, the constitutional, legal, and ethical right of these religious schools—their boards, faculties, staffs, students, and alumni— to decide how or whether to take religion into account in hiring faculty, and to do the same in other institutionally self-defining matters.

Most Catholic colleges and universities have not restricted faculty hiring to Catholic co-believers. That has brought many great non-Catholic scholars and teachers to Catholic campuses, and has made these schools especially welcoming to people of all faiths and of no faith. But it has also been associated with a loss of Catholic identity at many Catholic institutions of higher learning. Thus, in terms of their institutional casts and characters, the top-rated Catholic colleges and universities in America today range from the highly Catholic to the nominally Catholic.

By the same token, colleges and universities that are not now religious in character, whatever their roots may have been, have the right to define themselves in whatever way their boards, faculties, staffs, students, and alumni decide they should be defined. But intellectual honesty and civic comity require that religion be treated fairly. That is, however, not always the case.

America today is a country in which about four in ten adults describe themselves as born-again or Bible-believing Christians. Yet elite nonsectarian schools like Penn have almost no faculty who describe themselves as evangelical Christians or orthodox Protestants. Thus students at these schools are in something of a political and demographic bubble; they rarely if ever encounter faculty members who are orthodox religious believers. None of these schools have secular "faith statements" to which faculty members must subscribe, but when someone like me (a politically centrist Catholic Democrat) passes for being a "religious conservative," they might as well have one.

Like institutionalized racism, institutionalized antireligious bias cannot be corrected simply by changing laws, policies, programs, funding flows, or outward signs of respect for diversity. Where religion is concerned, higher education's playing field can only be truly and completely leveled when more key decision-makers at places like Penn—which, again, is a genuine model of well-meaning progress in this regard—become even more willing to publicly reason about religion; to forthrightly defend any decisions or practices that betoken secular, not nonsectarian, principles; and, in particular, to discuss differences about religion's role in concert with people whose orthodox Christian, Jewish, Muslim, or other religious identities may be rare on campus, but are not rare either in the country at large or in much of the rest of the world today.

In a nonsectarian institution of higher learning, religion is not sacred. In those schools, only liberal arts learning, rational debate, and democratic civility are and ought to be sacred. Thus religious studies can and should be as critical as the scholars leading a particular course or research project deem necessary. For instance, while Catholics may not accept the Gnostic gospels, there is absolutely no reason for a nonsectarian college or university scholar who studies them to defer in the least to the Church's position or to apologize for not taking Catholic apologetics at face value. People with orthodox religious views are free to be a part of the nonsectarian higher education community, and they are free to dissent from the views held or decisions made by other members of the community. But the right to participate fully in the life of the community comes with academic duties that apply equally to all.

In nonsectarian higher educational communities, the right to dissent or debate on matters of religion entails the responsibility to converse in ways that translate private religious convictions into publicly accessible reasons. For instance, as a Catholic debating a nonbelieving colleague about some public policy issue with high moral salience (for example, the death penalty), I might feel that he or she is "invincibly ignorant," but I must give empirical, historical, or philosophical reasons to explain why I believe I am right and he or she is wrong. And, no matter how twisted (or worse) I may feel his or her conclusions to be, I must remain civil. The only coercion permitted is that supplied by rational argumentation. In the academy, insights are shared for the illumination of all and never for the purpose of inciting only some.

But what is good for the orthodox religious goose is also good for the secular liberal gander. In a nonsectarian institution of higher learning, anyone who thinks, talks, writes, or behaves in ways that result in discrimination, intimidation, or harassment against religious individuals or groups should be considered as being every bit as much in violation of the letter and spirit of school policies as anyone who discriminates, intimidates, or harasses individuals or groups based on race, ethnicity, gender, or sexual orientation. For instance, university administrators at any level who display bias against religious individuals or groups in curricular or extracurricular matters should be held no less strictly accountable than they would be if they displayed any other misplaced, unfair, community-corroding, and potentially illegal biases.

Of course, the line separating intellectually grounded critique from ideologically motivated attack, or that separating academic challenges to religious orthodoxies from political ones, can sometimes be hard to draw. And, in a nonsectarian college or university, the benefit of the doubt must go to the critics, not the defenders, of any given data, doctrine, or dogma.

For the higher educational playing field to be leveled with regard to religion and to stay level, we need more honest dialogue, greater mutual forbearance, and a reflexive willingness to do unto others what we would want them to do to us, especially when those "others" represent religious ideas and identities that one shares only weakly or not at all. This is the nonsectarian, not secular, legacy of Penn's founder Franklin who wrote on his deathbed that he had "ever let others enjoy their religious Sentiments . . . [including] those that appeared to me unsupportable and even absurd. All Sects . . . have experienced my good will . . . [and] I hope to go out of the World in Peace with them all."[33] To Franklin's embracing sentiments, every member of a nonsectarian, not secular, college or university community, at least when functioning as a member of that community, should say a sincere "amen."

John J. DiIulio Jr. is the Frederic Fox Leadership Professor of Politics, Religion, and Civil Society at the University of Pennsylvania and Director of the Program for Research on Religion and Urban Civil Society.

5

The Ideals and Diversity of Church-Related Higher Education

Douglas Jacobsen and Rhonda Hustedt Jacobsen

Visitors to one East Coast liberal arts college are informed that the steepled, churchly looking building in the center of campus was never a chapel. While the school was founded by a religious denomination, the reason for building this "chapel" was purely aesthetic: It would give the campus a more quaint and traditional look. At most church-related colleges and universities, however, the old chapel really did once serve a religious purpose, and many still use their chapels for worship or contemplation today. At other institutions the old chapel now serves primarily as a setting for alumni weddings, but students stream into a large sports auditorium for required chapel services several times a week. These very different chapel configurations are a visible sign of the amazing diversity that exists among the nation's church-related colleges and universities.

It is difficult to make generalizations about any group of institutions so varied, but one thing these schools share in common is the fact that religion is not only allowed on campus, it is typically promoted in some way. During much of the twentieth century— during the years when secularization was a dominant theme in higher education—many of these schools felt defensive about their religious connections, perhaps even a little embarrassed. As a result, some church-related colleges and universities severed their religious affiliations. But religion is no longer embarrassing, and church-related higher education is flourishing in our present postsecular age.

This essay examines the historic ideals that drive these schools and how religion impacts the education that takes place on their campuses.

The Demographics of Religiously Affiliated Higher Education

Religiously affiliated colleges and universities play a significant role in American higher education. In 2004 (the latest year for which information is available), more than eight million students were enrolled in four-year undergraduate bachelor's degree programs in the United States.[1] Nearly two-thirds of these students (65.7 percent) attended publicly funded schools and the other third (34.3 percent) attended private institutions. Approximately 40 percent of those enrolled in these private schools—more than one-eighth of the total undergraduate population and representing well over a million individuals in all—were students at religiously affiliated colleges or universities.[2]

Religiously affiliated schools tend to be smaller than their public university counterparts, so this one-in-eight student ratio translates into a significantly larger proportion when comparing institutions. In fact, one out of every three bachelor's degree–granting colleges and universities in the United States—768 out of a total of 2,345 institutions listed in the United States Department of Education college database—claims a religious affiliation (figure 5.1).[3] American colleges and universities supply their own information to this database and each one decides for itself whether to list a religious affiliation. In some cases, historical connection to a religious body may not translate into current affiliation. For example, both Baylor University and Bucknell University were

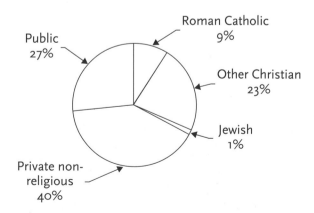

FIGURE 5.1. Distribution of Undergraduate Institutions by Religious Affiliation

founded by Baptists, but now only Baylor lists itself as religiously affiliated. Similarly, both Haverford College and Earlham College were founded by Quakers, but currently only Earlham describes itself as church related.

It is common today to describe the United States as a religiously pluralistic country. In fact, Diana Eck, who is director of the Pluralism Project at Harvard University, calls America "the world's most religiously diverse nation."[4] While that statement is true in the sense that virtually every religion on earth can now be found somewhere in the United States, it is also true that America remains a decidedly Christian place. This is reflected in the structure of religiously affiliated higher education. In terms of students, 99.6 percent of those attending religiously affiliated colleges and universities are enrolled at Christian institutions. In terms of institutions, 741 (96.5 percent) of the 768 religiously affiliated colleges and universities in the United States are Christian and the remaining 27 (3.5 percent) are Jewish. No other religions are represented. While there now are a handful of colleges and universities in America that have ties to other religions, no school describes that relationship as formal affiliation. Thus, for example, Soka University in Southern California says in its promotional materials that the school was founded on "Buddhist principles of peace, human rights, and the sanctity of life," but lists itself in the Department of Education database as religiously unaffiliated.[5]

This essay focuses specifically on "church-related" higher education, on the Christian colleges and universities that account for the overwhelming majority of religiously affiliated institutions of higher education in America. Our intention in adopting this focus is neither to marginalize the nation's Jewish institutions of higher learning nor to downplay the increasingly pluralistic nature of religion within higher education generally in the United States, and it is certainly not to encourage Christian hegemony. Rather, it is merely to acknowledge existing realities and to make clear that our observations apply only to the particular histories and contemporary challenges of Christian higher education in America.

Stereotyping Religious and Secular Schools

Americans live and breathe diversity, yet they long for simplicity. That longing for simplicity is reflected in the way people sometimes talk about faith and higher education using a bipolar frame of reference that ignores actual diversity. Their bipolar framework suggests that colleges and universities in America are either thoroughly religious or they are not religious at all. That is far from the truth—religion is present in many different forms and to varying degrees on public and private school campuses across the nation—but the stereotypes continue to be powerful.

It is this bipolar framework—extreme secularity versus extreme religiosity—that serves as the backdrop for Naomi Schaefer Riley's popular book *God on the Quad: How Religious Colleges and the Missionary Generation Are Changing America*. Describing the students who attend religious colleges and universities she writes:

> The 1.3 million graduates of the nation's more than seven hundred religious colleges are quite distinctive from their secular counterparts. And the stronger the religious affiliation of the school, the more distinctive they are. The young men and women attending the twenty religious colleges I visited in 2001 and 2002 are red [i.e., socially and politically conservative] through and through. . . . They reject the spiritually empty education of secular schools. They refuse to accept the sophisticated ennui of their contemporaries. They snub the "spiritual but not religious" answers to life's most difficult questions. They rebuff the intellectual relativism of professors and the moral relativism of their peers.

Riley calls them collectively the "missionary generation" and says their goal in getting a religion-based education is "to change the culture of Blue America from the inside out."[6] The juxtaposition is stark. Riley describes the schools she studied as being really religious; one might call them "religionist" institutions. By implication all the other colleges and universities in America are "secularist" wastelands.

Riley's book goes on to portray with considerable nuance the complex and fascinating realities that actually prevail at various religious colleges, but other commentators are happy to embrace the stereotypes. In fact, sharp distinctions between secularist and religionist alternatives are standard fare in the rhetoric employed by those who consider America to be embroiled in a culture war. Proponents on both sides of that conflict have a stake in keeping the distinction between faith and secularity as wide as possible in the culture at large and in higher education in particular. Examples are not hard to find. David Wheaton, a former tennis professional who is now a popular evangelical writer, speaks from the religionist side when he likens professors at mainstream colleges and universities to the serpent who tempted Eve in the Garden of Eden: "Just like their forefather, Professor Serpentine, they have rebelled against God and rejected His word. Their dismissal of, or in some cases their disdain for God, Jesus Christ, and the Bible spawns their ideology and fuels their cause—they want to dismantle your Christian faith and replace it with a biblically counterfeit worldview called humanism. . . . Your University of Instruction will turn into your University of Destruction. Guaranteed."[7]

Writing from the opposite ideological camp, the secularist Sam Harris has produced a best-selling book that calls upon thinking people everywhere to rise up and defeat the evil forces of religion. He assumes that religion is antithetical to human reason: "The central tenet of every religious tradition is that all others are mere repositories of error or, at best, dangerously incomplete. Intolerance is thus intrinsic to every creed. Once a person believes—really believes—that certain ideas can lead to eternal happiness, or to its antithesis, he cannot tolerate the possibility that the people he loves might be led astray by the blandishments of unbelievers. . . . On this subject liberals and conservatives have reached a rare consensus: religious beliefs are simply beyond the scope of rational discourse."[8]

Religionists and secularists both deal in stereotypes, and stereotypes often do have a kernel of truth imbedded in them somewhere. While there may be no genuinely secularist institutions in America (i.e., institutions where opposition to religion is an explicit goal), it is likely true that some faculty members at some colleges and universities actively seek to disabuse students of their faith. The same is true on the other side of the equation, where some schools embrace the religionist option. The recently established Patrick Henry College located near Washington, D.C., for example, describes its goal as "the transformation of American society" through the preparation of "Christian men and women who will lead our nation and shape our culture with timeless biblical values and fidelity to the spirit of the American founding."[9] The reason Patrick Henry makes news, however, is not because it is typical, but because it is not.

While there may be no such thing as a typical college, every institution of higher learning in America shares a commitment to reason and to some basic expectations and standards regarding the educational process. Church-related institutions share those commitments, but they pursue them in conjunction with respect for or fidelity to some specific religious tradition. Understanding the promise and perils of connecting faith and reason requires some familiarity with the long history of Christian higher education.

The Deep Roots of Christian Higher Education

The deep roots of American church-related higher education are in the medieval universities of Europe that came into existence during the eleventh through the fourteenth centuries. The emergence of these institutions signaled the end of the so-called "Dark Ages" when learning had been largely eclipsed.

Their rise was made possible by the reintroduction of various writings from ancient Greece and Rome (especially those of Aristotle) that had been lost in the West, but had been preserved by Muslim and Jewish scholars in North Africa, southern Spain, and the Middle East. Having regained that wisdom of the past, these universities sought to construct a complete and coherent understanding of reality by combining everything that humanity had discovered about the world with everything that God had revealed in the Bible and in Christian tradition. Pulling all these tidbits of knowledge together and using reason to draw out all the possible inferences, scholars toiled to produce a *summa*, or summation, of all knowledge both human and divine. Saint Thomas Aquinas is perhaps the best known of the many medieval university "scholastics" who worked on this task of using logic to bring together faith (understood to be the repository of accumulated Christian truth) and ordinary human knowledge.

But the scholastic ideal fell on hard times as the power of deductive logic came under attack and as unanimity about what constituted Christian truth dissolved. During the late medieval period, a new group of philosopher-theologians called nominalists suggested that, as a general guide to truth, careful observation of the world and simplicity of explanation were preferable to the often convoluted, complex, and sometimes seemingly counterfactual assertions of theologically informed logic. The universe did not always make logical sense—the world just *was*—and the task of scholarship came to be understood as the discovery of the world's quirks and anomalies as well as its beauty and order.

The second development that undermined the scholastic ideal was the Protestant Reformation of the sixteenth century. Protestants did not accept the Roman Catholic interpretations of God's revelations in the Bible and church tradition, and they began to formulate their own new versions of Christian faith. With the rise of various competing and to some degree contradictory understandings of Christian faith, it was no longer possible to speak of *the* Christian tradition. Now there were many traditions rather than one tradition, and attempts to summarize all knowledge human and divine were derailed by the lack of a preexisting Christian consensus. The best that scholars could hope for was a clear and relatively comprehensive view of reality that accorded with the teaching of one of the several Christian subtraditions that had emerged in Europe.

While this was a truncated ideal, it was enough to keep scholars busy for the next two or three centuries. Europe was largely segregated along the lines of religion, with one form of Christianity dominating in each locale (e.g., the Reformed Church in Holland, Lutheranism in Scandinavia, the Anglican Church in Great Britain, and Catholicism in most of southern Europe). The people of Europe were frequently at war with one another (and religion was a contributing factor), so it is not surprising that universities rarely felt compelled to look beyond the religious perspectives of their own local region. Surrounded by the like-minded, it was easy to assume that one's own viewpoint represented the fullest and best possible expression of religion, and this prejudice was sometimes reinforced by legal decree. In England, for example, dissenters (individuals who were members of Protestant churches other than the established Anglican Church) were not eligible for degrees from Oxford University, and that rule was not eliminated until 1866.

During the 1700s, however, a set of new philosophical and educational ideals began to percolate through Europe, and they slowly reconfigured faith, knowledge, and education. Taken together, these forces are known as the Enlightenment. The Enlightenment was a complex movement that assumed different forms in different European states, so that the English Enlightenment, for example, was led by moderate deists, many of them ordained clergy, while the French Enlightenment took a more radical and often explicitly anti-Catholic tone. Yet four convictions formed the basic core of all Enlightenment thinking: (1) more truth can be discovered than we know right now; (2) reason, and not authority, should guide the search for truth; (3) the search for truth is open equally to every rational human being; and (4) the purpose of education is accordingly not merely to transmit truth to a new generation, but to advance truth on all fronts even if this makes it harder to envision any overall pattern of unity in the structure of human knowledge. These convictions, however they were interpreted or applied, represented a massive challenge to older Christian conceptions of the university.

Newman's Vision

Writing from Ireland in the mid-nineteenth century, the Roman Catholic scholar and eventual cardinal John Henry Newman articulated a fresh understanding of higher education that combined these new Enlightenment ideals with the historic goals of the Christian university. His classic work *The Idea of a University*, first published in 1859, lines out the contours of a search for truth that welcomes the insights of everyone, allows faith a place in the dialogue, and preserves as much as possible of the old medieval ideal of the unity of all knowledge.

In keeping with the Enlightenment, Newman argued that the search for truth should be "free, independent, [and] unshackled" and, in addition, he suggested that religious authorities and others might, at times, need "to bear for a while with what we feel to be in error, in consideration of the truth which it is eventually to issue."[10] But in keeping with older medieval scholasticism, he also affirmed that ultimately all truth coheres and "we cannot separate off portion from portion, and operation from operation, except by a mental abstraction."[11] For Newman, God was part of that mix and he thought scholarship would be diminished in both scope and depth if God was ignored.

At the core of Newman's vision of the intellectual life was a rich and dynamic understanding of tradition, which he defined as the long, multigenerational process of exploring all the implications and ramifications of a complex idea. The unfolding of that process could itself be complex and sometimes convoluted: "At first no one knows what it is, or what it is worth. It remains perhaps for a time quiescent; it tries, as it were, its limbs, and proves the ground under it, and feels its way." But slowly, and with many incremental changes over time, tradition unfolded bringing new insights with it. Newman commented: "In a higher world it is otherwise, but here below to live is to change, and to be perfect is to have changed often."[12] Far from being a dead weight that slowed the growth of knowledge and insight, tradition was, for Newman, the dynamic force that prodded understanding forward.

Newman's vision of higher education is formidable. It makes the case that Christian colleges and universities ought to be places where inquiry is free and wide-ranging, where learning is holistic and interconnected, and where reflection is informed by a deep and lively sense of religious tradition. Virtually all contemporary church-related colleges and universities have adopted Newman's ideals to some degree. They have committed themselves to being places where genuine learning and unfettered inquiry can flourish alongside of and in dialogue with living traditions of religious faith and practice. But America is a very different place than Europe and it is necessary to examine the peculiar dimensions of American cultural, educational, and religious history before reflecting on the ways different religious traditions might interact with education at church-related colleges and universities today.

American Developments

Both faith and reason resonate differently in America than in Europe. When it comes to reason, Americans tend to value the practically minded more than the theoretical, and when it comes to faith, Americans generally prefer clear moral guidance to nuanced theological speculation. As a result, higher education in America has never been as elitist as in Europe nor has it been as grandiose in its claims. Whether the issue is either faith or reason, Americans want to know the practical implications; working out the theoretical kinks is not given the same priority.

Just as significant for church-related higher education is the fact that American religion is unfettered by government dictates or regulations. Americans can be members of whatever religions they choose. This commitment to religious freedom was remarkable from the start, and it remains so today. Equally remarkable is that America's religious diversity has never produced anything like the religious warfare that is part of European history. The notion of "friendly competition" may be a bit too upbeat, but it captures reality better than any war-derived metaphor. Religions compete in America, but they do not do battle. The diversity of church-related higher education in the United States is, in part, a result of that harmonious competition.

Religiously related educational pluralism and particularity were evident in America as early as the 1700s when Yale offered a staunchly conservative Puritan alternative to Harvard's growing liberalism and to Princeton's revivalist option. And then there were the Anglican schools, William and Mary in Virginia and later King's College (Columbia University) in New York, along with Ben Franklin's nonsectarian University of Pennsylvania in Philadelphia. The diversity was already significant before the nineteenth century when the religious composition of the country expanded and the church-related college market expanded with it. Methodists, Baptists, and Christian restorationists (like the Churches of Christ), along with many other Protestant denominations and a host of Roman Catholic religious orders, began planting colleges across the west almost as fast as Johnny Appleseed planted fruit trees.

Ethnicity often had as much to do with founding these schools as did religion. Dutch Reformed Christians founded Dutch-speaking institutions for the Dutch, and Norwegian Lutherans did the same for Norwegians. Literally hundreds of church-related colleges were launched during the nineteenth century, and almost all of them began as very modest endeavors, with perhaps ten or fifteen students meeting in a large old house at the edge of town and one or two not-very-well-credentialed "professors" in charge. But what was true of church-related schools was also true of other schools founded at the time: They all began small. Many of these schools did not survive, but the failure rate was probably less than 50 percent—not bad given their circumstances.[13]

Unlike today, there was no clear-cut distinction drawn during this time between schools that were religious or private in character and those that were public. In fact, it was rather typical for a church-related college "to petition a state legislature for some funding on the basis that it was a 'public' college."[14] While church-related schools were often launched with specifically religious purposes in mind, they usually thought of themselves as simultaneously serving the public good, and they opened their doors to all comers. Compartmentalization and specialization eventually increased, but until the end of the nineteenth century there was still a fairly fluid environment for all American colleges and universities.

Then, in the early twentieth century, a complex reconfiguration occurred in both the educational and the religious landscape. Higher education was transformed by the professionalization of the academy and the emergence of the modern university ideal. Being a college or, even more, being a university, became serious business. Wealthy patrons competed with one another over whose school was the greatest. Chicago, Cornell, Stanford, and other new universities vied with the older schools of the East Coast for prominence and acclaim. These "great universities" as a group were soon perceived as defining "real" higher education—and that education looked quite similar to how they did things in Germany. It was directed by scholars who had distinguished themselves by their academic accomplishments and not their faith, and the education these schools offered concentrated much more on the sciences and humanities than on religion. Religion was no longer assumed to be a first-order concern for any great university or college.[15]

At the same time, the modernist-fundamentalist controversy erupted in the church world, creating new religious tensions that cut across the older denominational divides. The core issue was straightforward. Various religious "modernists" had begun revising Christian doctrine in light of new scientific advances and scholarly ways of reading the Bible, and these modernist forays had prompted the formation of a "fundamentalist" opposition that saw any suggestion of doctrinal change as a form of apostasy. While this dispute was ignored by many people in the pews and while many church leaders wanted no part of either camp, the conflict had symbolic importance because it suggested that the grand complexities of American Christianity (at least in its Protestant forms[16]) could ultimately be reduced to a simple choice between liberal and conservative. That imagery was stark and in many ways unreflective of the continuing differences within religious groups, but it was compelling. Everyone from backcountry preachers to New York City journalists picked it up, and it became a common point of reference for defining religious and social developments in American culture.

The end result was that church-related colleges had to stake out their identities on newly professional educational turf as well as newly politicized religious turf. It was almost as if another act had begun in the play of American higher education, and the stage set had been rearranged. Many church-related schools tried to resist making any choices and to go on as usual. Others made a conscious decision to leave their religious roots behind, going with the flow of the increasingly secular norms of the higher educational mainstream. Still others opted to embrace their religious roots even more tightly and accept, however grudgingly, their diminished status within the academy. And in a host of different ways, other colleges tried simultaneously to honor the intellectual task while remaining religiously connected.

Contemporary Diversity

The diversity of church-related higher education in America today reflects both the older denominational identities of these schools and the different ways they have responded to twentieth-century developments—and that diversity is breathtaking. Table 5.1 displays some of this diversity in simplified form, but it provides only the broadest of brushstrokes.[17] For example, the Catholic label represents over fifty different religious orders along with other schools affiliated with local Catholic dioceses. The Baptist label is similarly simplified, clumping together American Baptists, Southern Baptists, National Baptists, General Baptists, Free Will Baptists, and Seventh-Day Baptists. All told, more than fifty distinct Protestant denominations are currently identified as having a formal affiliation with one or more schools, and in addition to these denominational schools, many others describe themselves as "multidenominational," "interdenominational," or "undenominational." Anyone reading the names of the largest schools affiliated with various Christian groups in America from Table 5.1 will immediately recognize that they represent a wide range of approaches to higher education. In particular, they have very different conceptions of what it means to be church-related and of how to connect faith with reason. Some of these schools have assumed that church-relatedness has to be described in clearly measurable terms such as mandatory chapel for students, statements of faith that faculty are required to sign, or strict codes of behavior that are enforced on campus. Yet religion can also exert its influence in subtle ways that are more qualitative than quantitative.

Richard McCormick, professor of ethics at Notre Dame, says, for example, that a great Catholic university is one that has some people on campus who "have assimilated Catholic culture so personally and deeply that their attitudes, habits, and values are thoroughly stamped by it." He describes these people as "walking symbols" of faith, winsome representatives of the school's religious identity. They are not pushing their faith on anyone; they are simply exemplifying it in their own personal lives. How many of these people are required in order for an institution to qualify as a "great" Catholic university? McCormick does not give a precise answer, but indicates that "it would be unrealistic to

TABLE 5.1. Church-Related Colleges and Universities That Offer Bachelor's Degrees

Religious Identity	Number of Schools That Offer Bachelor's Degrees	Largest Schools
Roman Catholic	**208** 28.1% of church-related colleges and universities 8.9% of all colleges and universities	DePaul University, IL St. John's University, NY Saint Louis University, MO Boston College, MA Loyola University Chicago, IL Fordham University, NY Georgetown University, DC Saint Leo University, FL Marquette University, WI Regis University, CO
Baptist	**106** 14.3% of church-related colleges and universities 4.5% of all colleges and universities	Baylor University, TX Liberty University, VA Mercer University, GA Campbell University, NC Wayland Baptist University, TX
Methodist	**95** 12.8% of church-related colleges and universities 4.1% of all colleges and universities	Duke University, NC Emory University, GA American University, DC Southern Methodist University, TX Hamline University, MN
Presbyterian	**58** 7.8% of church-related colleges and universities 2.5% of all colleges and universities	University of Tulsa, OK Arcadia University, PA Carroll College, WI Trinity University, TX Buena Vista University, IA
Churches of Christ/ Disciples	**52** 7.0% of church-related colleges and universities 2.2% of all colleges and universities	Columbia College, MO Texas Christian University, TX Pepperdine University, CA Chapman University, CA Harding University, AR
Lutheran	**43** 5.8% of church-related colleges and universities 1.8% of all colleges and universities	Concordia University, WI Capital University, OH Valparaiso University, IN Pacific Lutheran University, WA Augsburg College, MN
Other Christian affiliation	**179** 24.2% of church-related colleges and universities 7.6% of all colleges and universities	Brigham Young University, UT Brigham Young University, ID Indiana Wesleyan University, IN Azusa Pacific University, CA Ashland University, OH Biola University, CA Elon University, NC The University of Findlay, OH Olivet Nazarene University, IL Bob Jones University, SC

expect to find large numbers."[18] McCormick has confidence that a small number of truly saintly cxcmplars can season an entire campus with an aroma of faith that others will find inspiring and even enticing, and he would find it alarming and antithetical to faith were a college to stipulate specific rules of doctrine and behavior for its students.

Each church-related college and university has its own unique take on how best to pursue knowledge in a faith-seasoned environment. Some church-related schools believe it is their responsibility to actively advocate certain religious ideas and ideals, and they carefully craft curricular and cocurricular programs in that light. Other schools take a more neutral posture when it comes to inserting religion into the curriculum or other student programs. Most schools seek to combine these approaches, advocating religious commitments or values in some settings, while adopting a religiously neutral stance in other institutional endeavors.

It is important to note that schools that take a more neutral, hands-off approach are not necessarily being less faithful to their spiritual traditions. For some groups such as the Society of Friends (Quakers), it is a central tenet of their faith that religion must never be forced or coerced. For them, it would be inappropriate for a college or university to stack the religious deck. Their policy of religious neutrality communicates to students that they must decide for themselves what to believe without any official winks or nods from the school. Like many public universities and private nonreligious schools, non-advocatory church-related colleges and universities will have people on staff—chaplains, counselors, and other student life professionals—to provide students with unbiased information about religion and to assist students who find themselves embroiled in life-upsetting personal crises of faith. But outright advocacy would be antithetical to the institution's ideals.[19]

Religious Advocacy and Religious Neutrality

Defining and maintaining the ideal of religious neutrality can, however, be difficult. Does giving all religious groups the same support constitute being neutral, or can schools make reasonable judgments about which perspectives are welcome on campus and which are not? Would any school allow a religious group on campus that expressly preaches hate? Or what if an individual professor or other staff member begins to boldly advocate one particular religious or antireligious stance in the classroom? Should the school intervene and mandate neutrality? How does one prevent a religiously neutral approach from looking like it is simply not interested in religion at all? The questions can be multiplied. Neutrality is not as easy as it might first appear.

Neutrality may also, in some circumstances, be an impossible or even undesirable goal. Robert Orsi, professor of the history of religion at Harvard, points out that "it seems virtually impossible to study religion without attempting to distinguish between its good and bad expressions."[20] In our post-9/11 world, politicians, commentators, and people on the street, as well as college and university professors and administrators, routinely make distinctions between what they see as good and bad religion, or between what is more often called "true" religion and "extremist" religion. Who has not heard it said that "true" Islam is a religion of peace, and that Muslim "extremists" do not represent the real heart of this venerable tradition? Are such statements fully neutral? Of course, they are not. They recommend certain religious alternatives as superior to others and thus they are, in some sense, advocatory. Even those who are most committed to religious neutrality would likely have few qualms about this kind of modest advocacy.

But not all schools opt for neutrality. Some schools have decided that their calling is to be selectively and proactively advocatory, at least in some situations. Church-related colleges and universities are private institutions, and as private institutions they can legally advocate all sorts of things, including religion. Most church-related schools that engage in one or another form of religious advocacy acknowledge that ultimately faith is a personal choice and that religion cannot be imposed on anyone. But persuasion is not coercion. The presentation of one religious option in a manner designed to make it seem more attractive than other options is a form of persuasion. Schools taking a persuasive approach assume that college and university students are fully capable of assessing, and then either accepting or rejecting, whatever pro-religious perspective their institutions may want to advocate.

Religious advocacy can take many different forms. Some schools advocate very specific doctrines and religious rules of life; others focus on faith or values much more generally. Some church-related institutions ask their student life professionals to handle religious matters, trying to keep discussion in the classroom religiously neutral, while others think the classroom is precisely where religion ought to be addressed. Some religious colleges and universities restrict their advocacy to what takes place in theology or Bible classes; others think religion should be discussed across the entire curriculum. All of this can vary greatly in both content and intensity. Every church-related school has to make determinations about what is appropriate on its own campus based on its own particular religious tradition.

Tradition Enhanced Learning

Church-related colleges and universities are rooted in different traditions of faith and practice, and those differences are not inconsequential. Even at schools that are now only historically associated with some particular denomination or religious group, one can often still smell the lingering fragrance of that tradition on campus. For example, visitors to Swarthmore College, which no longer considers itself a Quaker school, might still detect a mix of peaceableness and feistiness on campus that seems distinctly Quakerish. The special contributions that church-related schools make to the broader academic enterprise—as well as the unique experiences they offer to students—are derived from these different traditions.

The word *tradition* is sometimes used as a synonym for religion, as when people speak of the Catholic tradition or the Jewish tradition or the Buddhist tradition. Tradition also describes the active process through which religions reproduce themselves over time and through generations. In order to keep these two notions clear, the religious historian Dale Irvin uses *tradition* for one and *traditioning* for the other. Traditioning involves "reinventing our traditions in order to make them relevant," and Irvin notes that "nothing less is at stake in this process than the meaning and identity of faith itself, for a truly irrelevant faith will soon die of its own irrelevance, and the identity of the community will pass into the arena of being a historical relic or part of the archive."[21]

Awareness of traditioning as a dynamic of religious faith is relatively new, at least among Christians. Until recently, "most Christians of the world have . . . assumed that both tradition and identity were given in an unambiguous manner."[22] But historical and postmodern perspectives have revealed the naïveté of that view. Traditions change and grow as they are handed down, branching and reconverging, advancing laterally and in depth, incorporating or actively rejecting insights from other traditions. But all is not chaos. Like a symphony that progresses through very distinct movements, but constantly reaches back to pick up early note sequences or syncopations, reincorporating them in new forms in the ongoing flow of the music, religions maintain their identities through traditions that creatively circle around a few key insights, mixing and matching those insights with an array of other new ideas, values, practices, and concerns that enrich the music and move the rhythm along.

It is these living traditions of faith, and not simple lists of doctrine and dogma, that enhance the education being offered at most church-related colleges and universities. This is where Newman's European vision of higher education as the tradition-informed search for knowledge begins to blend with the practical character of American faith and education. The goal is not to put strictures on what can and cannot be taught; the goal is to add something positive to the excellent education that every college or university in America seeks to offer and it is to make a practical contribution to the common good. Most church-related schools want to be involved in the growth of knowledge, and they also want to have a positive, practical impact on the world.

Schools that are rooted in the same religious tradition will likely share certain general approaches to education, but individual colleges and universities make adjustments as they respond to the particular needs and challenges of different constituencies. In the end, the schools may end up looking like very different institutions despite their shared denominational affiliation. Beneath the surface, however, one will likely find more similarities than are apparent at first glance since religious traditions have an abiding influence.[23]

Take the Lutheran tradition as an example. Martin Luther, the founder of Lutheranism, said that God is hidden in the world and that finding God almost always comes as a surprise. From the perspective of the Lutheran tradition, the world is a complex place where the deep truths of life are often buried underneath a welter of seemingly contradictory facts and assertions. Higher education in the Lutheran tradition comes with an expectation that truth is clothed in irony and overlaid with ambiguity. It follows that Lutheran schools often have exceptionally strong programs in the arts, music, history, and literature—academic disciplines that have the capacity to express the ironies and ambiguities of faith and life.

The Reformed tradition, harking back to the sixteenth-century Protestant reformer John Calvin, stresses the coherence of truth and its codifiable nature. Churches in the Reformed tradition, such as Presbyterians, assume that God has created a world where things operate decently and in order. Higher education in the Reformed tradition has accordingly given special attention to philosophy, trying to understand the logic of the world and the systematic structures of human thought. At Reformed institutions, one is likely to study not only science but also the philosophy of science; not only art, but philosophical aesthetics as well. And a business major might reflect on business as a way of life, assuming that it will contribute to the common good and not just to the individual's paycheck.

Schools that locate themselves in the Catholic Franciscan tradition or in the Protestant Anabaptist tradition are much more likely to direct student attention to addressing human needs. Saint Francis, who lived in the thirteenth century, devoted his life to serving lepers, the poorest of the poor, in northern Italy where he lived. Anabaptists, who have pacifist roots that go back to the sixteenth century, have been known for service to others (even their enemies) since the earliest years of their movement. It is not surprising that schools in these traditions emphasize fields of study like social work, psychology, and economic development, and they seek to inspire students who will undertake the often hard and almost always monetarily under-rewarded work of caring for those who need assistance.

Jesuit schools take their name from the Society of Jesus (the Jesuits), which was founded in the sixteenth century by Saint Ignatius Loyola. The Society of Jesus began as an order devoted to preaching the Christian gospel both in Europe and in foreign lands. As a preaching order, skills of communication and persuasion were essential; as missionaries, cross-cultural communication was highlighted. In more recent years, that cross-cultural concern is evident in emphases on global social justice. How can one communicate across cultures and not be touched by the misery of so many of the world's people? And how can one feel that misery and not seek to change the structures of the world that cause and perpetuate such pain and suffering? Many in higher education express concerns about justice, but students attending schools in the Jesuit tradition are likely to find that concerns about justice are deeply imbedded in the campus ethos.

In the mid-twentieth century, an emphasis on any religious tradition— whether Lutheran or Reformed, Franciscan or Jesuit—would have made little sense to most educational leaders. They would have seen religious tradition as almost by definition restrictive and sectarian, as something to shed or to move beyond as quickly as possible. But in recent years the notion of tradition as a potent—and often positive—force in human life and thought has been retrieved both within the academy and within the culture at large. It is assumed that no one operates from an entirely bias-free perspective, but rather that a person's life history, including participation in communities of tradition, will shape that individual's experience and interpretation of the world. Thus, it is now commonplace for scholars to acknowledge their location within a particular community of discourse when discussing topics that impinge on issues of meaning and purpose.

The gap between church-related higher education and mainstream nonreligious higher education has, in some ways, shrunk. Both kinds of institution value objective inquiry and critical rationality, and professors at both kinds of institutions may identify their particular communities of discourse. Leaders at church-related institutions usually recognize that tradition by itself is not sufficient, since higher learning requires an openness to new and even contentious viewpoints that may contradict or undermine prior affirmations. Most church-related colleges and universities are thus as committed to critical thinking and academic excellence as other schools, just as many public and nonreligious private colleges and universities are looking for ways to allow the discussion of purpose, meaning, values, and even faith into the classroom.

But the two domains have not merged. They continue to have different goals and they are circumscribed by different regulations regarding what is and is not appropriate. The tradition-informed instruction that is the stock-in-trade of many church-related colleges and universities would be clearly out of bounds at public institutions of higher learning where neutrality toward religion is the legal standard. Church-related schools have the freedom to experiment and to innovate in matters related to religion, and each of the 768 institutions that describe themselves as church-related has its own approach to higher education. In the process of making connections between a religious tradition and higher learning, some of them will produce environments that are less than hospitable to doubters and skeptics, and some of them will have little appeal to those outside of a particular religious community. Yet each one offers a distinctive educational alternative and together they provide important resources for understanding the variety of ways that living religious traditions and higher learning can interact.

Douglas Jacobsen is Distinguished Professor of Church History and Theology at Messiah College. **Rhonda Hustedt Jacobsen** is Director of Faculty Development and Professor of Psychology at Messiah College. They are coauthors of *Scholarship and Christian Faith: Enlarging the Conversation* (Oxford University Press, 2004).

6

Why Faculty Find It Difficult to Talk about Religion

Mark U. Edwards Jr.

Reticence about one's religious or spiritual convictions is the default mode today for most scholars in most secular colleges and universities—and even in some church-related institutions.[1] We faculty rarely mention our personal religious or spiritual convictions in our scholarship or teaching. Why not?

Most commonly religious academics say nothing because there is nothing to say; our personal beliefs are simply not relevant to the disciplinary matter at hand. We may have been motivated by our religious or spiritual convictions in selecting our field or in choosing our research topics. We may see research and teaching as a religious calling. Our religious or spiritual convictions may urge on us the requisite self-denial, diligence, and honesty needed to do such activities well.[2] But we commonly spend the bulk of our time—religious calling or not—on technical disciplinary activities. We read and explicate texts; we do careful and controlled experiments; we read and review the literature relevant in our field; we introduce young students to our discipline; and so on and so forth. Our explicitly religious concerns are not, or at least not directly, relevant.

Even if our religious or spiritual convictions do occasionally seem to have a bearing on our work, voicing these convictions may add only an autobiographical footnote to the scholarly or pedagogical task. After all, one does not have to be religious or spiritually inclined to, say, oppose some forms of human experimentation, to be morally critical when recounting the history of Nazism in Weimar

Germany, to raise questions about evolutionary psychology, or to find fault with Rational Choice theory. Other scholars may reach similar conclusions for reasons that have nothing to do with religious or spiritual conviction and everything to do with widely shared moral norms and with consideration of evidence, reasonable argumentation, and demonstrated results (even if these are often contested).

We may also be reluctant to bring up our religious or spiritual convictions because we're painfully aware of the unhappy history of discrimination, violations of academic freedom, and violent resolution of disagreements occasioned by religious traditions, and in the West especially by Christianity. Many elite research universities, steeped as they were in the pervasive Protestant ethos of America, discriminated against Jewish academics until well into the middle of the twentieth century.[3] Catholics were also suspect because they were thought to owe allegiance to what many liberal Protestants and secularists saw as a dogmatic, authoritarian, and "un-American" faith.[4] A similar history can be traced regarding the ways in which people of faith, sometimes within the academy but more often outside, have tried to limit academic freedom in the name of religious conviction.[5]

But history is history: What about now? What about cases where religious perspectives arguably are germane to what we do and might conceivably advance the scholarly or pedagogical agenda? Why are so many of us still reluctant to talk about religion? To understand the deep inhibitions the American secular academy has about explicitly religious discourse, we need to understand the power that the modern academic disciplines exercise as institutions and as intellectual projects.

The Origins and Character of Disciplinary Scholarship

Higher education today, indeed the academy as a whole, is structured along the lines of the modern academic disciplines. With the explosive growth of knowledge in the modern world, no one could any longer master the entire scope of human knowing. In response, a division of labor evolved within the academy that broke up the formerly unified scholarly task into a variety of smaller, more manageable fields of study. With time, those divisions hardened into the modern disciplines as we know them today, with each discipline slowly developing its own procedures, vocabularies, and theories that seemed specially pertinent to its own specific area of research and teaching. This same process also constituted the different disciplines as communities of practitioners who held one another accountable to the norms and standards of that discipline, so much so that how one approached a subject of study became as definitive for the disciplines as the subject matter being studied.

Many of today's modern professional disciplinary communities also arose as alternatives or even rivals to the religious communities of the nineteenth and early twentieth centuries with their seemingly antiquated ways of knowing. The disciplines championed modern rational and empirically verifiable means of finding truth. The goal was to explain the world as it is and as it had come to be without recourse to either mystery or miracle. Within the disciplines, God thus eventually became methodologically and interpretively unnecessary, regardless of the religious faith or lack of faith of the scholar involved. The natural sciences were first to take this path, with the social sciences and humanities quickly following suit.

During much of the nineteenth century, natural science's status within American colleges and universities had depended on its close association with Christian theology.[6] Above all, science provided evidence of design. Assuming that God had created the human mind in the image and likeness of the divine rationality, it was further assumed that the study of science disclosed the rationality with which the creator had endowed the creation. That assumption allowed and encouraged many scientists (many of whom were devoutly Christian), between the years 1830 and 1870, increasingly to limit their explanations of natural phenomena to "secondary causes" within nature itself rather than appealing to divine intervention from beyond nature. With time, the appeals to supernatural explanations diminished and finally disappeared altogether. In effect, what constituted an explanation of the world had changed. Now if scientists were unable to account for some natural phenomenon, their response was not to invoke God but to pursue further scientific inquiry. By 1870, most scientists had come to assume that all natural phenomena were amenable to naturalistic description and explanation even though many of them remained personally religious.

About the same time that these naturalistic assumptions were sweeping the field in the natural sciences, scholars of what might be termed the "human sciences" also began to declare their autonomy, in this case not so much from religion directly as from moral philosophy.[7] During most of the nineteenth century, moral philosophy was seen as the capstone of a collegian's education. As the Harvard moral philosopher Francis Bowen put it, moral philosophy was "a general science of Human Nature, of which the special sciences of Ethics, Psychology, Aesthetics, Politics, and Political Economy are so many departments."[8] It sought to pull together all that the student had learned in the set curriculum of the day and arrange it into a coherent Christian system of knowledge and duties. Moral philosophy focused on human motives and obligations, the social relations of human beings, the harmony of nature and scripture, the agreement of natural science with human morality, and the unity of the true, the good, and the beautiful. As an indication of its crucial integrative function, the yearlong course in moral philosophy, usually required of all seniors, was commonly taught by the college's president, who often was an ordained minister.

Over against this Christian moral understanding of human character and responsibility, the emerging social science disciplines of history, psychology, political science, economics, sociology, and anthropology allied themselves with the much more objective and empirical orientations of the natural sciences. They did so for two reasons. First, they had already largely come to share the conviction that the scientific method provided the surest avenue to attaining truth, and second, they wanted to acquire for themselves some of the prestige the natural sciences had accrued. The new human sciences quickly adopted a rhetoric and methodology that was rigorously naturalistic and, by the turn of the century, psychologists, sociologists, and anthropologists were employing their scientific methodologies to understand even religion itself in naturalistic terms.

Concentrating on the discovery of causal relationships and agents of change, social scientists became resolutely empirical even as they sought to discover "laws" of social behavior. During the Progressive Era, they often conjoined their zeal for scientific advance with a conviction that scientific progress would drive social improvement. The prediction and control promised by the scientific method would be put to service for social engineering. By the 1920s, the younger social scientists had embraced the "value-free" model of objective science. While they continued to see social utility arising from their research, they professed that a value-free approach was crucial to making their results socially useful.

Finally, even the humanities declared their independence from religion. Drawing on the long history of classical, liberal education (with its often conflicting functions), the predecessor courses to today's classes in the humanities hoped to promote Christian character by requiring students to read the classics, which were seen as "edifying" texts. In the early decades of the twentieth century, however, humanists began to champion a different kind of character formation. Instead of focusing explicitly on Christian themes, the goal was largely redefined to focus on general human refinement and familiarity with the highest achievements of Western culture. The arts, literature, and thought of Western civilization now became the core, and a new canon of "great books" in a sense replaced the Bible as the icon of cultural literacy. The so-called "culture war" of our own day with its "battle over the canon" draws, in an often confused and ironic way, from these earlier developments.[9]

Between the end of the Civil War and the onset of World War I, these new academic fields of study underwent yet another shift, becoming both increasingly specialized and increasingly professionalized as new ways of thinking about the world gave rise to new social arrangements within the world of scholarship and higher education.[10] Knowledge was exploding within the new disciplines and it was becoming obvious that it was impossible for anyone to be familiar with everything that was known and all the ways such knowledge could be acquired, even within a relatively limited field of study like biology or sociology or history. The enterprise of knowing the world necessarily became a community project, for only a community, through its many members, could encompass all the burgeoning knowledge and multiplying techniques for advancing knowledge. Specialization had become part of the natural sciences decades earlier, but specialization in the social sciences and humanities also began to create new disciplines and subdisciplines within their ever-expanding fields.

Each of these new academic subunits would eventually become the provenance of specially trained researchers—professionals—who were expected to tend their field alone and to let other fields be worked by scholars who were specially trained in those fields. No longer could a faculty member roam over whatever range of topics might attract his or her intellectual attention; the disciplinary scholar derived his or her authority by specializing in one clearly defined subject. This specificity of expertise, in fact, came to distinguish the academic professional from the wide-ranging amateur or dilettante who would have been seen as hopelessly unfocused by members of the new disciplinary guilds.

Increasingly, these disciplinary professionals were mentored and trained in only a handful of research universities. These top universities took the responsibility of ensuring that young scholars-in-training learned their fields thoroughly and imbibed both the methodologies *and the attitudes* that were proper to each of their professional fields of study. Intellectual "master pieces," known as dissertations, became means of certifying that these budding specialists were fit to join the lower ranks of the disciplinary guilds. By the end of the nineteenth century, the status conferred by the PhD was fast becoming a requirement for scholars wanting to become members of the faculty at most of America's colleges and universities.

Outside of and around the school structures of higher education, these new disciplinary professionals also began to organize themselves into academic

associations. They founded scholarly journals, they planned annual conferences to meet with one another and facilitate communication, they articulated
a range of professional standards that allowed members of each discipline to
evaluate one another and police the field, and they developed a number of new
practices (such as the scholarly footnote and the literature review) that allowed
them to acknowledge one another as fellow practitioners who understood the
inner workings of their specific academic community and who were contributing to the field. As professionals, they also asserted the right of self-regula-
tion (resulting in the American notion of "academic freedom") since no one
else was qualified to judge their work. By such means, each disciplinary field
constituted itself as a professional community, crafted ways to distinguish
itself from other disciplinary communities, and devised ways to maintain the
particular academic goods, standards, and practices that were deemed essential
to that discipline.

The Impact of the Disciplines Today

What is the legacy of this "disciplinization" of the academy for faculty as
professionals today? In contemporary American higher education, most of us
who are scholars entered into our disciplines through a lengthy process of
professional formation that profoundly affected how we see ourselves, what we
believe, and how we behave. This has a direct and important bearing on our
willingness to allow any explicitly religious perspectives into our scholarship or
teaching. We are members of a discipline, and for most of us, religion falls well
outside our self-defined spheres of expertise. To talk about religion, then,
would be to transgress the boundaries and standards of specialized excellence
that undergird our professional lives. It would run the risk of undermining the
most basic support structures that sustain our status as scholars. To understand
the threat that talking about religion represents, we need to recognize the depth
and breadth of the disciplinary formation we undergo as scholarly professionals.

The typical stages in academic professional formation look something like
this.[11] Our apprenticeship often begins in the undergraduate years, when we
choose a major, take courses within the major, begin entertaining the thought
that we might want to become professors ourselves, and are, perhaps, encouraged by our professors to continue on to graduate school. We learn by
observing our faculty role models and by doing research tailored to our novice
status. Our self-identity is shaped in the process. We begin to describe ourselves to others and to ourselves as a such-and-such major, and we imitate in

small ways the behaviors and convictions of full practitioners in the field. We feel satisfaction as we begin to exhibit the skills and values that constitute the disciplinary practice. Increasingly, our continuing progress within the field requires not only intellectual engagement but also emotional commitment; we come to care about what we're learning and we find that such caring motivates us to learn more.

In graduate school, this process continues and intensifies. During this advanced stage of apprenticeship, we learn how to discriminate between good academic practices and bad. We do this by reading our discipline's literature, becoming familiar with its paradigmatic stories, and by watching master practitioners: our mentors and teachers. And, of course, our firsthand experience is also part of the process. Gradually we become fully acculturated into the discipline and are then given relatively controlled opportunities to take part in the actual work of the field, researching and teaching under the tutelage of senior colleagues who suggest ways to improve and who critique our work when necessary. At first, most of us operate by following rules and maxims, but with time we develop a more intuitive sense of what is required. Sometimes we become, at least figuratively, journeymen and journeywomen through stints as post docs or teaching assistants. Later we continue our supervised development through probationary periods as instructors and assistant professors. Finally, as we master the field, we come to see and know and do our scholarship and teaching with a style that is clearly our own and yet still conforms to the hallowed traditions of our disciplines.

Even after achieving tenure, however, we still look forward to more: to another book or to more articles—to our masterpiece—which will finally show our disciplinary superiors that we are qualified to enter the ranks of being a full professor. And even after obtaining that goal, we continue to compete with other professionals in the field for grant funding, status, and choice positions at desired institutions. In a real sense, our professional formation never ends. As we move through the stages from apprenticeship to mastery and even to the status of respected definers of our fields, we become ever more identified with and emotionally invested in our disciplines. We come to think of ourselves— and others see us and treat us—as historians or chemists or sociologists.

Even as we seek to advance our own discipline through new approaches, new discoveries, and new interpretations or explanations, we internalize ever more deeply the traditions that have been handed down to us, and we use them as means of measuring our accomplishments and as springboards for further work. We make our discipline's take on its particular aspect of the world our own second nature, and that grafted-on nature opens up some forms of knowing but closes down others. We acquire a disciplinary *orientation* that shapes how we see, understand, and experience the subjects we study and, to the extent that this disciplinary orientation spills over into how we see and understand the world at large, it shapes who we are as persons.

In sum, the disciplinary communities we are part of as academic professionals represent powerful and coherent, if not necessarily always complete, ways of construing ourselves and our world. In this, the disciplines are very much like religious traditions and because of that we feel tension between the two. It is not just that talking about religion extends us beyond our spheres of expertise, which it does; religion also presents itself as an alternative that is potentially in competition with our disciplinary identity. Religions and disciplinary communities both select what they see and do not see; what they value and do not value; what they consider important and real and what they consider unimportant or perhaps even imaginary. They can both exhibit tendencies toward totalizing explanations, overlooking data that do not fit or dismissing interpretations that do not comport with their own views. And most religious and disciplinary communities form their members in ways that make it hard for anyone to be truly comfortable in both kinds of communities at the same time.

So, why would anyone try? Given the history of conflict and discrimination, and given the alternatives to religious ways of knowing that have been created by the various academic disciplines, why would anyone be tempted to allow explicitly religious perspectives back into scholarship and teaching? And if someone was so tempted, how could that person possibly explain such a sentiment to the many disciplinary colleagues who would be appalled by the idea? Why not simply keep the two apart? Why not relegate religion to the purely personal realm and bar it from the academy? Why try to talk about religious beliefs at all? Why? Because things have changed and it is no longer nearly as easy to keep faith and scholarship apart—especially for our students—and perhaps it is no longer as necessary.

What Has Changed?

During the last half of the twentieth century, the WASP hegemony over American higher education finally came undone. Faculties and student bodies became more diverse ethnically, socially, and religiously. A first response to the increasing diversity at American colleges and universities following World War II was secularization: Diversity forced the dismantling of any remaining vestiges of Protestant cultural supremacy. That secularism, in turn, increased the level of security felt by most minorities who always have to cope with majoritarian expectations. Finally, perhaps ironically, this new mixture of diversity and secularity has opened up a safe space where religious individuals (who now feel increasingly like minorities on campus) can once again go public with their religious convictions in ways that formerly would have been impossible, but that are now allowable within the secular diversity of campus life.

What has also changed is the heady confidence with which the twentieth century began—namely, that reason and the scientific method were the sovereign means for understanding the natural and social worlds. This older confidence has given way to newer, more provisional claims and greater awareness of the limits to human knowledge. In the present context, it is hard to see how the kind of objectivity that once seemed to set scholarship apart from the subjectivity of religion can be reconstructed.

Recall the history of how the intellectual content of religious belief and practice were formerly held up to "scientific" standards and judged deficient, and how, after that, moral claims similarly fell victim to rising scientific realism. Scholars in both the natural and social sciences eventually advocated "value neutrality" as the way forward. Religious claims to (dogmatic) truth and moral insight yielded to uncertainty and doubt, and growing uncertainty about religion reinforced the scholarly notion that religion was properly a private matter.

But the unraveling of easy certainties was not to be confined to the religious sphere alone. The critical tools that formerly undermined dogmatic religious claims have in recent years been turned on reason and the scientific method themselves. In many disciplines, confidence in the scientific method and detached reason, along with the related notions of objectivity and value neutrality, has waned as the rational and scientific approaches of earlier times have proved incapable of delivering all they had promised. Romantic and postmodern reactions have now complicated knowledge claims to the point where space has opened up for a dizzying range of alternative perspectives, from "intellectually fulfilling atheism" (biologist Richard Dawkins) to "warranted Christian belief" (analytic philosopher Alvin Plantinga).[12] Although the default assumption—at least on the coasts—remains that true intellectuals and scholars are not religious, the actual state of affairs is now far more complex. And, even on the coasts and in research universities, religious and spiritual academics are coming out of the closet.

Finally, there's the larger world where religious convictions and practices are now shaping political, economic, and social life in ways thought impossible not very long ago and with enough force that even those in the ivory tower cannot ignore them. And if national and international developments are not compelling enough on their own, more and more students are bringing their religious convictions and practices directly on campus and into the classroom. Many evangelical Christian students, in particular, have been socialized into political activism and they are becoming increasingly more vocal, but Muslims (of varying stripes) and members of other historically non-Western religions also proudly and publicly display their religious identities on campus. Religious conviction bursts through attempts to confine it to chapel services, dorm room discussions, and topical courses.

In these changing circumstances, the default mode will no longer do. After all, reticence is not the same thing as absence. Not mentioning religious convictions does not make them go away. They still wield influence, but perhaps without appropriate examination, discussion, and compensating adjustment. In other words, if the academy and the scholarly disciplines continue to ignore religion, they may be ill serving both faculty and students. For faculty in general, but especially for faculty who are religious, the current situation requires a reexamination of whether or not and in what circumstances it might be appropriate, allowable, or perhaps even necessary to talk about religious beliefs and practices within the academic context.

How Should We Proceed?

There are two separate, but not unrelated issues that present themselves. The first issue has to do with autobiographical self-disclosure on the part of faculty members: What, if anything, should faulty members say about their religiosity or their antipathy to religion? The second issue focuses on the curriculum much more directly: Is there a place for matters that have traditionally been relegated to faith or spirituality (issues such as metaphysics, morals, and what it means to be human) in the disciplinary classroom?

Faculty Self-Disclosure

In various seminars I have run at colleges and universities around the country, I have asked faculty whether any of them ever mention their religious convictions in class and, if so, why. It turns out that many faculty who are personally religious do tell students something about their own convictions for what they see as good pedagogical reasons. One example involves a political science professor who explained that in introducing a discussion on public policy regarding welfare, she always starts with a confession to her students that attending Catholic Mass is her secret "vice," and so, not surprisingly, her Catholicism informs her views on appropriate policy.

Asked why she does this, she explained: First, it lets her students know where she is coming from, and she thinks that is crucial information when dealing with welfare policy. Second, by disclosing her own religiously informed perspective, she invites students to reflect on their own commitments and how these commitments influence their views. She went on to add that self-disclosure of this sort requires a deft hand, perhaps a bit of disarming humor, and, most important, a willingness to entertain and encourage alternative perspectives.

In the subsequent conversation, colleagues from several different disciplines commented on this strategy and its potential pitfalls. Faculty members from the natural sciences were generally not convinced this strategy would be useful in their classes. One chemist, however, shared how she introduces the concept of "green chemistry" in her physical chemistry classes. Her pedagogical goal is for students to value innovative chemical technologies that reduce or eliminate the use or generation of hazardous substances in the design, manufacture, and use of chemical products. She typically disclosed some of her own personal, religious commitments regarding the environment as a means of getting the students to engage questions about the morally responsible use of chemical knowledge.

A physicist from another school said that he let his students know in passing that he was an evangelical Christian. He said he normally didn't elaborate on this statement, although he indicated he was willing to discuss it with students outside of class if they were interested. His primary goal, however, was simply to let his students know that at least one evangelical Christian (newscast stereotypes to the contrary) did not find a deep commitment to science and the scientific method to be in conflict with equally deep religious convictions. This generated a great deal of discussion in the seminar about whether science and religion actually are compatible and I suspect that not many minds were changed. By the end of the discussion, however, most of the faculty had a more nuanced understanding of the issues involved.

Of course, self-disclosure can sometimes inhibit pedagogical goals rather than advance them. Such self-disclosure by faculty can make students feel uncomfortable or even coerced, and the power differential between faculty and students in the classroom makes this a valid and serious concern. The green chemist said that a few students in her class had complained in their course evaluations about the fact that she had brought what they termed her "liberal politics" into a science class. Others took issue more specifically with her religious perspectives.

Clearly this is tricky ground and restraint is in order, but if we fail to discuss or even mention the role that deep personal convictions may play in career choices and our scholarly work, we may be tacitly encouraging our students to conclude that they don't have to worry about such things. Indeed, we may be forgoing a splendid opportunity to illustrate how hard it is for scholars to identify their own subjective inclinations and to compensate for any improper effects those inclinations may have on our work. We may also be fooling ourselves or misleading our students about how fair and objective we really are. Sometimes, for some faculty, the best reason we can honestly give for why we approach a particular issue in some particular way is, frankly, because of our religious convictions. In such cases, why not simply say so? To pretend otherwise may be disingenuous and unhelpful to the task of advancing understanding and knowledge.

Religious Questions Related to the Subjects We Teach

It seems to me that when the subject matter of the course itself raises questions that either border on or overlap with some of the traditional concerns of faith, then it might be appropriate or even required to invite religion into the classroom. In particular, religious traditions (and most spiritual worldviews) have a stake in how a person: (1) thinks about morality, (2) understands maximally comprehensive reality (i.e., metaphysics), and (3) understands what it means to be human. These three broad topic areas do not exhaust the sorts of convictions that characterize religious communities, but they do capture crucial areas where religious or spiritual convictions bear on interpretations advanced within the modern American academy. The first two areas—morality and metaphysics—arguably transcend strictly disciplinary considerations and therefore do not necessarily conflict head-on with any particular discipline. Claims about the nature of being human, however, raise greater direct challenges since they often involve not only moral and metaphysical claims but also empirical questions that fall properly within the domains of various disciplines.

In the brief compass of this essay I can only gesture at the types of arguments that may be necessary to secure a relaxation of the many disciplinary bars against explicitly religious considerations—much more could be said, and has been said elsewhere[13]—but some simple laying out of the issues may be helpful.

Moral Claims: Consider that scholars or teachers often make moral or ethical judgments about what should be studied or about the use to which scholarship should or should not be put. They also occasionally advance moral claims within the subject matter itself. Are such moral or ethical judgments appropriate? And if so, is it appropriate to identify the basis for the judgment as religious, if that is, in fact, the case for the faculty member advancing the claim? Does doing so violate the standards and practices of the discipline?

Moral claims draw on moral intuitions, maxims, and practices of moral reasoning shared by the larger society of which the academic discipline is but a part. What should be at issue, then, is not whether religious or spiritual claims are appropriate in terms of the standards and practices of the disciplinary community, but rather whether religious or spiritual claims meet the standards appropriate to the broadly encompassing community of moral inquirers in which disciplinary professionals have no particularly privileged position.

Not that moral questions have nothing to do with disciplinary standards or practices. When moral reasoning concerns disciplinary practices, the disciplinary domain will provide the context and grounds on which the moral reasoning proceeds. Consider, for example, debates over the morality of embryonic stem cell research. A microbiologist can specify when an embryo is likely to first experience sensations, but cannot, on the basis of his or her specialized knowledge, specify that an embryo is (or is not) a human life with full moral status when it has achieved this stage. Others have as much right to argue this point as the biologist, and whatever view on this issue is advanced, it must be argued by keeping in mind the (to be sure, contested) goods, standards, and practices of the larger community (or communities) of moral inquirers.

A critic may, of course, attempt to limit a discipline's membership in this encompassing community of moral inquirers. He may assert, for example, that the generally accepted disciplinary standards distinguish between facts and values and bar certain questions of value (that is, moral questions) in properly formed disciplinary arguments. Much could be said about this, starting with whether the fact-value distinction is even cogent given what we now know about situated human reasoning. Be that as it may, moral disagreements tend to arise in a discipline when considering disciplinary *practices* or when expressing a judgment about the *behavior or moral beliefs of those one is studying* (say, in history or anthropology). When making moral judgments about the behavior or beliefs of those we are studying, the scholar will be expected by colleagues to be sensitive to the considerations and associated literature within each discipline regarding cross-cultural understanding and judgments—a set of standards and considerations that developed over the years, in no small part, through engagement with the larger community of moral inquirers.[14] And in any case, at this point, we're discussing the cogency, soundness, and appropriateness of particular moral judgments, not whether religious or spiritual claims have any role to play. Arguments are resolved on the merits.

Metaphysical Claims: Scholars in the natural sciences and social sciences occasionally confuse science with metaphysics (or at least that branch of metaphysics that concerns itself with a maximally comprehensive view of reality). In short, they draw conclusions that exceed science's grasp. For example, a biologist may confuse methodological naturalism (which assumes that scientifically adequate explanations for a natural biological phenomenon are to be supplied by causes and factors that do not refer to the divine) with metaphysical naturalism that denies "that there exists or could exist any entities or events which lie, in principle, beyond the scope of scientific explanation."[15] In weighing this metaphysical (and nonempirical) claim, the scholar who is religious or spiritual may wish to point out that metaphysical naturalism is an assertion of philosophic opinion rather than a statement of fact, scientific or otherwise, and is not subject to scientific proof or disproof. To make this limited point, the scholar can simply draw attention to the unwarranted move from methodology to ontology. He or she may, however, want to go further and offer an alternative metaphysical view, one derived from religious or spiritual commitments.

A critic may reply, and with considerable historical justification, that in modern American higher education, the naturalistic comprehensive scheme *is* the accepted scheme according to which such disputes must be resolved. While having past practice on its side, a blanket assertion such as this raises the question *why* religious or spiritual alternatives should continue to be banned, especially given today's highly diverse and pluralistic academy. If the objector is willing to engage this question, discussion and argument may proceed on the relative merits and demerits of the contending schemes and their proper role in higher education.

Claims about Human Being: Issues of morality and contending metaphysical schemes all come together in (often hotly contested) views of human nature. For example, various social sciences such as psychology and economics may base their theoretic edifice on assumptions about "human nature" and "human flourishing" that are contested by various religious and spiritual traditions. These assumptions—for example, the model of the rational, self-interest–maximizing human being that underlies many economic models, or the assumption underlying some theories of psychology that psychological health consists largely in individual self-development and self-expression—may be "givens" within their respective field (or subfield). Even so, such assumptions are rarely empirical generalizations or tested propositions. Rather, they reflect a particular set of values that may not be shared by religious or spiritual traditions.

Various assumptions underlying metaphysical naturalism also bear directly on human being: the status of values, norms, and moral claims; the putative existence of minds and the more contested existence of souls; the compatibility of deterministic understandings of how nature works with assertions of free will and associated responsibility. Most religious traditions will contest only reductive explanations in the human sciences that explain human experience, including assertions of purpose, value, or meaning, solely in terms of underlying neurology or evolutionary selection.

To argue about morality or metaphysics takes the scholar outside his or her disciplinary community into new encompassing communities with their own standards and practices. Yet much that is asserted about human beings may give rise to legitimate inferences that can be tested empirically or subjected to rational scrutiny or both. When generalizations lead to testable hypotheses or rational inquiry, I see no reason why the appropriate disciplinary standards and practices should not apply, whether the generalizations arise from religious or spiritual claims or from, say, interpretive schemes that arose out of the European and American Enlightenments.

Conclusion

For reasons we've rehearsed, and others, there may well be sound and defensible grounds for introducing some highly select, explicitly religious or spiritual claims into classroom lectures or discussions. We may wish to disclose where we are "coming from" and encourage similar self-awareness in our students. We may want our students to be aware of certain moral, metaphysical, or anthropological issues in our discipline that are religiously contested and what the religious alternatives may be. (This is sometimes termed "natural inclusion." By natural inclusion, philosopher Warren Nord and other commentators mean that "courses...that deal with religiously contested issues should at least acknowledge the existence of the religious alternatives and engage them in conversation."[16]) In offering religious self-disclosure or practicing natural inclusion, we may well find ourselves bending (or breaking) our discipline's standards and practices regarding religion in various ways, and some colleagues will undoubtedly object, offering cogent grounds for their objections. We may also find we are pushing against some of our students' sensibilities and, in those instances, parents or outside interest groups may try to intervene. We therefore need to be ready to explain both why we have chosen to introduce religious perspectives into the classroom and why we have introduced them in the ways we have.

As responsible professionals, we have additional obligations. If we decide to bring religious or spiritual convictions into the classroom, we need to be adept at handling heated exchanges that may be construed as disrespectful by one group of students or another. And if we want our students to recognize the religiously contested issues and their religious alternatives, we owe it to our students (and to colleagues in our own discipline and in religious studies) to handle the religious alternatives with competence and fairness.

This last point raises two serious challenges: what to include and how to include it competently. The world today is characterized by religious and spiritual variety, and much of that global variety is now at home within the United States.[17] What religiously contested issues do we include? For example, some conservative Christians might wish the professor of an introductory biology course to acknowledge the (from their perspective) contested nature of evolutionary theory. Catholic Christians might prefer that the professor acknowledge the morally contested status of, say, embryonic stem cell research. Hindus may think it most important to acknowledge the religiously problematic character of vivisection and animal experimentation. If all these contested issues are included, an introductory biology course will rapidly qualify for cross-listing in religious studies and students will find themselves shortchanged when it comes to their education in biology.

And then there is the matter of competence. To be religiously or spiritually inclined does not automatically make one an expert on religious or spiritual perspectives. For natural inclusion to work responsibly, its practitioners need to acquire sufficient understanding and expertise that they can deal with the religious issues responsibly. Given the demands of disciplinary work, it may be unrealistic to expect scholars in other disciplines to devote sufficient time and energy to gain the requisite competence in religion. And without such study, scholars practicing natural inclusion run the substantial risk of making pronouncements about matters they understand only superficially.

We faculty need to exercise prudence and restraint if we decide to introduce religious considerations into our scholarship, teaching, and conversation with colleagues. We must guard against repeating the unhappy history in American higher education of religious intolerance, discrimination, and constraints on free inquiry and expression, and we must respect the sensibilities of our students.

We are professionals rightly answerable to our larger disciplinary communities, which foster and protect a worthy and important enterprise. But disciplinary communities have histories. They are the bearers of living traditions, and they develop over time.[18] This means the goods, standards, and practices of our disciplines are pliable, at least to some degree. They can be and sometimes should be put to the question and challenged, and if the time is right and the reasons good, they should change. With regard to the issue of religion, this may be one of those times. This may be a moment when the circumspect reintroduction of religious perspectives into the discourse of the academy is appropriate. If we want change, we must convince colleagues by word and deed that the change truly advances the community's pursuit of knowledge and understanding in a pluralistic and religiously conflicted world.

There may be times when we feel we simply need to be frank. There may be times when we feel obliged as disciplinary professionals to explain the explicitly religious considerations that motivate us and inform the scholarly arguments we advance. But we need to take into account more than merely letting our students and colleagues know "where we are coming from." The real test is whether talk about religion, exercised with careful candor, will serve the best and deepest educational interests of our students and help advance knowledge for our own time and for generations to come.

Mark U. Edwards Jr. is Senior Advisor to the Dean at Harvard Divinity School and is formerly President of St. Olaf College. He is author of *Religion on Our Campuses: A Professor's Guide to Communities, Conflicts, and Promising Conversations.*

7

Faculty Priorities: Where Does Faith Fit?

R. Eugene Rice

The distinguished philosopher and public intellectual Richard Rorty has written an essay entitled "Religion as Conversation-stopper."[1] Although I have been a professor of sociology and religion for years, I have spent most of the past twenty years focusing on "faculty priorities"—everything from the meaning of scholarship to tenure. Now, as I turn back to religious concerns—this time with a focus on the religious implication of faculty work—I find that I am doing so with considerable trepidation. Rorty is right. In academic circles religion is a conversation-stopper. In fact, for many it is a hot-button issue that triggers deep-seated antagonisms, tensions, and intellectual rifts within what many of us still call a "community of scholars." Addressing religious issues in the contemporary context also has the potential to further fray the sometimes fragile relationships that exist between the academy and the larger society. Despite these difficulties, conversations can no longer be avoided. Silence is not an option.

Faith and Meaning

In response to my own reticence, I have chosen to focus not on religion but on faith. Religion is increasingly understood to refer to organized religion and institutional dogma (belief)—sources of so much of the current strain. These more explicit religious issues need to be addressed; for example, the religious illiteracy evident in this culture is a national embarrassment. But I want to approach faith in its broadest and most inclusive form as the making of meaning—an activity in which all human beings engage. I take my lead here from William G. Perry Jr., whose *Forms of Intellectual and Ethical Development in the College Years*[2] helped me understand the way college students make meaning of their lives. His insights, many articulated a generation ago, are still germane as we struggle to address the widely expressed interest of contemporary students in making meaning of and with their lives. Faith, as I am describing it, is an umbrella term for this overall process of creating meaning in one's life, of nurturing a sense of connection with others and the world as a whole, and of developing a vision of reality that provides enough order, form, and significance for one to make decisions about life. Such faith is typically expressed in the stories, narratives, images, symbols, and concepts that give coherence to life, and those stories, narratives, images, symbols, and concepts can be framed in terms that are either explicitly religious or quite thoroughly secular.

In this essay I contend that teaching and learning now take place in a markedly different intellectual and social environment. The postmodern debates that have raged in and across many disciplines, the expanding global awareness, and the dramatic pedagogical changes that have taken place recently have not only made it possible to talk openly about the construction of meaning and purpose but also necessary. When the questions of meaning and purpose are pressed to their deepest level, raising ultimate concerns, they take on religious and spiritual implications, and these are issues that students now say they want faculty to engage. In addition, I suggest ways of addressing religious and spiritual questions that avoid the pitfalls of both literalistic dogmatism and cynical reductionism. The final section of the essay explores how faculty might open themselves and their teaching to these larger questions and argues that there are also professional boundaries that ought to be considered.

Faith and the Role of Faculty

The reluctance of faculty to address the larger questions of meaning, purpose, and faith in the teaching role has been publicly challenged by several major studies. Receiving the most attention is *Spirituality in Higher Education: A National Study of College Students' Search for Meaning and Purpose* by the Higher Education Research Institute (HERI) at the University of California, Los Angeles.[3] The HERI study found that contemporary students have a "strong interest and involvement in spirituality and religion, are actively engaged in a spiritual quest, and have high expectations for the role their universities will play in their spiritual and emotional development." More than two-thirds of the entering college students across the United States say that it is "essential" or "very important" that their institutions enhance their self-understanding (69 percent) and almost the same number indicate that they want their colleges to play a role in developing their personal values (67 percent). Nearly half (48 percent) say that it is "essential" or "very important" that colleges encourage their personal expression of spirituality. Students also reported, however, that most professors provide little opportunity to discuss spirituality in class and that their institutions typically do little to foster or encourage student interest in the larger questions of meaning and purpose.

Given this disparity between what students want and expect and what the American professoriate provides, HERI launched—with the support of the Templeton Foundation—a national study of faculty beliefs, attitudes, and behaviors: *Spirituality and the Professoriate.*[4] In contrast to the student perception that faculty are largely indifferent to spiritual questions, this study found that four in five faculty describe themselves as "spiritual person[s]" and that more than two-thirds view "developing a meaningful philosophy of life" as a very important or essential goal of higher education. While more than a third of faculty respondents say they are "not at all" religious, more than half the professors surveyed said that enhancing self-understanding (60 percent); developing moral character (59 percent); and helping students cultivate personal values (53 percent) are valid educational goals for undergraduate students. Yet when they were asked explicitly whether "colleges should be concerned with facilitating student 'spiritual development,'" less than one-third (30 percent) agreed. In these responses I see an effort on the part of faculty to identify professional boundaries around student concerns for the making of meaning. Serious questions are being raised about whether teachers ought to involve themselves in "spiritual development," but enhancing self-understanding and assisting students in the development of moral character and their own values are seen as legitimate faculty priorities.

Recently I participated in a Wingspread Conference sponsored by the Johnson Foundation called "Religion and Public Life: Engaging Higher Education."[5] Early in that meeting, a serious rift became evident between those pressing for greater faculty involvement with students' struggles to make sense of spiritual and religious questions and those, mostly senior faculty, who had reservations about that kind of direct involvement. In particular, several established professors of religious studies suggested that the key function of the professor is the pursuit of knowledge along with the cultivation of the scholarly skills required to do that, unencumbered by responsibilities for either character development or civic engagement. They argued persuasively that the new breed of "change agents" emerging in the university and present at the conference ought to leave them free to pursue their subject matter, and to rely on the open discussion of carefully chosen texts to raise the larger questions of meaning. They cited, as examples, Saul Bellow's *Seize the Day*, Augustine's *Confessions*, and Toni Morrison's *Beloved*, and they saw their job as helping students understand the questions posed by such texts. How students might or might not address the personal implications of those questions for themselves did not, however, fall within their conception of the faculty role. As one professor put it, "We don't want to be therapists or community organizers."

As that comment makes clear, there are important boundary issues dealing with faith and faculty work that need to be addressed. Do faculty have responsibilities in this area? If so, what are those responsibilities and what limits apply? In the contemporary context of American higher education with its rich diversity, these questions are only beginning to be asked. Clear answers are not yet available and, perhaps, never will be, but a review of the history of these concerns in higher education provides helpful background for understanding the situation in which we find ourselves.

From the Colonial College to the New American University

Faculty members in the American colonial period and throughout most of the nineteenth century had a clear mandate to address issues of faith. During that time, most institutions of higher education had explicit religious roots in the various denominations and emerging sects of the time; attending to the larger religious and spiritual questions of students was a central responsibility of both administrators and faculty. Toward the latter part of the nineteenth century, however, faculty priorities were fundamentally altered by the emergence of the new American university and by conceptions of scholarship imported by those doing advanced studies in Europe, particularly Germany. The dominant understanding of what was to be regarded as the work of the scholar narrowed and began to be defined increasingly as specialized, discipline-based research. With this conceptual shift came a new organizational structure of graduate education with its research laboratories and specialized seminars. Newly organized disciplines and departments began to assume a dominant place not only in the new research universities but also in the liberal arts colleges and the "land-grant" institutions that blossomed as the nation moved west. A powerful vision of the priorities of faculty began to take hold, one that has continually gained strength over the years and demonstrated enormous resilience, particularly in the graduate schools where new generations of the professoriate receive their credentials and where their understanding of what it means to be academic professionals is nurtured.

This new, modern vision of the priorities of the scholar was articulated best by Max Weber in a famous lecture entitled "Science as a Vocation," delivered in 1918 at the University of Munich (interestingly, at the urging of his students who wanted to understand what motivated his work as a scholar). Weber talked eloquently of the "inner desire" that drives the scholar to the cutting edge of a field and of the "ecstasy" that comes only to the specialist on the frontiers of knowledge engaging in advanced research. The assumption was that if you pursued a research passion with your whole heart, then the quality of teaching and what we now call "service" would fall naturally into place. As Weber understood it, the central moral obligation of the teacher and of the scholar alike was "to ask inconvenient questions"[6] and thus advance the frontiers of knowledge. It is the affirmation of critical rationality and confidence that the antithesis will lead to some kind of Hegelian synthesis—in the long run—that continues to set the priorities for the majority of faculty and shape their assumptions about their work in the classroom.

The Processes of Modernization and Secularization

A probing understanding of the place of faith in the lives and work of faculty requires that we review the assumptions—implicit and explicit—that have dominated their views of the processes of modernization and secularization in recent years. The HERI study of the professoriate cited earlier found that 37 percent of the faculty surveyed asserted that they are "not at all" religious. This number is far higher than found in the general population of the United States and undoubtedly accounts for the widespread assumption that faculty are resistant to addressing spiritual and religious questions. In the general population there was a significant shift in polling data related to church attendance in the late 1950s and early 1960s. Americans who attended college during these years were more likely to attend church and be more orthodox in their religious views. Among those surveyed a decade later, those with college educations were less likely to attend church and less likely to be religiously committed.[7]

The period between roughly 1957 and 1974 was a time of major transformation in American higher education—on many fronts. Pressed by the
post–World War II baby boom and the GI Bill, the demand for college education escalated rapidly. University systems in states such as California, New
York, and Illinois grew and expanded dramatically. The success of the USSR,
dramatized in the launching of *Sputnik* in 1957, generated a "cold war" that
fueled funding for science and technology. The conception of scholarship that
had formerly been defined more broadly was now narrowed, placing priority
on scientific inquiry and the products of technical, quantitative pursuits.
Money poured into chemistry and physics departments, and schools of engineering expanded. The land-grant colleges became state universities with their
own scientific research foundations and direct connections to the centers of
money and power in Washington, D.C.

Rational, scientific inquiry ruled the day and faculty gained in status—
particularly those in the sciences. This is what Christopher Jenks and David
Riesman were pointing to in *The Academic Revolution*, which appeared in
1968.[8] This positivistic vision of the power of objective, value-free rational
inquiry gained strength and prestige during this period of affluence and expansion. The modern professionalization of the social sciences in this growing market promised more than it delivered. In addition to rational inquiry, the
positivists called for freedom—moral and political, as well as intellectual
emancipation. What was delivered was what is suggested in Weber's famous
image of the "iron cage," populated, in his words, by "specialists without spirit
[and] sensualists without heart."[9] The accomplishments of the science and
technology of the period were in fact remarkable, but connections to any concrete sense of identity, meaning, or purpose were diminished. Moral considerations, spiritual interests, and religion—all the normative dimensions of
social life—were either disregarded or explained away as the result of more
important or more "real" factors.

Of the more than one-third of the faculty in the HERI study distancing
themselves entirely from any kind of religious or spiritual interests, a substantial proportion were undoubtedly among the positivists described above. At
the extreme edge, where the struggle between religion and science had become
particularly bitter, a scientific fundamentalism arose that has become increasingly dualistic in opposition to a growing literalistic, fundamentalist religion. By the end of the 1960s the environment that had inspired positivistic
confidence in rational analysis, scientific inquiry, and technological produc-
tivity was beginning to seriously erode. The universal claims that provided the
underpinnings for theories of modernization were being challenged and the
reason versus faith debate took a dramatic turn.

The Impact of the Postmodern Era

Postmodernism as an intellectual movement began to emerge during a time of serious cultural, social, and political turmoil. The Vietnam War was escalating and the protests were spreading across colleges and universities. Most institutions were losing their authority—family, church, corporations, government, and universities, including the faculty. The civil rights movement that had begun as a moral call for social justice and inclusion led by revered religious leaders also raised questions of identity and how one's social location shaped one's understanding of the world. Following a similar pattern, feminist leaders began to talk about "women's ways of knowing" as distinct and different from much of the thinking that flourished in the then still male-dominated academy. These were all legitimate concerns, and the demand that group differences and divergent ways of thought be respected eventually came together in the call for multiculturalism in the classroom.

Within higher education, the faculty development movement with its attention to improving undergraduate teaching assumed from the start that there were different ways of knowing and later built on Howard Gardner's arguments for the recognition of multiple intelligences. In the sciences, Thomas Kuhn argued that changes in thought were often based on shifting paradigms rather than on the straightforward advance of empirical research, and, in the social sciences, it was becoming clear that problems involving human beings were not as amenable to clear "solutions" as were problems in the "basic" sciences. Virtually everywhere one turned on the majority of campuses there was the assumption that reality was socially constructed and that human beings ultimately had to take responsibility. Well before the term *postmodernism* came into vogue, postmodern ways of thinking had become part of the culture at most American colleges and universities.

At its radical edge, postmodernism, following Nietzsche, ended with a form of nihilism that not only dismantled the values of Christianity but that also undercut the values of modernity itself: reason, freedom, and the autonomous self. Some postmodernists went so far as to argue—not entirely without evidence—that the positivist university exists primarily to support the established structures of power, especially in the areas of race, gender, and class. On the other hand, postmodernism also opened the door to a new recognition and appreciation of the particularity of a wide range of cultural traditions, including long-established religious views that had earlier been discounted. Nietzsche's nihilism was not the only response to the limitations of modernity. In opening the academy to a diversity of approaches to inquiry and new ways of knowing, opportunities for rethinking the place of faith in the academy and the options for faculty were introduced.

Symbolic Realism: A Different Approach to the Interpretation of Faith

Early on in his wide-ranging career, Robert Bellah was struggling with the limits of the modernization process, including the impact of secularization. This struggle has been thoughtfully traced in a recent *Festschrift* published in his honor entitled *Meaning and Modernization: Religion, Polity and Self.*[10] He not only confronted the dilemmas of modernity, and built on the insights that would later be identified as postmodernist, but also persuasively articulated an alternative; he called it "symbolic realism." As a student in his classes, I remember him quoting the poet Wallace Stevens with some frequency: "The final belief is to believe in a fiction, which you know to be a fiction, there being nothing else. The exquisite truth is to know that it is a fiction and that you believe in it willingly."[11] As a student with an evangelical Christian background I was both provoked and disturbed by the term *fiction.* Bellah was not a relativist, but the reference to the term reflected, not his disrespect for the power of religious and spiritual symbol systems, but the seriousness with which he took our human limitations. Bellah agrees with the poet Stevens that the patterns of meaning by which we choose to order our lives are social and cultural constructions—"the final belief is to believe in a fiction." Bellah goes on, however, to contend that the religious and faith symbols created by communities and individuals as ways of grasping what is ultimate about human existence can have a reality of their own. These transcendent meanings are powerful enough to serve as anchors for human life and to provide a sense of moral order—reflected in the last part of the Stevens quotation: "The exquisite truth is that you know it is a fiction and you believe in it willingly."

Bellah's work has important implications for aligning faculty priorities with student needs in a postsecular age. He provides a vision of religion that avoids both the literalism of fundamentalist faith and the smugness that so often accompanies the suggestion that religion is nothing more than a human creation and thus lacks any authoritative standing in the struggle to make meaning of human life. Bellah is an antireductionist who years ago made the claim that "the radical split between knowledge and commitment that exists in our culture and in our universities is not ultimately tenable. Differentiation has gone about as far as it can go. It is time for a new integration."[12] His insight is even more relevant today. Both the reductionism of the positivists and the nihilism of some postmodernists have proved untenable, just as Bellah predicted. What is emerging in their place is a deep spiritual hunger and quest for meaning, which is finding voice among college and university students across the nation. Higher education and the faculty need to respond.

A New Faculty, a New Context

Jack Schuster and Martin Finkelstein have recently published the results of their extensive research on college faculty in *The American Faculty: The Restructuring of Academic Work and Careers*, tracing what they have coined a "silent revolution."[13] In addition to the dramatic changing of the guard that is taking place as aging faculty retire and replacements are recruited, Schuster and Finkelstein trace structural changes in the number of tenure appointments, the use of part-time faculty, and the unbundling of the professorial role. There are other changes, however, that relate directly to the focus of this essay. We are entering a postsecular era that requires attention. The question is no longer whether issues of faith should be addressed in our work with students, but how? The pedagogical context within which faculty work has also changed. The students are different: more diverse, more globally oriented. Faith perspectives and their differences profoundly shape the patterns of meaning that inform what is learned: how it is framed and appropriated. Local and global questions of immense significance are constantly grounded in religious traditions and competing perspectives on faith. To not address these issues in our interaction with students is a glaring omission.

I recently published an essay entitled "From Athens and Berlin to L.A.: Faculty Work and a Changing Academy."[14] Los Angeles was chosen as the focus not because it is an American city, but because it is an international—a transnational—city. One visit and you are struck by the rich pulsating diversity—a stimulating cultural mosaic. Los Angeles is also plagued by the perplexing problems engulfing cities around the globe. It has become a template for unplanned, spreading, privatized growth and is on the verge of gridlock. Addressing these global issues in a way that respects the diversity of the population and honors democratic commitments and processes in pluralistic contexts will require considerable knowledge of disparate faith traditions and the capacity to communicate and connect across those differences.

In American colleges and universities there has been a widespread shift from a focus on faculty—who they are and what they know—to a focus on learning. This is reflected in the assessment practices of regional accreditation bodies as well as professional associations. Learning outcomes have become a leading, if controversial, concern. From China to Tajikistan, higher education is now recognized as the pivotal institution in a knowledge-based society. Globally, the university is seen as key to social and economic development. Learning outcomes are regarded as critical, indeed. More recently, in the United States at least, there is a growing emphasis that goes beyond learning to paying explicit attention to how students make meaning and find purpose in their lives. Many see this as a part of the rapidly growing concern with spiritual and religious matters in a postsecular world.

A Pedagogical Transformation

What has been apparent in the shift from a focus on faculty to a focus on learning is that the learning depends in large measure on the way in which the student constructs meaning from what is presented in the lecture or structured into the laboratory experiment or other learning context. The contribution of the professor—or instructional team, as the case may be—is important, but primarily so as it structures the context facilitating learning. In a very real sense, we have experienced a pedagogical revolution. It manifests itself in a variety of ways. I have identified three ways that I regard as particularly influential: relational learning, which includes collaboration with others, particularly with peers (e.g., learning communities); active learning (e.g., service learning, community-based research, undergraduate research); and technologically enhanced learning where the acquiring of information is significantly democratized.

In all of these relatively new approaches to learning, the priority is placed on the making of meaning. And, that depends in large measure on what the student brings to the learning occasion—their personal, social, and cultural situation. This requires that faculty become acquainted with the backgrounds of their students, including the ethnic, spiritual, and religious cultures out of which they come. Teaching and learning become reciprocal processes and are no longer considered a one-way street.

As the locus of control in the learning process shifts from the faculty (the "sage on the stage") to the learner, the significance of the faculty role is increased, not lessened, though radically different. This is particularly true when the goals of higher education incorporate liberal learning. Martha Nussbaum, the well-known philosopher and social commentator from the University of Chicago, and recent author of *Cultivating Humanity: A Classical Defense of*

Reform in Liberal Education, has this to say: "Our campuses educate our citizens. Becoming an educated citizen means learning a lot of facts and mastering techniques of reasoning. But it means something more. It means learning how to be a human being capable of love and imagination."[15] Her language is only one step removed from a call for spiritual formation.

Others are even more direct in calling for a spiritual dimension in student-faculty interactions, most notably Parker Palmer and Sharon Daloz Parks. Palmer is particularly outspoken in his public assault on the positivistic orientation of faculty and their disciplines. He says that positivistic "objectivism" requires the student to hold everything "at arms length" so that "you can dissect, you can cut it apart, you can analyze it to death." This dominant approach to knowing is also experimental: Discrete pieces can be moved around "to shape the world more pleasing to us." From Palmer's perspective, the impact of this objectivism is immense. "Very quickly this seemingly bloodless epistemology becomes an ethic. It is an ethic of competitive individualism, in the midst of a world fragmented and made exploitable by that very mode of knowing. The mode of knowing itself breeds intellectual habits, indeed spiritual instincts, that destroy community. We make objects of each other and the world to be manipulated for our own private ends."[16]

According to Palmer, this positivistic emphasis on rational empiricism has rendered the internal, subjective quest for meaning and purpose irrelevant to the academy and has moved it outside the purview of faculty. In the objectivist world there is no place for spirituality, unless it is compartmentalized and becomes itself an objective, externalized reality. Palmer's contention that this objectivist mode of knowing dominates higher education is, I think, overstated. While it may have been an accurate description of past practices, it does not take into account the postmodern developments that have had a large impact on a number of disciplines, particularly in the humanities and the social sciences.

Sharon Daloz Parks has proposed an alternative epistemology that builds on the assumptions of a postmodern academy, recognizing that every perspective is rooted in particular, personal, social, and cultural conditions. This different approach to knowing—to the search for truth—realigns the relationship between the academy and issues of transcendent meaning. This alternative perspective, as Parks puts it, "invites faculty and students to bring the competence of contemporary scholarship to the search for critically composed and worthy forms of faith within a relativized world"[17] where every human perspective is incomplete and certainly not value free. This alternative perspective gives voice not just to racial, ethnic, gendered, and class perspectives that have been marginalized by the dominant approach to knowing, but also recognizes the legitimacy and importance of the spiritual dimensions.

Like Parker Palmer, Parks contends that questions of meaning must be considered within the academy. The focus on academic objectivity rooted in Western epistemology has, over time, appeared to preclude a self-conscious search for value and meaning and, as a result, "commitment to the truth has been divorced from questions of the good." Reason and knowledge in the academy have for too long been reduced to consideration of processes that can be analyzed and replicated, that can be produced and controlled. Within this framework, it made sense to speak of the university as a "knowledge industry." Wisdom was not part of the equation. Parks contends that "wherever a strict dichotomy between the objective and the subjective has been practiced, we have become vulnerable to exchanging wisdom for knowledge, and moral commitment for method." When higher education is only a "knowledge industry," professors function as less-than-whole persons, and students concerned with exploring questions of ultimate meaning—a faith to live by—are abandoned.

Parks makes a brilliant case for faculty opening themselves and their teaching to the making of meaning, including the open exploration of different spiritual and religious perspectives. She goes on, however, to speak of the "professor as spiritual guide."[18] *Guide* is a strong word, and for me it crosses a professional boundary that needs to be acknowledged and respected. I want to explore that boundary in what follows.

Faculty Priorities: Courage and Humility

In his collected speeches entitled *The Vocation of the Teacher*, Wayne C. Booth, who served as professor of English and dean at the University of Chicago, identifies the personal qualities of a scholar as honesty, courage, persistence, consideration, and humility.[19] While all of these traits are important, courage and humility are especially crucial for faculty who choose to welcome questions of meaning and purpose into the learning process.

For faculty following this path, courage will be required in order to risk sharing one's own sense of meaning and direction in life and to relate one's own field of specialization to larger questions. At times, taking this path may involve articulating the spiritual and religious assumptions that inform one's own approach to teaching and learning, taking care that this is done in a way that does not impose one's own values on students. Autobiographical self-disclosure means sharing one's doubts and deeper questions, exposing one's own vulnerability. It also requires acknowledging that one's own position, too, is a constructed fiction—surely tried and tested in the light of the best evidence available and deeply felt experience, but a fiction nonetheless.

This kind of courage also requires being open to the perspectives and stories of others, which risks the loss of control or dominance in the classroom or in a relationship with a student. Self-disclosure comes with a price: the forfeiture of some of the protections afforded by the status and prestige that faculty have labored so hard to achieve and that are frequently invoked in the university environment. Jane Tompkins's moving memoir of awakening this kind of courage in her own academic experience speaks directly to the point. Particularly telling is her account of her painful struggle with pressures to "appear smart." She writes: "I realized that what I had actually been concerned with was showing the students how smart I was, how knowledgeable I was, and how well prepared I was for class. I had been putting on a performance whose true goal was not to help the student learn, as I had thought, but to perform before them in such a way that they would have a good opinion of me."[20]

To move away from seeing oneself as the expert in control in front of undergraduates takes one kind of courage, but the challenge is escalated when colleagues are involved. For junior faculty, it takes courage to attend to student ways of knowing in a fashion that one's departmental colleagues might find questionable—especially when you might be offending a colleague who will later appear on your tenure and promotion review committee. The title of Parker Palmer's influential book exploring "the inner landscape of a teacher's life," *The Courage to Teach*, takes on added meaning when seen in this light.[21]

The open discussion of teaching—of what works and what does not—is being widely advocated, most notably by Lee Shulman and the Carnegie Foundation for the Advancement of Teaching.[22] Teaching can no longer be a private matter; it needs to be made public. When a faculty member adopts a new approach to teaching and learning, it will require courage to present oneself honestly, without cant or pretense. When authority depends on expertise—on what you know—the temptations of hubris are hard to resist. It is regrettable but not surprising that the general public typically associate faculty with arrogance rather than humility.

Yet any faculty member who pursues questions related to meaning and purpose will need humility in addition to courage. Humility means knowing where one's expertise ends, and it also means knowing when to keep one's expertise to oneself. And in teaching, humility's most important function may be allowing students the right to decide for themselves how they will understand the world. How does a faculty member generate enough courage to disclose parts of her or his inner life in class and also possess enough humility to welcome student's explorations of alternative perspectives? That is no easy task.

In thinking about how faculty might best respond to students who are struggling with the making of meaning, I am again reminded of William Perry's seminal work. One of the things I find most helpful is Perry's emphasis on the need for providing a balance of support and challenge in coping with students' efforts to construct meaning. Most faculty assume that our primary purpose is to provide intellectual challenge. Perry counters by warning that we need to support students where they are developmentally, to honor the struggles they are facing, given the contexts and histories that shape their thinking. Being sensitive about when to offer support and when to challenge is particularly important when working with students who are engaged in their own making of meaning. To rigorously challenge a first-year student deeply committed to a dualistic religious perspective can easily drive her or him more solidly into a literalistic worldview. The students' openness to alternative ways of viewing an issue—their deeper learning—can get inhibited, not advanced. Addressing processes of this sort will take both courage and humility on the part of faculty.

Professional Boundaries

Faculty, particularly those in the liberal arts disciplines, see themselves as boundary crashers. Academic freedom is at the heart of the profession. In the dominant perception, progress is made by challenging established ideas, so that discipline-defined paradigms are broken open and new conceptions advance the field. The professional vision of "standing on the shoulders of giants" involves building on the best that has gone before; professional priorities are shaped by academic tradition, innovation, breakthroughs, and making your own contribution at the cutting edge of a field. Because academic freedom has held such a cherished place in the profession and represents a *raison d'etre* for the university itself, we have not addressed sufficiently the professional boundaries that set the professor off from closely related but different professions, or what I would prefer to call vocations.

My own age cohort, which began teaching in the 1960s, has been particularly negligent about clarifying the boundaries that separate, for instance, the politician from the teacher/scholar. I am confident our neglect of that boundary has been one of the factors contributing to the decline of public respect for and even the status of the American professoriate. The growth of intellectually sophisticated conservative foundations and "think tanks" has cleverly exploited the image of the "left-leaning, politically correct academy," thereby undermining academic legitimacy and justifying their own right-wing ideological pronouncements. Faculty have also failed to discuss, much less develop, guidelines for addressing religious and spiritual questions. Taking on these questions of meaning and purpose have been so potentially contentious that the topic has been assiduously avoided.

I have made the argument that raising critical questions is not enough. Max Weber's dictum: "The moral obligation of the teacher is to ask inconvenient questions" is important, but not sufficient. Faculty are more than boundary crashers. The cultivation of critical rationality is not enough. Students need to be exposed to other approaches to knowing, and sensitivity to the process of making meaning ought to be built into the teaching/learning process. This should be done with care, making sure that the teacher's spiritual and religious views are not imposed.

Religious indoctrination has no place in the college classroom. Being open to exploring the larger questions of meaning is essential, but this needs to be done in a way that respects the personhood of the students—their fundamental right and responsibility for constructing their own meaning without external coercion. Developmentally, this makes sense. Faculty who are open to the exploration of larger questions related to life's purposes need to be especially attentive to the differences in status and power in their relationships with students. Professors enjoy broad authority in the classroom over what is regarded as sound opinion in the discipline, and they need to be careful not to use that authority inappropriately in discussions related to spiritual and religious matters.

The struggles with issues related to diversity and inclusion in the history of the American university and college, whether the focus has been on gender, race, ethnicity, or religious affiliation, have at each point led to the expressed need for the academic institution to provide a "safe place" for vulnerable minorities. Excluding issues of faith from classroom discussion was one way to cope. An effective strategy for making the classroom a "safe place" for those holding minority perspectives was to avoid the topic. Many faculty found this to be a convenient way out.

We are all familiar with the history of excluding Jews and Catholics from American colleges and universities—even the maintenance of quotas. In *Joining the Club: A History of Jews and Yale*, Daniel Oren points out that there was only one Jewish professor in Yale College in 1950.[29] We have come a long way since then in unraveling this established hegemony. If open dialogue on questions of meaning is going to be welcomed, as the majority of students are urging, guidelines for making the classroom a safe place for carrying out discussions that touch on larger religious and spiritual issues will have to be established.

Na'ilah Suad Nasir and Jasiyah Al-Amin in their recent article "Creating Identity-Safe Spaces on College Campuses for Muslim Students" describe graphically how pressing this issue is for campuses that welcome students from a diversity of backgrounds.[30] Religion and spiritual faith are central to the identity of a growing number of students. To be able to explore that critical dimension of their lives with faculty across disciplines without being threatened is an important element of the academic experience and ought not be relegated to activities sponsored by the office of student affairs alone. Students are now calling for faculty to be more open to these probing conversations about meaning and purpose that give significance to their lives. This is an invitation that faculty can hardly refuse.

R. Eugene Rice is a Senior Scholar at the Association of American Colleges and Universities and former Director of the Forum on Faculty Roles and Rewards at the American Association of Higher Education.

PART II

Religion, the Curriculum, and Student Learning

8

The Religious and Spiritual Journeys of College Students

Larry A. Braskamp

What is the status of religion in the lives of college students? Have college students become less religious? Do colleges and universities have a secularizing influence on them? The popular impression is that students are dissolute and irreligious like those in Tom Wolfe's popular novel *I Am Charlotte Simmons*. Is that fair or accurate?

Contrary to this conventional wisdom, the latest research indicates that religion and spirituality are important, even central, concerns for college students. Many arrive on campus with deeply held religious convictions and established patterns of religious practice, and they are eager to explore how those convictions and practices relate to the subjects they intend to study and to the life choices they face. Religion is part of who they are, and they want it to be part of their education. What is more, there is little evidence to suggest that this interest in religious faith in any way undermines the educational purposes of higher education; faith and learning can go hand in hand. Of course, not all college and university students are religious and that needs to be acknowledged, but the more surprising finding in recent research is how pervasive faith is.

A well-rounded portrait of the religiosity of American college and university students needs to include both beliefs (spirituality, faith, and the interior life—the "being" aspects of religion) and practices (worship, meditation, and civic engagement—the "doing" side of religion).[1] This essay examines both dimensions of student religiosity.

A Pre-College Religious Profile of American Teens

In order to understand the spiritual and religious profile of traditional-aged college students, it makes sense to begin with whom they are before they come to campus. What kind of faith did they possess as high school teens? The recently completed National Study of Youth and Religion (NSYR), overseen by Christian Smith, Melinda Lundquist Denton, and other researchers at the University of North Carolina, provides that information.[2] This study focused on teenagers (thirteen to seventeen years old), collecting data through a detailed questionnaire completed by more than 3,000 students and parents and through follow-up interviews with more than 250 individual teens and parents. The basic finding was that religion is a significant part of the lives of high school students. More than half (51 percent) said religion is important or very important in their daily lives as opposed to only 18 percent who said religion is not very important or not important at all. The NSYR also found that, for the most part, the religious convictions of these teenagers parallel those of their parents. Given that fact, it is not surprising that the "character of teenage religiosity in the United States is extraordinarily conventional."[3] High school students are not the rebellious and irreligious youth often portrayed in the press, on TV, and in movies.

While the religious faith and practice of American teens are relatively conventional, they usually lack depth. At this stage of their lives, young people tend to take religion for granted; it is simply there and it is there for their own benefit. Smith and Denton label this religious disposition "Moralistic Therapeutic Deism"—a faith that focuses on a god who is present in times of need and trouble and who is supportive of their goal to be comfortable and happy and lead a good life. The god of moralistic therapeutic deism is not, however, a personal authority figure nor is this a god who is intimately involved in their lives in any deep way. Teen attitudes about religion are more affective than cognitive and do not stress theological concepts like grace, forgiveness, and justice. This is lived religion, rather than reflective faith. Smith and Denton found moralistic therapeutic deism to be so pervasive that they describe it as the "new mainstream American religious faith for our culturally post-Christian, individualistic, mass-consumer capitalist society."[4]

Having said all that, Smith and Denton note that teens who consider themselves religious differ from those who lack religious faith or are nonpracticing, concluding that "empirical evidence suggests that religious faith and practice themselves exert significant, positive, direct and indirect influences on the lives of teenagers, helping to foster healthier, more engaged adolescents who live more constructive and promising lives."[5] For teens, being religious is positively related to having a healthy sense of well-being. This reinforces other research about high school students that has also found that the "general direction of religious influence is positive. That is, more extensive religiosity typically (and modestly) contributes to better educational outcomes, better emotional health, more satisfaction in the family, and more voluntarism."[6]

Some researchers talk about a trend that indicates that a growing sector of the American population now considers itself "spiritual, but not religious." People following this trend have little interest in "organized religion" and are attracted to free-floating spiritual ideas and practices they can assemble together into their own personal bricolage of faith. Smith and Denton find scant evidence, if any, that this distinction is part of teenage faith. Teens have not, for the most part, separated out being spiritual—being generally reflective about the meaning and purpose of life—from following the religious teachings and practices of their religious communities. Most teens are not spiritual seekers at this stage of their journey in life; they are still religious followers trying to fit in. Given that fact, it is not surprising that the current generation of high school students is more like than different from their parents and elders when it comes to personal values and religious perspectives. "Any generation gaps that exist between teens and adults today is superficial compared with and far outweighed by the generational commonalities. . . . Most problems and issues that adults typically consider teenage problems are in fact inextricably linked to adult-world problems."[7]

This portrait of pre-college teens provides important information for those charged with the responsibility of educating college students, especially students who enter college immediately after high school. It highlights how much religious faith and practice are part of the lives of these students—even if that religious faith is still in the process of formation—and how significant a role parents play in shaping that religiosity. At the time they enter college or university, most students have not yet fully developed their faith or beliefs and those convictions have not yet been deeply woven into their character and identity. They possess a form of religiosity, but it is not yet fully their own. Thus they enter college—a period in their lives that is often filled with uncertainty, confusion, and rapid growth—at a vulnerable stage. They are just beginning to wrestle with internalizing their own sense of religiosity as they simultaneously face the "big questions" of life: How do I know what is true and good? Who am I? How do I relate to others?[8]

College Students in the 1990s and Today

Every generation of college and university students has its own distinctive profile, and that profile can change quickly. Comparison can be helpful, and one way to comprehend the particularities of contemporary college students is to contrast them with the generation just before them. Arthur Levine and Jeanette Cureton's study of college students in the mid-1990s provides that baseline.[9]

The students they studied have been called "Generation X," or "Xers" for short, a symbol of a generation without a name or identity—a generation in transition. That generation has been characterized variously as frightened, demanding of change, desirous of security, liberal in social attitudes, socially conscious and active, consumer oriented, hardworking, diverse and divided, pragmatic, and idealistic and optimistic about their own futures and our collective future. These Xer college students were the product of the society in which they grew up. The 1970s and 1980s were years of profound demographic, economic, technological, global, and social change, and for many this was also a time when religious practices were swept aside in a sea of change. This is indicated by the declining levels of attendance at weekly religious services on the part of high school seniors, a drop of 25 percent between the years 1976 and 1991.[10]

A decade later our society is still in a period of profound change—globalization is more intense, technology is more integrated into everyday life, diversity and pluralism are more apparent, and terrorism is now a daily reality—but the reaction is no longer the same. Peter Gomes, the campus minister of the Memorial Church at Harvard University for more than thirty years, offers this perspective:

> What has impressed me . . . about the young people during several generations, but most particularly in this most recent one, is not their intellectual ability . . . nor their boundless energy . . . [but] their moral curiosity, their desire to know, to be, and to do good. . . . They sense their own drift. They know that the traditional sources of guidance—family, church, school, and state—are all themselves in some disarray, and they are intelligent enough not to believe that true happiness is to be found in the culture of materialism and sensual diversion that is ceaselessly thrust upon them in their role as passionate consumers. . . . They want to be able to live their lives and to offer them, if necessary, for something worthy of sacrifice and ser-

vice; and they want to live so as to leave the world a better place than the mess that they have inherited.[11]

If Gomes is right, students today are ready for spiritual, moral, and religious growth and change in a way that Xers were not, and they want that growth and change to be part of their holistic college experience.

Broad generalizations about college students have their place, but it is ultimately impossible to develop any single picture that fully describes the complex mix of people and personalities that are presently represented on America's college and university campuses. In recent years, however, three different portraits of contemporary students have emerged, alternatively describing the generation as "Millennials," "Postmoderns," and "the Missionary Generation." These differing portrayals can all be supported empirically, but each is in some way a caricature that needs to be viewed in juxtaposition with the other two. Taken together, however, these three descriptions can help educators, parents, and students themselves converse more meaningfully about the roles religion and spirituality are currently playing in college life.

Millennials

According to researchers Neal Howe and William Strauss, Millennial college students have a distinctive profile that is unlike the students of previous generations. They describe this student cohort as "smart, ambitious, incredibly busy, very ethnically diverse and dominated by girls. . . . They make decisions jointly with parents ('co-purchasing' a college) and believe in big brands (with 'reputation' counting for a lot). And they are numerous, very intent on going to college, and have very demanding parents." They like the "teaching of values, including honesty, caring, moral courage, patriotism, democracy, and the Golden Rule," which reflects their generally Judeo-Christian perspectives.[12] Millennials are conventional in that they mostly accept the norms of their parents and the larger society. Because of that they are willing to become members of the larger society and its established organizations, rather than rebelling against them. In short, they are establishment-oriented joiners. Many are also "over-achievers," constantly busy and engaged, trying to look and be successful, and perhaps expecting too much of themselves and others around them. They are, consequently, often viewed as a stressed-out generation.

Relationships among Millennial peers are fundamentally different from those of previous generations due largely to technology like e-mail and cell phones. Relationships with parents are also different (and often closer) than was the case in the past with parents remaining involved in the lives of their college-attending children (often to the irritation of college administrators and faculty who sometimes call these over-involved parents "helicopter parents," always hovering nearby and ready to drop in at a moment's notice). Instead of encouraging their sons and daughters to resolve conflicts and challenges with their peers and faculty on their own, the parents of Millennials often intervene, limiting the opportunities for their sons and daughters to make decisions on their own, to accept responsibility, and to grow from these encounters. As a result their journey into adulthood has been slowed. Descriptions of Millennials rarely discuss the religious beliefs and activities of these students, but as joiners they have a predisposition to become involved (or over-involved) in all sorts of organizations, including religious organizations, sometimes to the dismay of faculty and administrators.[13]

Postmoderns

A second portrait paints today's college students as Postmoderns, a term of flexible meaning that may sometimes be overused as a description of contemporary philosophical, sociological, and psychological perspectives on life, but that still makes a point. Postmodern students are characterized as having a sense of entitlement, viewing themselves as customers who expect good services in return for their (or their parents') costly investment in college. They seek entertainment and instant gratification, have a short-term perspective, and are somewhat cynical and skeptical, while also being pragmatic.[14]

In general, Postmoderns do not have a deep sense of any universal moral or civil order; instead they honor individual values and freedom of expression. For them, truth claims are largely relative and personal preferences largely determine what is true and good. Even if they have grown up in families with traditional religious values and practices, they have also internalized the fundamentally secular values and priorities of the society at large. Postmoderns are generally widely traveled, having had numerous educational and social enrichment experiences early in their lives, and therefore, they understand the diversity of the world.

As a group, Postmoderns tend to be more self-oriented than civic-minded in their understanding of social roles and in their understanding of the common good. Like their Millennial peers, they are somewhat reluctant to take on the responsibilities of adulthood, and have sometimes been described as being in a stage of "protracted, delayed adolescence."[15] But in contrast to the Millennials, Postmodern students are often disengaged from formal curricular and noncurricular activities, not identifying with the reflective, tedious lifestyle of the academy.[16] For many Postmodern students secularism is their religion of choice, but it is not a deeply thought out perspective.

The Missionary Generation

A third way to describe today's college students is as representatives of the "Missionary Generation," a term coined by Naomi Schaefer Riley in her book *God on the Quad*. According to Riley, this new Missionary Generation is out to change the world and particularly to change the liberal culture of so-called "Blue America." To a large degree this is an evangelical Protestant phenomenon, but conservatives within other religious traditions also participate— Catholics, Jews, Mormons, and even Buddhists.[17]

For Missionary Generation students, religion is central. They seek external authority, relying on the Bible or some other authoritative source of truth and wisdom to guide their lives. They hold traditional values about the family and about personal behavior. They welcome structure and rules to live by, basing them on explicitly religious principles and worldviews. They are serious students who study hard, but who reject the "study hard, party hard" lifestyle touted by some of their peers.

Missionary Generation students think of their lives in terms of calling and vocation, with a strong desire, indeed a sense of obligation, to use their God-given gifts and talents to make a difference in the world. While they are a rather homogenous group—mostly white, mostly Christian in their religious perspective, mostly lower to middle class, and mostly politically and socially conservative—they are not mere clones of one another when it comes to religious beliefs and social issues. They range from Religious Right Republicans to relatively left-wing "counterculture conservatives." Most members of the Missionary Generation are interested in evangelism—in "sharing" their faith with others—but the way they do that tends to be much less "in your face" than was the case with earlier generations of evangelical students. Instead of preaching their faith, students from this generation tend to let the way they live do the talking for them.[18]

A large number of Missionary Generation students attend church-affiliated or other religious colleges and universities, but many also attend mainstream schools and public universities. How do they behave in the classroom and engage with social issues? Based on a survey of students at ten explicitly Christian colleges, those who identify themselves as evangelicals or as theologically orthodox Christians say that the heart as well as the head needs to be used in faith and academic study. Highly evangelical students view themselves as "spirit-filled" in a way that some faculty and other adults perceive as bordering on anti-intellectualism. That is, these students emphasize the heart and *not* the head when making decisions, forming commitments, and drawing conclusions about what is good and true. In this regard, members of the Missionary Generation are similar to Postmodern students who also consider their personal values, chosen as a matter of personal preference, to be as valid as anyone else's.[19] As for social engagement, evangelical students are actually more apt than their peers to be concerned with issues of social justice, and they often support equal rights and gun control while opposing increased funding for defense. This is not necessarily what one would expect given evangelical stereotypes. In fact, on a number of important indicators, today's evangelical students are less conservative than evangelical believers of the past.[20]

One theme that is common to all three portraits of contemporary college students—Millennial, Postmodern, and Missionary—is that they seem less reflective than previous generations. Thomas Hearn (former president of Wake Forest University) has, in particular, described today's students as lacking "any sense of discovery, adventure, wonder, possibility, or any thought that they might find around some corner of their minds an unknown passion leading in some new direction."[21] If Hearn's harsh critique is accurate, it should come as no surprise since the general American public is also known for its short attention span, practicality, and democratization of knowledge. Turning things in a positive direction, however, it might be that what Hearn sees as unreflectiveness is, in fact, something else: a commitment to tolerance and nonjudgmentalism. Today's college students clearly do tend to be tolerant and accepting of divergent points of view, and this applies to their attitudes toward religion. If a previous generation advised keeping politics and religion out of polite conversation, that rule no longer applies on campus—and it especially does not apply to religion. Talking about religion is common and it is often welcomed by the current generation of college students.

Religious Development during College

Up until the early 1990s, conventional wisdom about the impact of college on the religious development of students was uniform and unidirectional. Generally it was believed that as students experienced college they would break away from prior religious beliefs, reduce the intensity of what religious beliefs remained, and lessen their participation in religious activities such as worship and meditation. It was also assumed that they would become more "liberal" in their personal values and perspectives on social issues, and less dogmatic in their assessments of truth and goodness. However, researchers who have conducted a variety of national multiple-campus surveys over the past decade have concluded that such a pattern no longer holds sway. What we see now is much more complex and multidirectional.[22]

When Students Enter College

A survey of over 100,000 students at 236 diverse institutions, conducted by UCLA's Higher Education Research Institute (HERI)[23] found that students entering college during the fall of 2004 reported high levels of interest in spirituality and high levels of involvement in religious activities, while simultaneously reporting high levels of religious tolerance and acceptance of difference. In terms of specific beliefs and practices, 83 percent said they believed in the sacredness of life, 80 percent had an interest in spirituality, 76 percent were searching for meaning/purpose in life, 74 percent discussed their life philosophies with friends, 69 percent looked to their religious beliefs for guidance, and 64 percent viewed spirituality as a source of joy. Regarding a number of more traditionally religious concerns, 79 percent said they believe in God, 81 percent attended religious services, and 69 percent prayed on a regular basis.

Clearly this is a religiously or spiritually oriented generation of students, with many students expecting to advance in their personal spiritual development during the college years. More than two-thirds (69 percent) said it is essential or very important that their college experience enhance their self-understanding, 67 percent wanted their school to help them develop their personal values, and 48 percent said very explicitly that they want their college experience to encourage their personal expressions of spirituality.

Entering college students not only bring their faith to campus with them, they expect to "grow" in their religious and spiritual lives while in college. They know that they do not yet possess the depth of spirituality or religion they desire, and they readily acknowledge they don't yet fully know what they feel about faith, what they believe, or how they should live. Thus 65 percent say they occasionally feel distant from God, 57 percent question some inherited beliefs, and 48 percent feel angry with God. Finally, despite the parent-child continuities of religious belief and practice discovered by Smith and Denton in their survey of teenagers, just over 50 percent of entering students say they disagree with their families about religious matters. This generation anticipates that college will be the time when they make up their own minds on spiritual and religious matters.

Part of what is significant in this HERI study is that it can differentiate between students' views of spirituality and of religiousness, and it can make distinctions between religious commitment and religious engagement. That is, researchers can separate out the beliefs, values, and core commitments of students from their actual involvement in religious, spiritual, or meditative activities. What researchers discovered, however, was that these concerns were interrelated. For example, their measure of "spirituality" overlapped 78 percent with "religious commitment" and 71 percent with "religious engagement." Perhaps more surprising is that students who express a strong personal commitment to religious values are also typically very tolerant of those who do not share their beliefs, with more than 80 percent saying that "non-religious people can be just as moral as religious believers." Almost two-thirds of students (64 percent) also acknowledge that "people can grow spiritually without being religious."

Entering students who express a high commitment to religious or spiritual perspectives on life differ from those with little or no commitment to religion on many, but not all, social and political issues. With regard to politics, religious students are three times as apt to view themselves as political conservatives while skeptical students are much more likely to call themselves political liberals. On social issues, religiously oriented students are more apt to oppose abortion, same-sex marriages, the legalized use of marijuana, and casual sex than less religious students; religious students are more likely to support affirmative action and abolishing the death penalty than their less religious peers. Perhaps understandably, the least spiritual students are more apt to be involved in a search for meaning in their lives than the more religious, and this relatively less spiritual group also embraces a more ecumenical worldview than their religious counterparts. Most students, religious or not, described themselves as engaged in charitable activities and as compassionate.

According to the HERI data, students who report higher levels of spirituality and religiousness are more likely to be willing to seek counseling if needed, to find meaning in times of hardship, and to report being at peace or being centered during college. Perhaps not surprisingly, students entering college with a greater sense of spirituality and religiousness also report lower levels of participation in common college activities that can decrease physical well-being, that is, drinking beer, wine, or liquor; smoking cigarettes; and staying up all night. Overall, the more spiritual and religious students maintain a healthier diet and are actually more engaged in charitable causes and social activism than other students.

The overall conclusion of the HERI research team is that entering college students "are searching for deeper meaning in their lives, looking for ways to cultivate their inner selves, seeking to be compassionate and charitable, and determining what they think and feel about the many issues confronting their society and the global community."[24] They are, in other words, spiritual seekers. Since this is not the profile seen in high school students, it would seem that this quest for answers actually emerges early in the college experience. It is important to note, however, that over the past four decades college students have placed a decreasing emphasis on developing "a meaningful philosophy of life" and an increasing emphasis on being "very well off financially." In terms of specific numbers, a focus on "having a meaningful life" decreased as a primary goal from 86 percent in 1987 to 39 percent in 2003. Conversely, the percentage of students who desire wealth rose from 42 percent in 1967 to 74 percent in 2003. While today's college students are spiritual seekers, they are not oblivious to financial concerns (which is perhaps a reasonable response to the debt so many of them now accumulate during their college years).

The Impact of the First Year

Several studies have tried to assess changes in attitude and practice that occur during the first year of college. For example, a different UCLA-sponsored survey administered to 3,680 students at 50 colleges at the end of their first year revealed that religious involvement (attendance at religious services, participation in religious clubs, prayer and meditation) had declined noticeably over the course of the school year, and they were less likely to rate themselves as more spiritual than their peers. At the same time, however, students ending their first year expressed more commitment to integrating spirituality into their own lives. Commenting on these seemingly divergent findings, the researchers concluded that this pointed toward "a disturbing disconnect between students' expectations for their lives and reality."[25]

Another study that surveyed 408 first-year students at eight Methodist colleges at the beginning and end of their first year in college discovered a similarly mixed pattern of change. Over 90 percent of entering students reported that they had attended a religious service or performed volunteer work during high school, and nearly as many said they had spent time in prayer or had discussed religion or spirituality with their peers. Over three-fourths (76 percent) indicated that they had taken part in a high school youth religious club or group with nearly half (46 percent) indicating frequent or very frequent participation. Three out of five students said they had read or meditated on sacred or religious texts with, once again, nearly half indicating that they had done so frequently or very frequently. In short, these students came to college with a high level of self-reported religious activity. Then what happened?

Nearly two-thirds (63 percent) of the students indicated that their religious or spiritual beliefs had been strengthened during the freshman year, even though more than 90 percent said their religious activity had decreased to some degree. Forty percent said they had begun to more seriously question their religious beliefs during their first year of college, and about three in four attributed their own religious change to the positive influence of peers.

Clearly the first year is an important one for the traditional college student. Many students begin to question their childhood religious beliefs and convictions while reducing their engagement in religious activities. Still, the majority see themselves as more religious and spiritual by the year's end. This gap between being less engaged yet more spiritual may reflect an intensified struggle in their journey of self-discovery and search for meaning and purpose. At least, that is the conclusion of many who write about college student development.[26]

The Collegiate Religious Journey

An ever-enlarging number of studies indicate that students maintain a keen interest in matters of religion and spirituality through their undergraduate years. One study of college juniors, for example, showed they place a high value on integrating spirituality into their lives, with more than 70 percent saying they discuss religion/spirituality with friends, they view themselves as spiritual beings, and they pray on a regular basis. Three-quarters of these juniors indicated that they are searching for meaning and purpose in life and that religious and spiritual beliefs have shaped their identity. By this point in the college trajectory, however, at least one in five students expresses a high degree of skepticism about religion and spirituality, and one in four says he or she is indifferent regarding the existence of a "Supreme Being."[27]

Similar results were obtained in a national survey of 1,200 students conducted by Harvard University in the spring of 2006. Seven in ten of the survey respondents reported that "religion plays an important role in their lives." One in four indicated they had "become more spiritual since entering college" and only 7 percent said they had "become less spiritual."[28]

This picture is largely confirmed by an ethnographic study undertaken by Conrad Cherry, Betty A. DeBerg, and Amanda Porterfield. They report that at the four schools they investigated—three private and one public—spirituality and religion are alive and well. Their book, *Religion on Campus*, characterizes students "as spiritual seekers rather than religious dwellers . . . constructing their spirituality without much regard to the boundaries dividing religious denominations, traditions, or organizations."[29] Students at the four institutions reported participating in a variety of spiritual and religious activities, reflecting the pluralistic nature of their spiritualities and the diverse ways in which they express beliefs. The three private colleges maintained a campus environment that largely encouraged religious life and spiritual questing, and even the state university provided a faith-friendly climate and numerous specific opportunities for religious/spiritual exploration and discovery to take place. Students generally perceived their campuses as being supportive of rather than hostile to their own spiritual searching.

What this seems to indicate is that students do not necessarily become less spiritual or less religious during college, but they do learn to reflect on their religious beliefs in a more questioning, inquisitive, and critical manner. Over time, college students develop more complexity in their thinking about what is true and good, their own sense of self, and their social relationships. In the religious realm, this complexity may entail a movement away from childhood faith practices. Sometimes this means students move away from faith altogether, but often it means students have developed more nuanced ways of expressing their spiritual and religious convictions.

Where Influence Happens

How exactly does the college experience impact students? What facets of college life are most influential? Dividing the campus environment into the four domains of culture, curriculum, co-curriculum, and community can help make sense of some complex dynamics.[30]

Culture

Does the culture of a college—its shared values, character, mission, identity, and campus ethos—have an impact on the religious and spiritual development of students? The simple answer is "yes," but the impact is mixed. A recent national survey shows that about one-third of both first-year students and seniors indicate that their collegiate experience has contributed "quite a bit" or "very much" to "their deepened sense of spirituality," and students at denominational colleges report that their college experience has had an even more pronounced impact on their spiritual development.[31] A study focusing explicitly on Lutheran schools similarly found that a greater proportion of students enrolled in these church-related colleges and universities reported having developed a sense of purpose and having integrated their faith with other aspirations in life than was the case with students at public universities.[32]

While most studies show church-related colleges as having a positive influence on the spiritual development of students, it should be noted that other studies found that a college's particular church affiliation was not a significant predictor of student religious development.[33] Conversely, students at elite, secular colleges do seem to be more apt to show a decline in religious commitment and engagement than students at other colleges.[34]

Some of the observable differences between students at church-related and secular institutions may not be related all that closely to what takes place on campus. That is, the existing reputation of a college or university may lead students to self-select certain schools over others. In these cases, the culture of the campus functions largely as an attractor of certain kinds of students, and that mix of students itself then becomes the primary shaper of other students' experiences. Once on campus, students who consider themselves "born-again" are more likely to remain religiously engaged throughout their entire college careers. This suggests that intensity of religious commitment may be more determinate of religious practice than mere affiliation with a church denomination.[35]

Curriculum

The curriculum, as the academic enactment of a college's culture and mission, is intended to help students synthesize and apply classroom, field-based, community, and service learning to their personal development, including helping students find purpose and meaning in life. Based on limited research, it appears that enrollment in academic courses focusing on religion assists students in developing more complete and complex understandings of themselves and their beliefs.[36] And many students expect the religious studies classroom to do this—to be a "site and resource for religious meaning and personal transformation."[37] But knowing more about religion does not automatically equate with spiritual or religious development. Studying Catholicism is not the same thing as being a Catholic.

If there is one thing that stands out with regard to the curriculum, however, it is the dearth of support students find for their own spiritual or religious journeys in classes, course work, and conversations with faculty. A recent UCLA poll indicated that juniors at forty-six diverse institutions expressed a strong desire to become more engaged in their religious/spiritual journeys, but few students receive any guidance or direction related to this concern in their classes or from their professors. Over half of college students report that their professors never offered them any opportunities to discuss the meaning and purpose of life, and nearly half were dissatisfied because their college experiences did not provide them with any "opportunities for religious/spiritual reflection."[38]

Cocurriculum

Students with high religious engagement in high school are apt to be similarly engaged during the first semester in college, and this in turn influences a relatively high degree of involvement in religious activities in the second semester. But having strong religious beliefs—having a strong interior commitment to faith—was not a significant predictor of high engagement in religious practices and activities. Thus habits of the hand (i.e., behaviors) were more significant for many students than habits of the heart or head in keeping them connected with spiritual and religious concerns. This "suggests that involvement is a more potent indicator of engagement than perceptions, attitudes, and beliefs. Religious involvement . . . is primarily behavioral, rather than perceptual."[39] To the degree this is true, the cocurriculum is a critical factor in the spiritual and religious development of college students.

In many colleges today, cocurricular experiences are largely the province of student affairs and campus ministry professionals. Over the past century they have increasingly assumed the responsibility for those aspects of student development that are not directly academic, but are instead social, moral, ethical, civic, spiritual, or religious in nature. Participating in campus activities alongside faculty and peers who have strong religious commitments helps develop, maintain, and strengthen students' entering religious beliefs.[40] College students with curiosity about exploring and developing their spirituality find social approval for regular church attendance in their dorm-mates' involvement in church activities, and peers who regularly attend church services strengthen other students' religious beliefs.[41]

It is important to note that involvement in religious activities is positively correlated with involvement in other college events. Thus college freshmen and seniors at a wide range of colleges who "frequently engage in spiritually-enhancing practices also participate more in a broad cross-section of collegiate activities."[42] In general, religiously involved students have a more positive attitude toward their colleges than do their peers. Furthermore, religious involvement does not seem to sap energy from studying and pursing academic matters. A recent review of the research concluded that "spirituality-enhancing activities do not seem to hinder, and may even have mildly salutary effects on, engagement in educationally purposeful activities and desired outcomes of college."[43]

Community

The college or university community includes everyone at the institution—faculty, student affairs professionals, the ministry office (if a college or university has one), administrators, staff, and students—and relationships with people from all of these different sectors of the school are potentially part of a student's education. Relationships with others—with other fellow travelers whether they are faculty, staff, or other students—can be very important in the journey of college students as they grow and develop religiously and spiritually.

Research by Ernest Pascarella and Patrick Terenzini confirms what we all know: that student-faculty relationships are critical for well-rounded student development.[44] Obviously this includes the roles faculty can play in the faith development of students. At church-related colleges (especially those with decidedly evangelical identities) students often develop strong personal relationships with faculty, and these relationships tend to include discussions of their personal lives. Faculty at these schools frequently see themselves as mentors and role models, and they willingly accept the responsibilities that entails. Not surprisingly, even at nonchurch-related colleges and universities, it is often (but not always) faculty with strong faith commitments who are more apt to enter into student relationships in which religious and spiritual issues are manifest.[45]

Other students are also significant conversation partners as students sort through matters related to spirituality and religion. For example, peer interactions were more influential than parental pressure in determining whether Muslim women students felt accepted or alienated when they veiled themselves on campus.[46] But "community" can also be experienced in other ways. African American students, for example, have noted that local church congregations often provide important opportunities for them to explore their spirituality, which in turn helps them persist in college.[47] In general, students desire social support from others when they are under stress or duress, and stress is a normal part of college life. But even students who are relatively stress-free value their relationships with others as they sort through their religious and spiritual priorities. A sense of community is important as students make important life decisions during their years in college.

Conclusions

The development of religious beliefs and engagement during the college years is complex and not easy to profile. Students are diverse and that must never be forgotten. But some general conclusions can be drawn from the empirical evidence and from the perspectives of educators who have been working with and observing students all their lives.

First, it is apparent that many students have an interest in religion and spirituality throughout college. Students are searching for meaning and community. While this search often leads them away from the organized religious practices and beliefs of their past, it is generally not a journey away from faith and spirituality, but rather a journey toward a more complex spiritual and religious identity. At the end of college, students typically are less tradition-bound in their practice of connecting to a greater source, a supernatural Power, or a personal God than they were at the beginning. They have experimented with a variety of avenues and approaches, and they have become somewhat more consumer-oriented in their religiosity, selecting from a variety of forms of worship and spirituality the ones that best meet their unique needs and lifestyles.

Second, the popular distinction between being "religious" and being "spiritual" is not particularly helpful in understanding the religious and spiritual journeys of today's college students. Rather, college and university students often value both the inner life of faith (spirituality) and the outer life (religion). Some people would even argue that separating spirituality and religion may not even be possible. Rather, being and doing are inextricably connected. The language of "vocation," which is being adopted at many colleges and universities, provides one way of combining these two concerns. The notion of vocation assumes that students grow and develop by having meaning and purpose in their lives, which ideally leads to a life of service to others.[48]

Third, being deeply spiritual and/or religious requires serious thought, study, and critical self-reflection, and sharing one's perspectives with others enhances personal growth and development. As Scotty McLennan, dean of Student Life at Stanford University reminds us: "Potpourri religion is usually not very deep and sustaining; digging shallow wells in a field usually will not produce water."[49] Religious traditions have merit because they have been tested and refined and can thus provide an important intellectual as well as inspirational foundation. The serious examination of religious practices and beliefs can help students become more rigorous, intellectually critical thinkers.

Fourth, the religious profile of contemporary traditional-aged college students suggests that religion and spirituality are integrated into their overall sense of identity and personhood. This underscores the need to view education holistically. Students develop as whole persons. Their cognitive skills and their ability to think with more complexity develop in conjunction with changes in emotional and social maturity, sense of self-identity and moral purpose, and interpersonal relationships. In this holistic process they are continuously asking "big questions"—How do I know? Who am I? What relationships do I want with others?—as they seek out valid forms of knowledge and places to stand in the midst of uncertainty. Spiritually and religiously this means evolving away from strong dependence upon authority figures toward more interdependence with others, and social relationships with others who are different from them. In their journeys toward self-authorship, the challenge and support of fellow travelers are essential.

Students themselves are seldom able to give well-reasoned, thoughtful, and integrated responses to the life questions they face or to answer those questions with much self-confidence and conviction, but, like many of the rest of us, they continue to address them anyway. A holistic approach to student learning and development—an approach that includes some form of spiritual and religious development as an integral part of a school's culture, curriculum, cocurriculum, and community—can help students as they negotiate their way through the complex journey that is college.

Larry A. Braskamp is a Senior Scholar at the Association of American Colleges and Universities and former Vice President for Academic Affairs at Loyola University Chicago. He is coauthor of *Putting Students First: How Colleges Develop Students Purposefully.*

9

The Different Spiritualities of the Students We Teach

Robert J. Nash and DeMethra LaSha Bradley

As people who co-teach seminars on the topic of religious pluralism at a professional college of education and social services, we have learned one, fundamental principle through the years: There is as much spiritual difference *within* most particular religious narratives or traditions as there is *between and among* different religious groups. This principle was reinforced for us at a national conference we recently organized and ran for the American College Personnel Association on the topic of how to talk constructively about religious pluralism on college campuses. Conference participants included faculty members, campus ministers, student affairs professionals, and students (both graduate and undergraduate) from a variety of schools, and no two participants narrativized or practiced their beliefs (or nonbeliefs) in exactly the same way. Even among the seemingly most similar, there were always elements of difference.

This same sense of religious difference has become a low but growing rumble on most American college and university campuses, and in our classes and other venues we have witnessed how this rumble can sometimes intensify into a loud growl. We worry about the potential for that growl to transform itself into a dangerously divisive force at America's mainstream colleges and universities in the years ahead. Many college students find it difficult, if not impossible, to separate their religious identities from the other identities they possess. For some, religious identity is the primary indicator of who they are. As educators, we need to recognize that religion is part of the multicultural composition of our schools, and we need to develop ways of fostering intelligent, respectful conversations on our campuses that include religion as part of the discussion.

Students come to college with the honest hope of learning more about the world, themselves, and others and, as whole persons, all of that is blended together in the different ways they narrativize their lives. When students first get to campus they arrive with their life-to-date narratives already in hand—narratives that contain distinctive mixes of belief and unbelief—and when they leave campus those narratives will invariably have been altered in some way. In this process of change, there is no road map that applies to everyone. Each student is unique.

Having said that, however, we believe it is helpful to analyze some of the most common spiritual narratives we have heard from our own students. Spiritual narratives represent different generally religious orientations toward life, but these orientations do not necessarily line up with the doctrinal and behavioral differences that divide the various historic religions from one another. Spiritual narratives are personal. They make sense of personal experiences and articulate personal convictions autobiographically. In what follows, we briefly identify and describe some of the most common student spiritual narratives, and we then make some observations about how to orchestrate meaningful conversations on campus, both inside and outside the conventional classroom space, involving students who represent these different spiritualities.

Spirituality and Spiritual Narratives

Whether Christian, Muslim, Jew, Buddhist, or Hindu, or whether theist, agnostic, atheist, or polytheist, students come to college with all shapes and sizes of spirituality.[1] By spirituality, we mean the following: a penchant, probably hardwired into all humans, to ponder the imponderable, to ask the unanswerable questions about the meaning of life, especially its omnipresent, unavoidable pain, suffering, and death—conditions that paradoxically coexist with life's unalloyed joys, pleasures, and satisfactions. More succinctly, spirituality begins with the question raised time and time again by such philosophers as Leibniz, Schelling, Schopenhauer, and Heidegger: "Why is there something rather than nothing?"

Among our students, the spiritual questions that surface most frequently include: Does my life really matter to anyone but myself? Why am I plagued at the most inopportune times by a longing for something more, even when it seems that I have it all? Why am I so restless? Is there really some purpose or rationale to life that can produce stability or a sense of permanence? Why, in spite of all the corruption and selfishness in the world, do I still cling to the possibility that I, and others, can live our lives with dignity and integrity? Is there any larger reason why I am alive—beyond satisfying my basic physical and psychological needs? Why do my pleasures and joys seem so fleeting? Why do people have to make war, oppress the have-nots, and impose their intransigent beliefs on unwilling others when a live-and-let-live philosophy of life seems so intuitively right?

Some of our students answer these questions by constructing narratives of meaning that are quite private and personal. Others are much more public about their spirituality, sometimes locating themselves within the frameworks of conventional religious traditions. Some students are grounded in doctrinal certainty; others are nagged by incessant doubt. The spirituality of our students manifests itself in many ways. All our students, however, need some sense of personal identity, a semblance of a community life in which they can participate, a reasonable way to discern what is right and wrong conduct, and a starting point for explaining those aspects of life that seem either enigmatic or ultimately unknowable. We have found in our teaching that these spiritual narratives cut across all age, gender, racial, ethnic, and socioeconomic groups. And there seems to be no way to reduce these narratives to something else. They are what they are: narratives of spiritual meaning and practice.

We try to respect the spiritual narratives of all our students. There are no right and wrong answers here: Each person's life has its own integrity. Our goal in the classroom is simply to invite each person fully into the conversation. To that end, we have found that our students are more likely to talk openly about their spirituality if we structure classroom discussions as mutual, open-ended conversations where we share our meaning-stories rather than as debates intended to convert or convince. We often start by asking: Would you tell us a little bit about your spirituality (emphasis on the *your*)? And each answer we receive expands our understanding of spirituality beyond what we knew before.

For some of our students, their spirituality is as instinctive as breathing. They do not need to think about it; they just do it. But, when they do take time to reflect on their spiritual acts and attitudes, those acts and attitudes themselves often become much more treasured and appreciated. For other students, however, spirituality seems to be a goal they are working toward. Like an exercise routine, they seek to incorporate spirituality into their lives by conscious choice and intentional habit. Many of our current students are especially attuned to the possibility of cultivating a form of spirituality that will provide them welcome surcease from the career rat race. Finally, some students describe their spirituality mainly as an impulse—something they act on in the moment with very few preset limits on what direction that impulse might take.[2]

Varieties of Student Spirituality

While it is impossible to reduce all the complexity of student spirituality to any simple list of alternatives or taxonomy of types, we have discovered that most students explain themselves using a relatively limited number of different general spiritual narratives.[3] Each student obviously has his or her own particularity to add, his or her own unique story to tell, but different versions of a handful of prominent narratives have come up again and again in our workshops and classes. We group them in five categories here: (1) orthodox believers; (2) mainline believers; (3) spiritual seekers; (4) spiritual humanists; and (5) spiritual skeptics.

Orthodox Believers

The orthodox believers we have met come in a wide variety of religious and philosophical stripes. With only a few disturbing exceptions, most remain humble but unyielding in their claims to be in possession of some absolute, revealed truth that most of their classmates and we obviously lack. Their confident, sometimes gentle sense of certainty attracts, more than repels, many of us. In classes and discussions, a small coterie of anti-orthodox skeptics, however, always manages to remain unconvinced, and they often have great difficulty concealing their disdain for any expression of uncompromising orthodox belief. The core narrative for orthodox believers is this: There is a Truth that is unimpeachable, immutable, and final, and it can only be found in a particular book, institution, prophet, or movement. The mission of the orthodox believer is to deliver this Truth to others as an act of love and generosity. While orthodox believers are usually religious students (often describing themselves as fundamentalists, evangelicals, or true believers), we have sometimes found a similar attitude among orthodox atheists who appear as certain about the nonexistence of a God as their theist counterparts are about God's existence.

Orthodox believers in our classes, despite their many differences, are certain that they are in possession of unimpeachable and absolute truth. Moreover, they are convinced of their moral responsibility to communicate this truth to others. Some publicly proselytize. Others are content simply to exemplify. Some openly recruit. Others are committed mainly to explain and teach. Still others believe that they have a duty to tell their spiritual stories whenever they can, because these stories have been so personally transformative. Some believe unequivocally that because their stories represent the whole truth, it is their spiritual right to convince others of this truth. More and more of them pride themselves on being "reborn," "saved," "chosen," or "enlightened." And then there are those who simply bow their heads in prayer, or sit in silent contemplation and meditation, and quietly thank their creator for bestowing such wondrous gifts of grace upon them.

When the topic of spirituality comes up, orthodox religious students generally describe their spirituality as directly linked to their religious beliefs. Thus doctrinal beliefs are primary and spirituality is secondary to how they understand themselves. Based on what we have heard in the classroom, free-floating spirituality is, for the orthodox believer, a threat to doctrinal certainty. One older, orthodox student said this to us after an encounter in class with someone she considered to be quite "liberal" in his religious beliefs: "I am a conservative Protestant and proud of it. I studied for the Baptist ministry some years ago, but I left because even they considered me too conservative. I am now a member of the Coalition for Christian Outreach and the Southern Baptist Church, and I've tried to loosen up a little bit. But I just can't. I am very happy here in this fundamentalist church. I'll admit that I'm an 'exclusivist' when it comes to my religion. I think that's the derisive word that came up in class. I won't—maybe I can't—change. Conservative Christianity is the home where the full truth of Jesus Christ lives. I hope to live forever in the fullness of this truth."

Mainline Believers

This is the spiritual narrative in which most of our students have spent their early lives. Mainline spirituality is a common denominator among the various Christian communities in the Western nations, but it is also present in certain Islamic, Buddhist, Hindu, and Afro-Caribbean religious communities as well. What distinguishes mainline believers from orthodox believers is the following: Mainliners seek a moderating balance between the traditional rubrics and rituals of their churches or religious organizations and their own freedom to interpret sacred texts and worship God in their own, unique ways.

Mainline students are rarely dogmatic or literalist. They want a secure sense of place in a specific religious community, but not at the expense of their spiritual individuality or their personal autonomy. Mainline believers are usually quite well versed in the beliefs and rituals of their religions, but they have also given themselves the right to express those beliefs and rituals outside the usual venues of worship services and other traditional religious activities. They tend to focus more on the feelings activated by religious rituals, and they look to re-create those feelings outside of the formal worship service. It is as if the traditional institutional beliefs and doctrines they follow are acknowledged as wonderful faith structures, but mainliners want to decorate and appoint those structures in their own way.

The key words of the mainline spiritual narrative are *unique, expressive,* and *individualistic.* Students who speak from this perspective readily acknowledge the traditional doctrines and rituals they espouse and practice, but they are also quick to add that they put their own special "twist" on some of these traditional beliefs and practices, and it is this special twist that mainliners typically describe as their own spirituality. Here is one mainliner's way of describing her spirituality: "I am basically a person who is very happy being a Reform Jew. I have a great fondness for my temple, my rabbi, and my community. I would say that being a Jew is all about being a believer in Judaism. I was concerned throughout the semester that being a mainline religious believer just wasn't sexy. I have no complaints about my religious community. I am not in the middle of some religious identity crisis. I don't need to look to the East or to atheistic secularism. As far as I'm concerned, religion is all about growing up in a particular religious community, making friends, attending services, finding a spirituality that makes you happy. Sometimes you lapse, sometimes you don't, but you've always got something to fall back on. If this isn't enough, then tweak your religion a bit to fit your needs, or find another religion. It's really pretty simple."

Spiritual Seekers

Many students today are seekers. They are not yet sure where they will end up in their journeys of life and, for one reason or another, they do not feel spiritually at home in any existing traditional religion. They are looking for something better or, at least, better suited to them. This is an eclectic category and it is impossible to develop one description that fits all the seeker students we know. There are, however, three main variants of this strand of student spirituality: wounded seekers, mystical seekers, and social justice seekers.

Some of our students situate themselves within what can only be called *a spirituality of wounded seeking.* These include both believers and nonbelievers who have had a tragic personal history of being severely harmed—both physically and psychologically—in the religious communities of their youth.

This woundedness might stem from the overzealous efforts of well-meaning, yet still injurious, clergy, lovers, parents, relatives, and friends who, wittingly or unwittingly, impose guilt and suffering on those who doubt, question, or rebel from their childhood religious affiliations.

A spirituality of wounded seeking can also derive from religious promises not kept, expectations that are unrealistic, hypocrisies that are all too apparent, or the ubiquitous problem of *theodicy* in theistic religions. In our experience, in fact, theodicy has been the major cause of lost faith among those students who see themselves as wounded seekers. They are simply unable to explain and justify the presence of terrible suffering and evil, both in their own personal situations and in the world at large. How, they wonder, can organized religions claim that God, Allah, or Jehovah is an all-good, all-wise, all-loving, and all-compassionate supernatural being when wars, pestilence, natural disasters, and senseless accidents and misfortunes are all around us all the time?

In our classes and workshop, wounded seekers are usually well represented. We frequently hear them make these sorts of comments: "I am a recovering Catholic, and I'm very angry. All I've ever felt from my Catholic upbringing is guilt, regret, and sadness. There is so much hypocrisy in this church, and also in others that I've heard about here. I really resonated with that speaker yesterday who said that religion should 'empower,' not 'infuriate,' people. I know that I should grow up, stop my whining, and get a life, but I am just so sour on religion that I've become totally dysfunctional in this arena. Is there really any religion that doesn't wound its members?"

A different narrative of seeking that is becoming more popular among our students is the *mystical narrative*. A core group of mystical seekers exists among all the traditional and nontraditional religions that we know, and they have become a formidable presence in our classroom. What these spiritual mystics have in common is their dissatisfaction with both orthodox and mainline forms of religious belief and practice, which they often see as hegemonic or oppressive. Some turn to the East, some to alternative American religions such as Native American, Wiccan, or Neo-Pagan, some to folk religions, and many to private forms of spirituality. The mystical narrative appeals to our student seekers because it is rooted in a love of mystery, stillness, and attunement. Many mystical students are suspicious of the fitful, ambitious, hard-driving, high-achieving Western dream of success. They seek, instead, a spirituality of calmness, flow, mindfulness, and stillness. For them, a life of frenetic, materialistic activity is the ultimate nightmare to be avoided.

One aspiring mystical seeker at our recent conference expressed things this way: "I'm a floater among all the religio-spiritual stories I'm learning about at this conference. I love knowing that being mindful and fully present to my life can be spiritual. I am learning from the speakers that the meaning in my life will best be found only when I let go of my need to find some absolute, out-of-this-world truth to live by. I want to find the stillness, the compassion, and the calm presence in the center of all this craziness. To do this, I've got to keep my mouth shut and open my eyes and ears to the wonders and mysteries of life."

A third type of spiritual seeker that is showing up more frequently in our classes is the *social justice seeker*. Students attracted to this spiritual narrative generally reject the orthodox and mainline hopes of a heavenly kingdom to come. Instead, they want to build the kingdom of God on earth in the here and now. Their faith is activist, not doctrinal or meditative. They seek the liberation of oppressed peoples, equal rights, and social justice for everyone who is being discriminated against or treated unfairly. Radical social transformation on behalf of the least among us is the main theme of this spiritual narrative.

We have known many social justice seekers, and the attitude they share is captured well in the following student comment: "That liberation theologian who spoke today put her finger right on it. She said that 'religion historically has been prescribed as a happy pill meant to blunt the pain of racism and injustice in society.' She challenged us with the question of the day, as far as I'm concerned. She asked 'How effectively does your church and its theology speak to oppressed peoples and their struggles for liberation and self-determination? If your church ignores this question, then it is worse than irrelevant. It is evil.' "

For social justice seekers, religion only makes sense when it addresses human rights and exhorts believers to criticize and confront existing structures of power and privilege. Some social justice activists remain in the faith traditions of their youth, but they usually want to reform their religious groups in the direction of paying less attention to the needs of those who possess power and more attention to the poor and powerless. Other social justice seekers reject their inherited traditions and become public critics of religious structures that serve the status quo. And some, if they become frustrated enough, go on to become humanistic skeptics, agnostics, atheists, or postmodern pluralists who totally give up on religion and sometimes lose all hope that the world can ever truly be changed for the better.

What holds these three very different kinds of seekers together is the simple question: Why? Why do so many people hurt? Why have I been so deeply hurt by the people closest to me? Why do I find peace in nature or in my relationships with others, but not in the conventional teachings and structures of my childhood religious community? Why is my society so desensitized to the needs of the unfortunate? Why do I so often find the process of seeking itself more satisfying than that which I seek?

Student seekers are looking for meaning and purpose in life: They are hoping to find a rationale for living. These are people who have questioned and have even, in some cases, abandoned their parents' religions, ethnic heritages, politics, and nationalities in order to discover for themselves a more compelling religio-spiritual basis on which to build their lives. Because of that, seekers often question orthodox and mainline spiritual narratives. They find it hard to understand how anyone can be content with the neat and tidy answers of traditional religion.

Spiritual Humanists

Humanism is a belief system with deep roots in the great *secular* histories of the world, but elements of humanism are also apparent in all the great *sacred* histories of the world as well. The basic tenets of humanist spirituality include a naturalistic, as opposed to a supernatural, philosophy of life; a belief that consciousness does not survive death, because consciousness is a function of the material brain rather than some immaterial soul; and a conviction that human beings alone have the power and responsibility to solve their own problems without assistance from any mythical, superhuman beings.

Humanist spirituality assumes that people possess genuine freedom and that they have to become the masters of their own destiny. Humanist morality, accordingly, represents a here and now secular ethic dedicated to freedom, social justice, happiness, and social progress. Within this spiritual narrative, truth is an ideal that needs to be constructed and reconstructed over and over again rather than being a permanent dogma that can be discovered and obeyed. Democracy is usually thought of as the political system that is most compatible with the humanist vision of a flourishing social and economic order, and reason and the scientific method are typically seen as the best means of creating a better future. As convinced as they may be of their own beliefs, spiritual humanists also know they always need to be ready to question even their own most basic assumptions and convictions.

Many of the students who fall into this category can be called *existential humanists*. For these students, individual freedom and authenticity are the central features of their spirituality. Those students who identify with existentialist spirituality are convinced that the traditional God of monotheism or the gods of polytheism are no longer viable choices for creating an authentic life. The loss of religious, moral, and spiritual absolutes in the modern, secular world has pushed them to the existential abyss that Sartre portrayed in his plays and philosophical writings. They see each of us as "condemned to freedom," in the sense that it is our responsibility, and our responsibility alone, to make meaning. For these students, as for the nineteenth-century existentialist Nietzsche, God or the gods have disappeared forever, if they ever existed at all. Now, it is up to each one of us to get on with our lives on our own. The way of living an authentic life is to take full responsibility for all of one's conscious choices and to shape and define oneself by the pattern of those decisions.

One existential humanist we know explains this posture by saying: "I try not to figure everything out the way most of you are trying to do. The point for me is that there is no point. Finding meaning is all well and good, but I think living my way into meaning is even better." Commenting on the film *American Beauty*, another proponent of this view said: "A character in the film says 'Sometimes there is so much beauty in the world that I don't know whether I can stand it.' This is all I really need to know and to feel in order to make meaning. It's not *why* this beauty exists, it's *because* it exists that makes it so important to me." Existential humanists, for the most part, take life as it comes and try to make the best of it, and making the best of it involves finding personal meaning (or creating it) by how we choose to respond to what comes our way.

While some humanists are spiritual existentialists, other humanists adopt a rather different *spirituality of scientific empiricism*. Scientific empiricists come in various forms. Some are believers; others are not. They can be believers, nonbelievers, deists, theists, agnostics, or atheists. As a spiritual stance, scientific empiricism is methodologically open with regard to whether or not a God or the gods exist. Students who lean toward a spirituality of scientific empiricism typically call upon the evidence of astrophysics, organic evolution, biology, and the brain sciences to either support or repudiate various forms of theism. Most scientific empiricists, however, openly admit that no evidence could ever be found that would constitute incontrovertible proof for them that there is or is not a God.

If God is forever questionable, however, the world is not, and the world itself can be a source of deep spirituality for these students. Some scientific empiricists come close to being nature worshipers, in the sense that they stand in awe before the "miracles" of the natural world. Others are overcome with the majesty and grandeur of an ever-expanding cosmos. We may, in fact, be alone in the universe, utterly bereft of supernatural assistance and assurance, but the universe is a wondrous place. It is not such a big leap from that sense of natural wonder to an ethic of responsibility for our little planet and the people who live on it. Because of that, many scientific empiricists feel an almost religious call to use their knowledge of the natural sciences to create a better and more humane world for all people (or for all living things).

An acquaintance of ours who would clearly identify with this option describes empirical scientific spirituality as follows: "I am a scientific realist, a person trained in laboratory science. The scientific method has always been important to me. Don't tell me how to live my life until you can demonstrate that your advice is scientifically sound. Someone . . . talked about 'numinous moments,' and 'loss of rational boundaries.' This is all well and good, and even I can understand what this person was getting at. But, in the end, the objective truth of one's experience of these numinous moments can only be determined by rational evidence. Right? Isn't there a beauty to this type of verification that can provide a kind of awe and reverence?"

Being true to one's own personality and character is central to both the existential and the empirical variants of humanistic spirituality. While mainline believers enjoy some of the same creative freedom as the humanists, they ultimately ground their identity in foundational beliefs derived from sources outside themselves. In contrast, humanists are up front in announcing that their pursuit of a personal authenticity has everything to do with how they choose to orient themselves and move about in the world. They are quick to assert that it is the choices they make, and not the predetermined plans laid out by any higher power, that shape their lives. These students are proud to be the authors of their own lives. This self-authorship, which they sometimes refer to as the quality of *authenticity* (a term derived from the same root word as *author*), is what gives their existence meaning.

Spiritual Skeptics

Finally, we have noticed a growing number of spiritual skeptics in our courses. Some of these skeptics are militant atheists. Some are postmodern doubters. Some call themselves "spiritual libertarians" or "spiritual pluralists." Some are freethinkers. Some are "apatheists," students who are completely indifferent to religion, who maintain they could not care less whether there is or is not a God or gods. With the eighteenth-century French mathematician Pierre Simon Laplace, they might well declare they have no need whatsoever for the "deity hypothesis."

While it might seem counterintuitive to conflate skepticism and spirituality, it actually makes perfect sense to do so with our current "postmillennial" undergraduate and graduate students. Skepticism can be a healthy form of faith when it remains genuinely open to truth claims made by the world's greater and lesser-known religions. Skepticism is, in fact, part of the history of

Judaism, Christianity, Islam, and many Eastern religions and philosophies. To some extent, Maimonides, Paul Tillich, and Irshad Manji were all skeptics, but skeptics who chose to remain inside their respective religious and spiritual communities.

At base a skeptic is an inquirer, nothing more and nothing less. Skeptics are methodological questioners, wonderers, challengers, and doubters. This spiritual orientation lends itself to testing the claims of politicians, storytellers, and all those self-proclaimed prophets and messiahs who claim to be exclusively in possession of theological truth. Skepticism takes no ultimate, absolute, or supernatural claim for granted. In the past, skeptics like Hume and Kant successfully challenged many arguments for the existence of God. But in doing so, these skeptics of the past actually helped restore the centrality of faith, especially if we think of faith in terms of Kierkegaard's or Pascal's "leap of faith." Whether intended or not, what these skeptical philosophers did was shift the burden of religious belief from the head to the heart, thereby legitimizing feeling as an alternative, and respectable, path to God. Even though they openly challenged doctrinal certitudes, moral absolutes, and grand supernatural narratives, they helped revitalize religion by keeping it honest and closer to the heart.

Spiritual skepticism is not always, however, a friend of faith, and it does not need to be. Spirituality represents the deepest way we respond to reality as we know it, and if someone sees reality as void and empty, that has to be part of his or her spirituality. Thus some of the skeptical students we know are very assertive in their claims that we are utterly alone in the universe, beyond final Divine revelations and interventions, and have been left to our own human devices. What makes this kind of skepticism spiritual is that it clings to courage and hope as necessary human virtues, even in the face of gnawing pessimism, cynicism, relativism, anarchy, and despair. The key to happiness in a world without ultimate meaning is, for those students who subscribe to a spirituality of extreme skepticism, to learn how to accept their own vulnerability and mortality, and nevertheless to then live with intelligence, dignity, style, and grace.

One of our relatively articulate student skeptics explained, "You know, just because I call myself a postmodern skeptic, it doesn't mean that I demonize all religion or spirituality. In fact, I'm a pluralist, admittedly more secular than religious, but still a respectful pluralist. As a result of this course, I have actually become genuinely open to religious diversity. But I want the right to be able to raise concerns and doubts about what others are claiming to be absolutely irrefutable religious and spiritual truths." Another skeptical student said, "I ask all believers if their beliefs are really enough each and every day to get them up and out of bed in the morning. I ask this, because I myself want something to get up for each day. Moreover, I don't always want to be a 'lone wolf,' a 'free agent,' going my merry way questioning everything, committing to nothing; acting cynical and being a negative force with everyone. But neither do I want to cling to some fantastic religious beliefs merely because I'm lonely, or afraid, or in need of cheap comfort."

In our classroom, spiritual skeptics never play favorites when it comes to religious or spiritual beliefs. They are never shy about asking every believer and nonbeliever the same provocative and evocative questions. As unrelenting questioners and honest listeners, they contribute immensely to our classroom learning community. While, at times, some skeptics can be irritating and smug, most whom we know are willing to challenge others by first questioning their own beliefs. Spiritual skeptics are not typically hostile. Most of them, in fact, are quite comfortable sharing their own quasi-spiritual narratives of doubt, wonder, and Socratic dialogue. Their motto might well be Alfred Lord Tennyson's: "There is more faith in honest doubt than in most of the creeds of the world." At their best, they play the role of Socrates, because, like him, they admit that when it comes to ultimates, they really know nothing at all.

Talking among and between Spiritualities

It can be difficult to engender conversation in the classroom (or outside the classroom) among and between students who embody different spiritualities, but there are ways this can be done.[4] In light of the religious tensions that exist on our campuses, in our nation, and around the world, this is also a necessary task. It is not something we can avoid, but represents instead a critical challenge to American higher education. Most of us, however, have little or no experience in leading such dialogues about religious and spiritual difference. Where does one begin?

When inviting students to talk about their spirituality, we first of all encourage them to speak *from* their religious and spiritual narratives, not *for* their narratives. In doing this, we try to convey the clear message that we value the differences within and between their various narratives. When speaking about matters of faith and spirituality, it is everyone's particular voice that matters. Traditions do not dialogue; people do. Perhaps not surprisingly, we find that our teaching is most successful when everyone is committed to listening to one another's narratives with respect and generosity.

We work hard to create a safe space in our classes where robust dialogue can take place. That kind of safe space is not, of course, built overnight. It requires time, patience, and strenuous effort, as well as a willingness to be personally tested. One important ingredient is student interest. Enthusiasm, we have found, is a great motivator. If students are engaged, they will make sure good conversation happens. Background knowledge is equally important, so we try to be as informed as possible and to add information to the conversation when appropriate. The most critical element, however, may be the sage advice to "lead by example." To that end, we try to model how to ask honest and probing questions of one another—questions that have no hidden agendas and that are not self-promoting. As co-instructors, we hope that our own mutually respectful interchanges will model the type of conversation we want to happen with our students.

Particularly in class settings, we counsel our students to question one another in ways that allow the other person or persons to look smart, not stupid. The classroom is not a war zone where the last, bloodied soldier left standing is the victor. Instead, we describe our classroom as a no-fire zone where everyone should be safe from both unfriendly *and* friendly fire. An important ground rule in this regard is that everyone should be afforded the initial respect of attributing the best possible motive to what is said. The initial positive attribution is intended to foster what the comparative religions scholar Diana Eck calls "constant communication—meeting, exchange, traffic, criticism, reflection, reparation, and renewal."[5] For meaningful dialogue about religio-spiritual differences to take place, charity and generosity are key and necessary virtues.

In our no-fire conversational space, we encourage our students to take nothing at "face value." There will always be other interpretations of what is said when people engage in dialogue about their religio-spiritual narratives. Narratives of meaning are tied closely to the unique experiences of each person, but the words we use to describe those experiences are limited in number. In conversation about spirituality, it is inevitable that the same words will take on different meanings for different students with different narratives. Think, for example, of these words: *God, faith, meaning, church, tradition, postmodern, East, West, prayer, worship, mindfulness, social justice,* and *transcendence.* All of these words, and a host of others that we use in religiously oriented conversations, are indeterminate. They carry many meanings, not one clear meaning, and always insert a degree of inexactness, uncertainty, and vagueness into the discussion. In religious dialogue nothing is ever settled once and for all—but settling on one answer is not the point.

Conversations about religious differences are by definition open-ended. Because of that, we encourage our students to be open-minded, but not so open-minded that nothing is ever challenged. In fact, we urge them to ask clarifying questions when religio-spiritual narratives are being discussed. We tell our students to question one another, asking for more detail or depth of description. Our goal is to get as many people as possible engaged in the dialogue, which helps keep the conversation as a whole fair and reciprocal. Sometimes we ask students to paraphrase what they have just heard a class-mate say, and we then ask the classmate to agree with, or correct, that para-phrase.

Questions can be probing. For example, in one recent class, a mainline student was asked: "How is it possible for you to still maintain a strong faith in an all-loving and compassionate God when there are tsunamis, wars, birth defects, and terrible, inexplicable suffering all around us?" After responding to this genuinely curious, well-meaning question, the student then returned the question to the questioner for his own reactions. What resulted from this back-and-forth was an engaging and sensitive conversation between a wounded ex-believer and a mainline believer on the classical problem of theodicy. It wasn't long before everyone else had gotten their opinions about good and evil out on the floor too.

As co-instructors, we have learned that conflict is inevitable in these types of dialogues, so we are always prepared for the worst. The goal is not to avoid all conflict, however, but to deal with it well; conflict can be hugely beneficial for the learning process. Nonetheless, how conflict is handled—how one facili-tates a continuing conversation after a controversial comment has been aired—is crucial. These inevitable clashes are one of the main reasons we work so hard to establish ground rules for dialogue at the beginning of the semester. By revisiting those ground rules both during and after a difficult exchange, we have found we can often calm down a potentially explosive situation. One of the benefits of this approach is that students begin to realize that conflict in and of itself need not be a conversation stopper and that civil discussion can continue even when the topic is difficult and tension-laden.

Reflecting on the numerous dialogues in which we have engaged our students both inside and outside the classroom, the following guidelines summarize most of what we have learned about facilitating constructive re-ligio-spiritual conversations either in the classroom or in other campus set-tings:

- Acknowledge at the outset the difficulty of embarking on these con-versations, stressing that talking about religious and spiritual differ-ences is rarely easy. Why is this the case? Because for many people, including college students, religio-spiritual concerns are part of their core identities.

- Don't forget to mention, however, the many positive benefits that can come out of these conversations, including enhanced understanding of different religio-spiritual stories, learning ways to communicate better about difference, and maybe even cultivating a richer and deeper personal narrative of meaning.
- Reiterate as often as necessary that your role is to create and facilitate a safe yet invigorating space where difficult but meaningful conversation can take place.
- Encourage active, generous listening by frequently asking individuals to paraphrase what someone else has just shared with the group. And then give the original speaker a chance to respond to the reframing.
- Remind those involved in the conversation to suspend any initial negative reactions they might have to what someone else has said that are based on religio-spiritual stereotypes, false information, or phobias of any kind. Ask them to look instead for the best, not the worst, way of making sense of the narrative. Always be willing to question what you believe, and to believe what you have previously questioned.
- Most of the time, *process* will be at least as important as *product* in these conversations. Think of religion and spirituality as verbs, not nouns; as ways of living, rather than as a fixed set of truths to believe. The main question for both instructors and students ought to be "Am I actually *living* what I believe rather than *believing* what I'm not living"?
- Provide times for feedback throughout the semester at strategically set times so that everyone is aware of what is working and what is not. This requires humility on the part of the instructor, a willingness to admit that the group process could always be better, and the courage to make changes when students offer insightful suggestions.
- Learn to love and to live in the questions of life and thereby model how to accept and return questions. As the poet Rainer Maria Rilke once said: "Love the questions . . . be patient toward all that is unsolved . . . do not now seek the answers which cannot be given you because you would not be able to live them . . . perhaps you will gradually, without noticing it, live along some distant day into the answer."[6]

Robert J. Nash is Professor of Integrated Professional Studies at the College of Education and Social Services of the University of Vermont and the author of *Religious Pluralism in the Academy: Opening the Dialogue.* **DeMethra LaSha Bradley** is a Student Life Professional at the Center for Student Ethics and Standards at the University of Vermont.

IO

Spirituality, Diversity, and Learner-Centered Teaching: A Generative Paradox

Elizabeth J. Tisdell

Good teaching is filled with paradox; so is good living. After all, we cannot really embrace life in all its mystery and complexity without dealing with the tension of its opposites and contradictions. As Parker Palmer suggests, embracing the paradoxical tensions of life often pulls us open to the spirit and to new possibilities.[1] The Trappist monk Thomas Merton noted that paradox was also part of the spiritual life. Drawing on the famous story of Jonas and the whale in the Hebrew Scripture, Merton described his own spiritual journey as "traveling toward destiny in the belly of a paradox."[2]

Like Merton and Jonas, I too live in the belly of a paradox in my role as a professor who works mainly with adult students at a state university, teaching courses that deal with diversity. Even though the academic setting is secular, I find I simply cannot teach in a culturally responsive or learner-centered way without encountering the spiritual, since the secular and the spiritual overlap in the lived experiences of my students. Some would argue that spirituality has no place in secular higher education—that the sacred and the secular are opposites and should be kept apart. I believe, however, that the experiences of many students (as well as many faculty members) are at least partly characterized by a secular-spiritual dialectic that can open up new possibilities for culturally responsive teaching. An encounter with the spiritual is almost unavoidable in culturally responsive teaching even if the educational setting is clearly secular.[3]

The Spiritual-Secular Dialectic and Higher Education

In his analysis of learner-centered teaching, Douglas Robertson notes the many paradoxes that are inherent in teaching that seeks to facilitate student learning and engagement. These tensions include control of course content versus going with the flow; facilitator role versus evaluator role; and a focus on the subject versus a focus on learners' needs.[4] Rather than seeing this as a problem, Robertson argues that "these enduring, deep-seated contradictions in the learner-centered teaching role have the potential to be transformed into generative paradoxes, or contradictions in which both sides of the opposition are true and both sides feed rather than fight each other."[5] Robertson does not discuss the tension between the secular and the spiritual, nor does he even mention spirituality. But clearly the secular-spiritual dialectic also has the potential to become a generative paradox for learner-centered teaching. If one teaches in a way that genuinely takes into account learners' needs and the multiple ways they construct meaning, one cannot help touching on the spiritual. Indeed, even in a secular setting, the spiritual and the secular can "feed rather than fight each other."

Teaching touches on the spiritual in many settings, but in my experience teaching for diversity in a way that is culturally responsive to the varied identities of student learners almost always includes the spiritual. Teaching for diversity means taking into account the ways in which both individual learners and different cultural groups construct and value knowledge—and some cultural groups place more emphasis on the spiritual than others. Cynthia B. Dillard, Daa'lyah Abdur-Rashid, and Cynthia Tyson[6] make this point in their discussion of what it means to be African American and female in a secular American academy that is still largely white and relatively male. In considering the epistemologies that frequently ground scholars of color, they note: "Many scholars and activists involved in the reformation of the academy have worldviews deeply embedded in the spiritual. The heretofore silencing of the spiritual voice through privileging the academic voice is increasingly being drowned out by the emphatic chorus of those whose underlying versions of truth cry out 'We are a spiritual people!' "[7]

Dillard, Abdur-Rashid, and Tyson are not saying that white people are not spiritual. Rather, they are suggesting that as a result of both the influence of the Enlightenment and the separation of church and state in the United States, the secular academy has focused almost exclusively on a form of rationality that explicitly excludes the religious and the spiritual. But many cultural groups are not as epistemologically grounded in Enlightenment rationality as white culture in the United States. For these other groups, the cutting off of the spiritual from the academic seems more foreign than it may seem to their white Euro-American peers. But with the ever-increasing cultural diversity of higher education and the need to be culturally responsive to all learners, it is important for the academy to reconsider the role of spirituality in constructing knowledge.

In recent years the role of spirituality and religion in higher education has begun to attract more attention. Various studies have addressed cocurricular concerns[8] and some have examined curricular matters as well.[9] With a few exceptions,[10] only minimal consideration has been given to how spirituality can inform teaching specifically about and within differences of race, gender, and culture. This has been the focus of much of my own work,[11] and what I have found is that ironically there may be more freedom to incorporate spirituality (understood in a very broad sense) in classrooms in secular universities than is the case in colleges or universities connected with a specific religious tradition. In the secular setting of the public university with its diverse student body, it may be easier to have the two sides of the spiritual-secular paradox feed rather than fight each other because there is no institutional pressure to adhere to a particular religious tradition. My own spiritual and cultural story, and its relationship to my scholarship and teaching, sheds light on how I have come to this conclusion.

Spirituality and Cultural Identity in My Scholarship and Teaching

I have always been interested in spirituality, but the development of my academic interest in the relationship between spirituality and culturally responsive teaching has been more of a journey. That journey is, of course, partially rooted in my background as one who was reared Roman Catholic, in a family that valued education. For me, and for most schooled in the Catholic tradition (perhaps unlike members of some other Christian denominations), there has never been a conflict between being a Christian and pursuing the life of the mind. Furthermore, the tradition of Catholic social teaching suggests that faith without works is empty. Thus, it is a tradition that emphasizes working for social justice and that places less emphasis on proselytizing. (This is different from many evangelical Christian traditions, which tend to emphasize giving verbal witness to their faith.) My grounding in Catholic social teaching about justice may explain why I have centered my research and teaching around issues of social justice that challenge power relations based on gender, race, and culture.

My work as an educator has also been informed by my own spiritual search for meaning, justice-making, healing, and wholeness, both for myself and others. While my current spirituality is informed by a variety of spiritual traditions, it remains heavily rooted in what is foundational to my own particular religious background: the teachings of Jesus as interpreted through the Roman Catholic tradition in which I was reared, and particularly the way that tradition connects spirituality to social justice. How I see my vocation, or role as a person in the world, and as a teacher, is very much grounded in the paraphrased passage of Isaiah 42 (also repeated in Luke's Gospel): "to bring glad tidings to the lowly, to heal the broken hearted, to comfort those who mourn, and to set the captives free."

How I have lived out this vocation has taken different forms over the years. Since completing my doctorate in 1992, I have been an education professor teaching mostly graduate students and doing research related to challenging systems of oppression based on race, gender, and culture in higher education. While I currently teach in a doctoral program at a public research university, I have taught in the private sector as well. My master's degree is in religion, and before completing my doctorate, my earlier years in higher education (from 1979 to 1989) were spent working as a Roman Catholic campus minister and adjunct religion and math instructor, for three years at a large state university and for seven years at a Jesuit university. Thus I have worked in different types of institutions of higher education in different capacities.

The institution in which I work at any given time, and my particular role in it, determines how I live out the message of Isaiah 42, and whether or not I ever explicitly talk about that message, or about the underlying spirituality that motivates my work. As a campus minister it was appropriate for me to do so. In my current position teaching doctoral students, it is not usually directly relevant to my work, so I talk about the explicitly Christian aspects of my own spirituality only in rare circumstances. However, given that my recent research has been in the area of spirituality, culture, and higher education, I do discuss the topic of spirituality in a less personal sense. This includes references to academic studies of spirituality drawn from the fields of psychology, sociology, religious studies, and education as well as my own research.

While I tend not to discuss *my own* spirituality in a very direct way in teaching about cultural issues, it is neither possible nor desirable to wholly avoid the topic. In teaching about cultural issues, I expect students to explore and share aspects of their own cultural story, and they have a right to expect me to be similarly forthcoming. So I talk about growing up in a white, Irish American, Roman Catholic family with all its rituals and rules, because that is an important part of my own cultural story. More important, telling my cultural story in this way gives students the freedom to tell their cultural stories in ways that include religion and spirituality if they are part of those stories.

I have taught in a number of highly multicultural and religiously pluralistic contexts and in those settings students in my classes were naturally presented with a wide range of cultural stories that often included cultural and religious difference. In my current teaching context in central Pennsylvania, where the vast majority of my students are white and of Christian background, there is less cultural diversity in the classroom than in other institutions where I have taught, so I make sure to include readings by and about members of other cultural groups. Further, most of my students are or will be teaching or working in a multicultural and religiously pluralistic context reflective of the larger world. As religion scholar Diana Eck explains, there are now "more Muslim Americans than Episcopalians, more Muslims than members of the Presbyterian Church USA, and as many Muslims as there are Jews—that is, about six million.... [And] Los Angeles is the most complex Buddhist city in the world, with a Buddhist population spanning the whole range of the Asian Buddhist world from Sri Lanka to Korea, along with a multitude of native-born American Buddhists. Nationwide, this whole spectrum of Buddhists may number about four million."[12]

While it is probably obvious by now that I have always seen my work with cultural issues and inclusion in higher education as rooted in my own spirituality, it is only recently that I have approached the subject of spirituality and culturally responsive teaching as a topic of scholarly research. What I have learned is that it is virtually impossible to teach for social transformation in a way that confronts systems of oppression only by taking into account rational modes of thought. People have incredibly emotional experiences of both oppression and privilege, and those experiences deeply affect who they are and how they think. Furthermore, many people experience the process of recovering from and reclaiming parts of their oppressed identity as a spiritual exercise, and many speak about it in those terms. It seems that for many, spirituality has a role to play in transformative learning and, even in secular higher educational settings where rationality has typically been more strongly affirmed, we need to allow the language of spirituality to be part of the conversation.

Defining Spirituality, Religion, and Culture

While it is clear there are overlaps among spirituality, religion, and culture, it is important to acknowledge there are differences as well. Thus, I want to be as clear as possible about what I mean by "spirituality." Drawing on both scholarly literature about spirituality in education and on definitions of spirituality as used by participants in my research, I describe the domain of spirituality as follows: (1) Spirituality and religion are not the same; but for many people, there is some overlap between the two. (2) Spirituality is always present though often unacknowledged (particularly in public institutions) in the higher education environment. Spirituality is about: (3) a connection between people and what they refer to as the Lifeforce, God, a higher power or purpose, or the Great Mystery; (4) ultimate meaning-making and a sense of wholeness, healing, and the interconnectedness of all things; (5) the ongoing development of one's identity (including one's cultural identity) moving toward what many authors refer to as greater "authenticity"; and (6) the ways in which people construct knowledge through largely unconscious and symbolic processes as manifested in image, symbol, music, and other expressions of culture and creativity.[13] Finally, (7) spiritual experiences often happen by surprise.

How all of this relates to the classroom and specifically to culturally responsive education deserves some clarification. First, drawing on spirituality in the secular higher education classroom is *not* about pushing a specific religious agenda. It is about drawing on people's passions, and it is about forms of knowing that involve mystery, intuition, inspiration, faith, and spiritual experience, which typically focus on the wholeness and interconnectedness of all of life.

For some people, this kind of spirituality has nothing to do with any specific religion. But for others, spirituality is grounded quite clearly in a specific religious tradition, though sometimes informed by several other spiritual or religious traditions as well. Spirituality and religion are not the same, but for people who grew up religious or who are currently religious, there is always some overlap between the two. Clearly, religions do provide guidance on how to live a spiritual life from the perspective of that tradition, making meaning through sacred stories and symbols that tell ultimate truth, as well as through allegories, metaphors, art, ritual, and ceremonies that communally celebrate life's most important transitions such as birth, entry into adulthood, commitments of love, and death.[14] These are the spiritual parts of religion. But religions are also organized communities of faith, usually with an official belief system, written creed, and codes of regulatory behavior, determined by those with the power and authority to do so. These are the political parts of religion that are *not* particularly related to spirituality, and this is probably what people are rejecting when they describe themselves as "spiritual but not religious."

There is a cultural dimension to both religion and spirituality that is important to highlight here, particularly in relation to how people construct knowledge through image, symbol, music, art, and unconscious processes. As both James W. Fowler and Sharon Daloz Parks note, people construct meaning in powerful ways through image, symbol, and ritual.[15] Symbols, music, art, and ritual gestures are nearly always cultural—in complex ways they both draw from and have an influence on the communities in which we live or have lived—a point that neither Parks nor Fowler discusses. For Latino writer, religion scholar, and educator David Abalos, however, the cultural dimension is central. In his discussion of how members of particular cultural groups can create and sustain positive social change on behalf of themselves as individuals and their cultural communities, he suggests they need to reclaim four "faces" of their cultural being: the personal, the political, the historical, and the sacred.[16]

Reclaiming these four faces spirals one inward and outward simultaneously, and this paradoxical movement is at the heart of good teaching. Going deeper into one's self while connecting more meaningfully with the larger community is part of what higher education should be about, since the task of higher education, at least in part, is to help people to develop their critical thinking skills, to see the world from multiple perspectives, and to be contributors to a multicultural society.[17] Reclaiming these four faces also reintroduces spirituality into the educational mix. Paying attention to the cultural aspects of education necessarily includes the possibility that spirituality may become part of the conversation, even in ostensibly secular settings like public universities.

Spirituality, Paradox, and Culturally Responsive Education

In a broad sense, my own teaching often draws on the four faces that Abalos describes. I want students to examine their personal connections to whatever topic we are studying, to put it in a historical and cultural context, to explore what it means for educational practice or for society at large, and to relate it to their personal passions as well as the good of the whole society. To one degree or another, this process invites learners to a journey of reclaiming the personal, historical, political, and sacred faces of their own lives as they construct new knowledge in light of who they are and what they already know.

Teaching in this way (and writing about my teaching) also makes me continually revisit how these four faces are connected in my own life, calling me to spiral back to reclaim my cultural and spiritual roots and to reexamine significant spiritual experiences, time periods, and learning episodes in my life. One particular event that I have been thinking about recently took place in the summer of 1982 when I was living in the Quaker community at Pendle Hill, Pennsylvania. I was twenty-seven years old at the time (other participants ranged in age from twenty-three to seventy-two) and I was a campus minister.

The six-week gathering at Pendle Hill was part of an institute called "Formation for Ministry in Community" led by a team of five that included Parker Palmer and the now deceased Dutch spiritual writer Henri Nouwen. At that time Parker Palmer had just finished writing *The Promise of Paradox*[18] and he often referred to the role of paradox in the spiritual life.

My experience at Pendle Hill and the notion of paradox have taken on great significance in my life and in my teaching over the years. It was there at Pendle Hill that I first began to name the mystery of paradox and to appreciate living with the tension of opposites, allowing that tension to pull me open to creativity, spirit, and new possibilities. Sitting together in Quaker silence every morning with my colleagues, I began to appreciate the power of communal silence, partly for the value of solitude itself and partly because of the paradoxical way in which solitude can actually encourage solidarity with others. Solitude can motivate action in and for the world. Thomas Merton, who was a hermit, monk, and a literary activist, knew this—he understood the paradox of socially activist solitude—and what I lived and learned about paradox during my Pendle Hill experience has informed my living and teaching ever since. Trusting in the tension of paradox has given me the courage to take risks, personally and academically. It has given me the courage, while working in a secular university, to actually do research about what I'm passionate about: the role of spirituality in culturally responsive education. The research has, in turn, affected both my beliefs about teaching and my actions in the classroom.

In the course of my research, I have found that the insights of women and people of color often provide more helpful information about social realities and culturally responsive teaching than do the comments of white, male, Euro-American students and colleagues. This makes sense given that the curricula and institutions of higher education were largely created by and for Euro-American men. Academia is already quite culturally responsive to white American men so they rarely feel its resistance, but this is not the case for many people of color, immigrants, and women. Rather than flowing with the currents of American culture at large and higher education in particular, they often experience resistance, and because of that resistance their ability to map the contours and sharp edges of American academic culture is more highly developed. Thus what I have learned about the role of spirituality in culturally responsive education has often come from conversations with colleagues and students who are not representative of the dominant culture. Each person's story is unique, but elements of the personal, political, historical, and sacred have contributed to all of their developing perspectives around spirituality and how it informs their lives and ways of teaching. Those perspectives have then been carefully and conscientiously appropriated for use in the classroom to help students wrestle through the meaning-making that is so essential to culturally responsive education. I highlight four aspects of spirituality: (1) dealing with internalized oppression and reclaiming cultural identity; (2) mediating among multiple identities (such as those associated with race, gender, class, sexuality); (3) accommodating information about other religious, spiritual, and cultural practices while retaining individual authenticity; and (4) connecting unconscious knowledge construction processes to image, symbol, ritual, and metaphor that are often cultural in character.

Understanding and reclaiming one's cultural identity is a process. A part of that process for those who are members of nonmajority cultures is dealing with one's internalized oppression, a strongly held but mostly unconscious belief in the superiority of those more representative of the dominant culture. According to many cultural identity development models, people must unlearn this internalized oppression in order to develop a positive cultural identity.[19] Doing so often cuts so close to the center of personhood that it unavoidably involves the spiritual. Thus many people experience the process of reclaiming their cultural identity and unlearning their internalized oppression as a spiritual process.

One such example is provided by Penny, a Jewish woman, who reported that in her growing up she "felt uncomfortable around people who looked and/ or behaved in ways that were 'too Jewish'." She continued, "When told I didn't 'look Jewish,' I replied 'Thank you.' . . . In brief, I had learned to internalize societal attitudes of disgust at those who were 'too Jewish'; I had learned to hate who I was, and I did not even know it." She went on to describe the process of reclaiming her Jewish heritage, culturally and spiritually: "My spirituality is all about how I relate to my world, how I make meaning of life. From Jewish prophetic tradition and mysticism (via the Kabbalah) comes the concept of *tikkun olam* or the repair and healing of the world. This aptly expresses my core motivation in life, toward social justice, toward creating a life that is meaningful and makes a difference. I believe I get this from my Jewishness/Judaism, which for me is a blend of culture and spirituality." For Penny, dealing with her internalized oppression and reclaiming her cultural identity brought her back in touch with her spirituality. Dealing with her personal and cultural history put her back in touch with her core self and helped her reclaim what David Abalos describes as her sacred face.

All of us (including our students) strive to make sense of our historical, political, personal, and sacred faces. It is a challenge for every human being. But those who have to negotiate their identities against a new cultural backdrop must deal with even greater challenges. Aiysha, for example, is a Muslim woman of East Indian descent. She was born in East Africa, and then lived in

England and Canada before finally immigrating to the United States. Moving this much, and finding herself a member of a privileged group in some contexts but a member of an oppressed group in others, has forced Aiysha to learn how to negotiate her own developing identity in a constantly shifting cultural context. These moves and identity shifts, along with her education and the fact that she is now a professor helping others deal with these issues, have forced her to think about the development of her religious and cultural identity as an immigrant and a Muslim in the United States. She has developed the ability to cross cultural borders and to speak to many different groups fairly comfortably at this point in her adult life, despite continuing pressure to simply "blend in."

In reflecting on the experience of being both Muslim and of East Indian descent, Aiysha says: "Before it was just a matter of fact for me. Now, it's still a matter of fact, but it's also a matter of pride. I've taken the attitude 'This is *who I am*. If you are going to know me . . . you're going to know the whole of me, not just parts of me." She also notes that this new sense of "the whole" is related to her spirituality, to her growing sense of having a more "authentic" and centered self, and she draws on that sense of spirituality as she mediates among her multiple identities.

Like immigrants in a new land, people who are gay, lesbian, or bisexual also need to negotiate their identities in a dominant culture that is different and sometimes hostile. The spirituality of their childhood religious traditions, which are often less than accepting of gays and lesbians, can make that negotiation more, not less, difficult. Harriet, a nurse in her early fifties, who is a lesbian from a working-class background, grew up and still lives in the rural South. Harriet also grew up Pentecostal, and in explaining how the Pentecostalism of her childhood intersects with her social class and her Southern culture, she noted: "It has to be understood in the context of being your culture. It's not [just] your religion or spirituality, because it's everything you *are* and what you *do* and *how you live your life*. . . . It's your way of life!"

Harriet described the painful process of coming to terms with being a lesbian in light of her religious upbringing. In her early twenties she had a pivotal spiritual experience in a worship service, which she describes as a physical healing from injuries sustained in an accident. That healing also helped her come to terms with her lesbian identity as part of her own personal experience of God, though she knew she was not going to find public acceptance of that identity in the Pentecostal church. Explaining how she made meaning out of all this she noted: "Well, this was a turning point for me. . . . Why would God heal me if I was this person that was condemned to hell? God wouldn't do that for me, and I thought 'Okay, this is my sign that it's okay for me to be a lesbian.'"

The authenticity of her identity, confirmed through this particularly significant spiritual experience, gave her courage to embrace who she is and, over time, to develop a positive identity as a lesbian and to reaffirm her Southern, white, working-class roots. In the end, Harriet opted to stay in the South doing social justice work despite some life-threatening encounters with homophobia and heterosexism. Over the years, she has developed a more positive sense of spiritual identity that includes both attending the local Unitarian church and being involved with various women's spirituality groups. Together these connections help fuel not only Harriet's spirituality but also her social justice work related to issues of race, class, gender, and sexual orientation in the rural community where she lives.

As a means of sustaining herself in this sometimes difficult work, Harriet has adopted Harriet Tubman—who was herself a deeply spiritual person—as her role model. She says: "Sometimes I think, 'What can one person do?' One person can do a lot! . . . And when I get depressed, I look at [Tubman] and just think about 'if she could do it, I could do it!' " Her own spirituality and the cultural resources of Tubman's spiritual example are important sources of strength for Harriet as she mediates the multiple aspects of her identity, including her class background, sexual orientation, and Southern heritage.

Penny, Aiysha, and Harriet are all adults who have spent years as professionals in adult or higher education. They, like many others educators I have met, have crossed cultural boundaries as they have shaped their identities and charted their professional careers. To some degree, Penny, Aiysha, and Harriet had no other option; their life histories put them naturally on a boundary-crossing trajectory. Others, however, have opted to cross cultural boundaries voluntarily. One such person is David, who is currently involved in the Vedanta tradition, an East Indian form of Hinduism. David specifically went looking for a spiritual tradition that would help him develop what was missing in his own Irish-Anglo Catholic upbringing. Similarly, Maureen, a professor in her mid fifties, left her Methodist church in order to become more involved in one of the Yoga traditions.

Spiritual boundary crossing can also occur as a side effect of other life choices. For example, Patricia, a professor and a clinical psychologist in her early forties, is a white Euro-American who had been married to a Muslim man from North Africa for fifteen years. Her close personal relationships with her husband and his family, as well as with many other people of color and those from other countries, have forced Patricia to rethink her own spirituality. She explains: "What my experience with Islam and Muslim people did for me in a very concrete way was to make me realize that I don't accept Christianity as the only way to spiritual fulfillment." She further explains: "Probably the strongest value-related influence in terms of my Christian heritage is individualism. I'm Euro-American, and individualism was just a really powerful thing in my family...so my spirituality has taken a very individualistic form. That's probably the Christian heritage piece." Patricia notes that her current eclectic, individualist spirituality—an amalgamation of Christian, Buddhist, Muslim, and Hindu practices and beliefs—is a result of her own spiritual search and the result of deliberately crossing cultures. Those spiritual dimensions in turn have an effect on the way she fulfills her professional roles.

My observations are drawn largely from conversations with educators who have successfully progressed through college and graduate school and who are now working with a new generation of students or are involved in grassroots community service. They have traveled farther down the road than most college students, and they have had more opportunities for self-reflection and for transformation. Perhaps that explains why most of them no longer define their current spirituality strictly in terms of the religious traditions in which they were reared. However, most of them mention aspects of those childhood religious traditions that continue to be important.

These aspects tend to focus on unconscious connections and cultural forms of knowledge that include music, image, metaphor, and sacred story. For example, Harriet says she still occasionally attends Pentecostal church services because "I miss the music." Greta, a German immigrant who was reared Catholic, and who has mostly negative things to say about the religion of her youth because of what she termed its oppression of women and sexual minorities, says that the resurrection of Christ serves as a powerful metaphor in her life: "Easter—there's always some resurrection. You go to hell, you die and you're really at the bottom of mystery, but then you get resurrected."

Anna is an African American woman who moved away from the Christian religious tradition of her childhood long ago, but the music and person of Aretha Franklin remains an important spiritual symbol for her. Anna explains, "I grew up in a black community doing and understanding and experiencing things of black culture, so when I say Aretha takes me back, she takes me back to my childhood and the things that I understood then—things like music and dance, and the way of walking, the way of talking, the way of knowing, the interactions, the jive talk, the improvisations, you know all those things that I learned coming up—the music of the church, the choir that I sang in, all of that. And because I was raised in that community with that knowledge, her music takes me back even farther than I know, because I don't know where all of those things come from." For Anna, Aretha Franklin's music is a source of great inspiration because it connects her both to her ancestors and to their (and her own childhood) spirituality.

Music, symbol, art, metaphor, and poetry often connect with spirituality, and those constructs often are key elements in courses in the humanities, education, and the social sciences. Professors who open the door to spirituality by drawing on these forms of knowledge construction—and much of what we discuss in the classroom will do just that—also open the possibility of truly transformative education for our students. This transformation can lead students into dealing with internalized oppression and reclaiming cultural identity; mediating and rethinking multiple aspects of their identity based on race, gender, ethnicity, or sexuality; accommodating information about other religious, spiritual, and cultural practices; and exploring the ways they have constructed knowledge through a variety of images, symbols, rituals, and metaphors that are cultural in character. These dynamics of personal and cultural learning are not pertinent to every college or university course, but they are part of what is going on in many higher education classrooms, and they are a part of culturally responsive education.

Practical Conclusions

So what difference does any of this make? Clearly, by drawing on the connections between spirituality and culture, educators can enhance the scope and impact of what they do. If good teaching is attuned to the multiple dimensions of learning, it makes sense to structure one's teaching in a way that facilitates multifaceted learning. In my own courses, I accordingly incorporate image and symbol in the knowledge construction processes alongside other more traditionally academic ways of learning—that is, through critical interaction with academic texts, and examination of research that is part of doctoral study. Narrative is another important element. Thus I usually begin my classes that focus on cultural issues with an assignment that asks learners to read narratives by members of many cultural groups, and then to write aspects of their own cultural story (and, as explained above, I also participate in this exercise by providing them with a written version of my own cultural story). I also request that they bring a symbol of their culture with them to class and to talk about what that symbol means to them.

Students from different cultural backgrounds explain their cultural stories and symbols using their own terms, and by doing so they develop expertise in defining and describing their own cultural experience. Occasionally students will employ explicitly religious language or symbols to make their points, and this is perfectly legitimate. It is important to remember, however, that art, poetry, music, and other art forms that touch on the spiritual for some people will not be understood as spiritual by everyone. Whether or not one experiences something as "spiritual" is largely a matter of one's personal interpretation and response. While spirituality is a central part of human experience for some people, it will not be so for everyone. Because of that, it is important to not push a religious or spiritual agenda on anyone, especially in a secular higher educational setting. It is equally important to stop pretending that the spiritual is simply off limits. If we are serious about the multifaceted character of learning as our students actually experience it, spirituality will sometimes be an unavoidable part of the process for some people, particularly in culturally responsive education. Further, given that spiritual experiences often point toward the wholeness and interconnectedness of all things, it may be that a certain kind of openness to the spiritual is necessary within some higher education contexts. This has nothing to do with forcing spirituality on anyone. Rather, openness to the spiritual embodies and represents an openness to human affectivity in general and to learning that touches the heart. In learning that hopes to be transformative, this kind of attention to and respect for the knowledge of the heart is crucial whether one identifies it as spirituality or not.

Drawing on multiple modes of knowledge, including knowledge of the heart as well as the knowledge that comes from critical reflection on text and research, also has the effect of creating a greater sense of community within the classroom, and this is an important part of emancipatory teaching.[20] I encourage students to get to know one another and to work with one another. I want everyone in the classroom—both my students and me—to together explore the world through the multiple perspectives of people of different races, ethnicities, cultures, genders, and class groups. Too often in higher education, students engage in learning in strict isolation, but significant learning is often not solitary, nor are activities that facilitate social transformation; after all, social transformation is, by definition, communal. Thus, while it is important to read and analyze course material, it is also important to encourage learners to work collaboratively on some projects. As an example, in my own work with graduate students, who are themselves educators, such projects typically include written collaborative scholarly book reviews, as well as creative presentations that often incorporate cognitive, affective and symbolic/creative dimensions that model how themes of the book can be used with real communities in a way that is culturally responsive. This is part of what Diana Denton refers to as creating trans-traditional community in the classroom.[21]

When one draws on multiple forms of knowledge production including the rational, the affective, the symbolic, and the communal, it often leads to a greater sense of personal wholeness, deeper learning, and more freedom to express oneself authentically. This heightened sense of authenticity, which some call "spiritual," is expressed in both the individual and collective work of the classroom community in multicultural secular higher education settings. It is expressed in increased cognitive understanding because of engagement with readings from a variety of cultural perspectives; it is expressed in affective responses and connections to one another and to those in the community who are quite different from oneself; and it is expressed in the music, poetry, dance, drama, and other forms of art that a learner creates—art forms that often come out of some previously unknown depth of one's soul and that emerge as a result of new engagements with one's own and others' spiritual and cultural experiences. These modes of expression often take people by surprise, simultaneously creating new possibilities for their work in the world. This is what Laura Rendón describes as the mutual engaging of the "scientific mind with the spirit's artistry,"[22] and it can take place in both religiously affiliated colleges and in secular universities.

Over twenty-five years ago Parker Palmer suggested that we don't think our way into a new kind of living; rather, we live our way into a new kind of thinking.[23] What I have offered here is part of my own journey of living my way into new kinds of thinking within the "secular" academy, though of course, my point here is that learning happens by embracing the tension of the paradox in the midst of the dialectic of the sacred and the secular. Spirituality is present in virtually every class because spirituality is part of the lives of many of the students we teach. In culturally responsive teaching, that usually becomes evident very quickly. This does not mean that every class has to focus on spirituality in addition to whatever else the main topic of the course might be, but it does mean cultivating openness to the spiritual. It also means living the tensions of the many generative paradoxes of good teaching that Robertson[24] describes, as well as the paradox of the secular-spiritual dialectic. The generative paradox that presents itself when the sacred and the secular are brought together can be a powerful learning experience. Surely, allowing students to explore that paradox can be part of good teaching at any institution of higher education.

Elizabeth J. Tisdell is Associate Professor of Adult Education at Penn State University, Harrisburg, and author of *Exploring Spirituality and Culture in Adult and Higher Education.*

11

Taking Religion Seriously in Public Universities

Warren A. Nord

As a broad generalization I think it fair to say that public universities do not take religion seriously.[1] While most public universities offer students some opportunities to study religion, these opportunities are almost always optional. Some study of religion is often included in survey classes dealing with history and historical literature, but students can usually avoid these classes. Even in classes where religion is addressed, religion is not always taken seriously. For example, most universities offer a scattering of elective courses that address religion from the perspectives of various disciplines (e.g., philosophy, sociology, psychology, or political science), but such courses are often reductionistic, explaining (away) religion in terms of the basic categories of the host discipline. Even in departments of religious studies (which exist on a minority of public universities) religion is not always taken seriously, as we shall see. I would estimate that only about 10 percent of undergraduates in public universities take a course that takes religion seriously.[2]

What does it mean to take religion seriously? A course takes religion seriously if students study one or several living (rather than dead) religious traditions in some depth, while being open to the possibility that religious categories provide credible ways of making sense of the world and their lives so that religion is presented as, in William James's language, a live option. A university takes religion seriously when it requires students to take at least one course that takes religion seriously.

I will propose four arguments for taking religion seriously (in my sense of the term) in public universities. First, a student cannot be liberally educated without some serious study of religion. Second, taking religion seriously is part of the university's obligation to address the moral education of students. Third, while everyone agrees that the Establishment Clause of the first amendment to the Constitution permits the study of religion in public universities (within certain constraints), I argue that it actually *requires* the study of religion (again within certain constraints). Fourth, the public nature of public universities imposes a civic obligation to take religion seriously. I'll conclude by briefly sketching what higher education would look like if religion were to be taken seriously.

The Liberal Education Argument

In common usage, education is liberal when it is broad as opposed to narrow. Rather than being highly specialized or merely vocational, liberal education provides breadth by requiring students to learn both about history and about cultures other than their own. It requires them to take coursework in a variety of subjects, learning about the world from a diversity of perspectives.

Whatever one thinks of the truth or value of religion it is uncontroversial to claim that religion has been influential in history, and even in public schools, where fears of controversy run rampant, it is widely acknowledged that students have to learn something about religion in the context of studying history and historical literature. At most public universities, however, it is all too easy for students to avoid this kind of historical engagement with religion as broad historical survey classes or Western civilization courses have given way to a welter of specialized courses that often ignore religion. Even when students do learn about religion in the context of studying history, they often conclude, not unreasonably, that religion is nothing more than a historical artifact. When religion is discussed outside the arena of history, in a psychology or sociology class for example, the goal of the course is often to explain religious behavior in the categories of secular social science. Rather than inviting students into a genuine engagement with living religion, such courses may actually discourage students from taking religion seriously.

If, however, a liberal education is a broad education, why shouldn't religious categories for making sense of our world be taken seriously? After all, religions address many of the most important human concerns and questions and they continue to be extraordinarily influential in many people's lives. In the absence of a powerful argument to the contrary, it would seem that religious ways of making sense of the world deserve a place within a truly liberal education.

There are four common arguments to the contrary. The first is that public universities are constrained from taking religion seriously by the First Amendment. I argue below that this represents a serious misunderstanding of the First Amendment. A second counterargument draws on lingering concerns about Protestant hegemony in public higher education. It is important to remember that the history of higher education is, in part, a history of emancipation from religious orthodoxies and authority, but that emancipation was accomplished in public universities long ago and it is not about to be reversed. The problem now is the marginalization of religion. For much of the twentieth century advocates of a third counterargument took the gradual secularization of civilization to justify the secularization of higher education (so that religion deserves no more than historical attention). But the secularization thesis is in deep trouble. Some of its former advocates now argue for a desecularization thesis and others admit that major repairs are necessary if the secularization thesis is to survive.[3] A fourth argument against taking religion seriously is that while it may be important to study religion as either a historical or sociological phenomenon, religious ways of making sense of the world are not intellectually respectable. This argument requires a longer response.

No doubt the primary reason that religion has been thought less than respectable is that it does not measure up to the rigors of modern scientific method; religion is a matter of faith rather than reason. But should this settle things educationally? Theologians have their own conceptions of what is reasonable, and few claim that faith is blind. Of course, universities don't impose scientific standards of reason on philosophy, politics, literature, art, or ethics. Moreover, postmodernists have told us that all efforts to establish metanarratives, including those of modern science, are misguided, and if this is the case then surely the conflict of religion and science can't justify the exclusion of religion from the academy.[4] And we should note a remarkable new dialogue among theologians and scientists over the last several decades that has undercut much of the traditional antagonism between science and at least some kinds of religion.[5]

It remains true, of course, that intellectuals are somewhat less religious than the public, but there is certainly no consensus, even among university faculty, that religion is intellectually disreputable. What might appear to be a consensus is the result of exiling religious dissenters from secular orthodoxies to divinity schools, seminaries, and religiously affiliated liberal arts colleges. Or perhaps I should say the *vocal* dissenters are exiled, for most keep their religion to themselves. Indeed, it would appear that faculty in colleges and universities are almost as likely to believe in God as are other folks; a 2006 study found that more than three-quarters of college faculty members believe in God or a Higher Power of some kind.[6]

This does raise an interesting question. As George Marsden has noted, "Keeping within our intellectual horizons a being who is great enough to create us and the universe . . . ought to change our perspectives on quite a number of things. One might expect it to have a bearing on some of the most sharply debated issues in academia today. . . . Why, in a culture in which many academics profess to believe in God, do so few reflect on the academic implications of that belief?"[7] The likely answer is that specialization and the secular *Zeitgeist* of higher education enable and encourage a truly remarkable degree of intellectual compartmentalization.[8]

Quite apart from this silent majority, however, there continues to be a lively religious counterculture that is intellectually respectable in the following sense. It is shaped, in part, by scholars and intellectuals, many with advanced degrees from our most prestigious research universities, who understand and in many ways work within the dominant culture, but who also draw on theological traditions to rethink and reform the conventional wisdom of our time and place. While it may be true that some religion is mindless and disdains intellectual respectability, much religion isn't and doesn't. Most religious scholarship has not gone the way of astrology or lapsed into purely private and irrational faith. Theologians and religious scholars continue to grapple in informed and sophisticated ways with secular modernity and postmodernity. No doubt many scholars in the dominant intellectual culture find their efforts irrelevant, worthless, or perhaps even dangerous; indeed, I suspect that many assume that all religious thought is simply a variation on fundamentalist anti-intellectualism. But such naïveté does not justify excluding religious voices from the curricular conversation; to do so is both uninformed and illiberal.

Not only is there no consensus on the intellectual respectability of religion, there is no consensus, even among secular scholars, concerning many of the great issues about which religions have ventured answers—the origins of the universe, the origins of life, the origins and nature of consciousness and mind, what it means to be human, free will, morality, justice, and sexuality, to name but a few. It is not as if secular thinkers have solved all these problems to everyone's satisfaction without religion. But if there is no consensus that secular ways of making sense of the world are adequate, and religious ways of making sense of the world continue to be influential (among intellectuals as well as among the public), and if we've not solved many of the enduring great problems of civilization, then it would seem reasonable that religious voices be included in the curricular conversation.

The problem is not only that in excluding religion we are excluding a significant way (or range of ways) of making sense of the world, it is also that we make it difficult for students to think critically about secular ways of making sense of the world. One of the most important purposes of liberal education is to nurture critical thinking. It is critical thinking that makes intellectual progress possible and it is the core of what we mean when we speak of the examined life. What do they know of England who only England know? Or, we might ask, what do they know of secular ways of making sense of the world if secular ways of making sense of the world are all they know?

It is often held that a liberal education requires that students take coursework in a variety of subjects, but we teach disciplines much more than we teach subjects (which are open to various interpretations, to different disciplinary approaches). And almost always, these disciplines employ purely secular categories for making sense of their subject matter. Take economics, for example. Not only are religious perspectives completely ignored in economics courses (in spite of a rich twentieth-century literature in economics and moral theology), but students are typically taught neoclassical economic theory that makes economics into a "value-free" social science, one in which there is no room for religious or spiritual or even moral categories of interpretation. The point is that students do not learn the *subject* of economics, which is replete with moral and spiritual issues and problems and is open to various interpretations (conservative and liberal, secular and religious[9]); instead they learn to think about the economic domain of life only in terms of contemporary social science. And this is done almost entirely uncritically.

There are, of course, religious as well as secular ways of making sense of virtually every subject in the curriculum—nature and psychology, ethics and politics, literature and art, as well as economics. But it is virtually never explained to students that these religious views exist. As a result, public education (both K–12 and higher) unrelentingly and uncritically nurtures a secular mentality.[10] This borders on indoctrination.[11] It is true, of course, that much secular and scientific scholarship is compatible with much, perhaps most, religion. The problem is that we don't just teach discrete scientific facts and secular theories. Instead we teach students to think, to interpret their experiences, in secular categories—categories that often conflict with and marginalize religious categories.

A part of what is at issue is the difficulty of thinking about and assessing rival frameworks of interpretation, philosophical systems, or worldviews. In fact, quite apart from religious alternatives, there is little agreement among scientific naturalists, traditional humanists (that is, scholars using the categories of the humanities), and postmodernists. Here, then, is another reason to be wary of excluding religion from the curricular conversation: It is not at all obvious how to assess worldviews, and when this is the case, humility is a particularly important educational virtue. The great scholar of comparative religions Ninian Smart argued that worldviews are inherently debatable and because of that there is "neither a God-given nor a humanity-bestowed right to teach a debatable worldview as though it is not debatable, nor to neglect the deeply held beliefs and values of other people on the ground that you consider them foolish."[12]

I would add that it is not enough simply to introduce students to alternative cultures, traditions, theories, or worldviews like items on an academic cafeteria line. If a liberal education is to serve its critical purposes it will initiate students into an ongoing interdisciplinary conversation about how to make sense of the world. As things stand now, at most universities students are free to choose among a dizzying array of (often narrowly focused, highly specialized) courses that are unlikely to cohere in any meaningful way and that cumulatively may leave them largely culturally illiterate and unable to think critically about any of the alternatives. Texts and teachers rarely acknowledge that their subject matter may be interpreted in fundamentally different ways. And in spite of a widespread acknowledgment (in principle) of the value of interdisciplinary studies, undergraduates are too rarely required to participate in interdisciplinary discussion. As the literary critic Gerald Graff has put it, college curricula are typically separatist "with each subject and course being an island with little regular connection to other subjects and courses."[13] As we actually practice it, education is essentially a sequence of monologues, something closer to serial socialization than to a conversation; it is more a matter of training students than educating them. Graff's proposal, one that I endorse, is to "teach the conflicts"—indeed, to use this as an organizing and connecting principle for a liberal education.[14]

The Moral Argument for Taking Religion Seriously

As traditionally understood, a liberal education must have depth as well as breadth. It should provide students with some understanding of good and evil, suffering and flourishing, justice and injustice, love and beauty. And it should address the ways in which people find meaning in life: How should we live our lives? What could be more important? I will call this the moral dimension of education. I do not mean anything narrow or moralistic. What I have in mind might also be called the existential (or even the spiritual) dimension of education.

In his very helpful book, *Orators and Philosophers: A History of the Idea of Liberal Education*, Bruce Kimball charts the history of two quite different, sometimes competing ideals of liberal education.[15] The first—which he calls the liberal arts ideal—is grounded in the classical canon. It assumes that moral truth and the ideals of civic virtue are to be found in classical literature. It is largely a literary education and its goal is character formation for future public leaders. As a result of its classical focus, a liberal arts education necessarily binds students to the past, to tradition. While Kimball traces the liberal arts ideal back to the Greek rhetorician Isocrates, Cicero is its patron saint. It was the educational ideal of late Greece and Rome, the early Middle Ages (where it took on Christian hues), the Renaissance, and early America.

A second conception of liberal education—which Kimball calls the liberal-free ideal—takes Socrates as its patron saint, and centers on the continuing search for truth. It values free, critical inquiry and tolerance; it is skeptical. It pays scant attention to the classics but is instead concerned with philosophical inquiry and scientific experiment. It assumes no truth from the past, but is constantly looking for new truths. A liberal-free education underwrites the idea of progress and has the goal of liberating students from tradition, rather than binding them to it. The liberal-free ideal was foreshadowed in Greek philosophy and in the philosophy of the high Middle Ages, but it came into its own only with the scientific revolution, the Enlightenment, and nineteenth-century research universities. It has been the dominant form of liberal education in American universities since the end of the nineteenth century.

Kimball's two conceptions of liberal education correspond to two complementary approaches to morality and moral education. There are, on the one hand, conservatives who believe that tradition quite properly guides and constrains us. The task of culture is to mold character and nurture virtue. Liberals, on the other hand, are inclined to see tradition as restrictive and oppressive. The cultural task is accordingly that of criticizing tradition and of reforming or even overthrowing those ideas and institutions that have governed society in the past. A liberal arts approach to education tends to support a conservative understanding of morality, rooting students in historical narratives while nurturing traditional moral and civic virtues. A liberal-free education supports a more liberal understanding of morality, stressing liberation and nurturing critical thinking about inherited values and narratives. Both approaches are essential to our moral development—to everything there is a season—and some study of religion is necessary for each.

The strength of the conservative or liberal arts approach is that it recognizes that we must all rely to some degree on the virtues we acquired from our parents and teachers as children and on the wisdom of the traditions within which we find ourselves embedded. To some it will sound old-fashioned to talk about the wisdom of our traditions, but if there is such a thing as moral progress in the world (no matter how slow and halting) then it is reasonable to place some trust in them. They need not be simply dead weights around our necks.

Human beings are not autonomous, morally unencumbered, atomistic organisms. We are born into communities and defined by webs of rights and responsibilities; we are part of ongoing stories or narratives that give meaning and direction to their lives. Of course, we often disagree about how to construct our historical narratives and which literature to heed. Still, we don't disagree about everything. We can usually agree that it is essential for students to appreciate the importance of honesty, integrity, and compassion, and we agree that studying literature can do a great deal to nurture these virtues in students. We agree that students ought to be initiated into the American constitutional and democratic tradition; we want them to acquire the virtues of citizenship and an appreciation of the obligations they have as citizens who are part of a society committed to liberty and human rights. And (though this may be a little more controversial) students should understand the overlapping traditions— political, philosophical, *and* religious—that have shaped Western civilization and ground the moral and civic identities they have inherited.

This kind of character education is essential for children before they reach the age of reason, but even beyond that elusive age it is fitting and important that students continue to be educated in the moral and civic practices and traditions that shape our public life and civilization.

The virtue of a liberal arts education is that it locates students in the thick moral, civic, and religious traditions that give them ground on which to stand when confronting the alternatives available to them (including the materialism and often mindless individualism of popular American culture and the relativism of so much of our intellectual life). The great danger is that such an education will be narrow and dogmatic. It is not just that traditions may turn out to be fundamentally mistaken (most everyone agrees that historically this has often happened, sometimes with devastating consequences); it is that if students are not given the resources and encouragement they need to think critically about the traditions into which they have been initiated then education degenerates into mere training or indoctrination and moral progress becomes difficult if not impossible. One cannot be a morally responsible person if one practices business as usual by uncritically accepting one's cultural or subcultural tradition. A liberal arts education must be balanced by a liberal-free education in which students learn to think critically about both the world (i.e., the subjects taught in their various courses) and about how to live their lives in it.

We are the heirs of a rich and sometimes conflicting moral heritage, embodied in and given shape through art and literature, and through various theories and traditions, institutions and ideologies, philosophies *and* theologies. A properly moral education will engage students in thinking critically about the major ways humankind has developed for making sense of their lives. As part of a properly liberal education, religious options should be presented to students as live options for living their lives, as well as for the critical perspective they provide on secular ways of thinking and living embedded in most of their coursework.

There is no small irony in the fact that for all the importance we commonly attribute to morality, ethics courses are nonexistent in public schooling and are typically offered only as electives in higher education (though courses in professional or applied ethics are now often required in professional schools). It can only be astonishing, on reflection, that we require students to learn about the most abstract, complicated, and obscure scientific theories but leave them completely ignorant of all moral theories. How many students have *any* understanding of utilitarianism, Kantian moral theory, social contract theory, or liberation theology? How many have even heard of John Rawls or Reinhold Niebuhr? Of course, the fact that the study of ethics is compartmentalized in philosophy departments (and professional schools) typically means that religious voices are left out of the discussion. (Why not include Reinhold Niebuhr along with John Rawls, liberation theology along with utilitarianism?) While courses in the history of ethics may include religious thinkers (but never later than Kierkegaard), recent and contemporary religious voices are almost always left out.

It makes no sense to hold that either the conservative ideal of moral education, which requires that students be located in the context of traditions, or the liberating ideal of moral education, which requires that students learn to think critically about the major ways in which humankind finds meaning in life, can be pursued apart from the study of religion.[16]

The Constitutional Argument for Taking Religion Seriously

It is uncontroversial that it is constitutionally permissible to teach about religion in public universities, at least when done properly. No Supreme Court ruling, indeed, no Supreme Court justice, has ever held otherwise. It is utterly uncontroversial that students may be taught about the role of religion in history, that they may read religious texts, and that they may be taught about the role of religion in contemporary politics and culture. Indeed, there clearly is no constitutional problem with taking religion seriously (in my sense of this phrase). I want to argue, however, that taking religion seriously is not merely allowed in public universities, it is constitutionally required.

The relevant case is *Abington Township v. Schempp* (1963) in which the Supreme Court distinguished between devotional Bible reading, which, because it is a religious exercise, is unconstitutional, and academic study of the Bible (and religion more generally), which is constitutional. Writing for the Court, Justice Tom Clark noted that "it might well be said that one's education is not complete without a study of comparative religion or the history of religion and its relationship to the advancement of civilization. It certainly may be said that the Bible is worthy of study for its literary and historic qualities. Nothing we have said here indicates that such study of the Bible or of religion, when presented objectively as part of a secular program of education, may not be effected consistently with the First Amendment."[17]

The Court did not define what it means to study the Bible or religion objectively, but its meaning is clear both from this case and from its history of Establishment Clause jurisprudence. The Court has consistently required that the state be neutral in matters of religion—in two senses. It must be neutral among religions (it cannot favor Protestants over Catholics, or Christians over Jews or Buddhists); and it must be neutral between religion and nonreligion. Schools and universities cannot promote religion; they cannot proselytize; they cannot conduct religious exercises. But just as public education cannot favor religion over nonreligion, neither can it favor nonreligion over religion. Justice is a two-edged sword. As Justice Hugo Black put it in the seminal 1947 *Everson* ruling (which has shaped the Court's Establishment Clause jurisprudence ever since), "State power is no more to be used so as to handicap religions than it is to favor them."[18] Similarly, in his majority opinion in *Abington v. Schempp* Justice Clark wrote that schools cannot favor "those who believe in no religion over those who do believe."[19] And in a concurring opinion in *Schempp* Justice Arthur Goldberg warned that an "untutored devotion to the concept of neutrality" can lead to a "pervasive devotion to the secular and a passive, or even active, hostility to the religious."[20] Arguably, this is just what has happened.

The purpose of the Establishment Clause is to promote what the distinguished legal scholar Douglas Laycock has called "substantive neutrality." Such neutrality requires government "to minimize the extent to which it either encourages or discourages religious belief or disbelief, practice or nonpractice, observance or nonobservance."[21] In regard to the curriculum, "government must be scrupulously even handed, treating the range of religious and non-religious views as neutrally as possible."[22]

Clearly it is permissible to teach students to take religion seriously, to convey to students that it is a live option, so long as religion is not privileged but treated neutrally along with nonreligious ways of making sense of the world. A substantive neutrality would appear to make a stronger claim, however. If students are taught secular ways of making sense of the world and their lives that conflict or stand in some tension with religious alternatives, then they must also learn something about those religious alternatives or the state is privileging nonreligion. No doubt, as I've said, many of the particular claims made by scientists and secular scholars can be reconciled with much religion. But, arguably, public education nurtures a secular mentality; we teach students uncritically to interpret experiences and evidence in secular rather than religious categories. It is at the level of philosophical presuppositions or worldviews that we find the tensions and conflict.

The only way to be neutral when we disagree is to be fair to the alternatives—and then not take sides. Because public universities teach students ways of thinking about the world that stand in some tension (or even conflict) with religious alternatives, they must also teach students about religion in some depth. That is, given the Supreme Court's long-standing interpretation of the Establishment Clause, it is mandatory in public universities to require some study of religion if students are required to study disciplines that cumulatively lead to what Justice Goldberg called a "pervasive devotion to the secular."[23] Of course, students must learn about a variety of religions; neutrality also means that public schools and universities cannot promote or privilege a particular religion over others.

I should add that the Supreme Court has never drawn this implication from its commitment to neutrality. Neither has it denied it. But what else could neutrality mean?

Academic Freedom

The courts have made it clear that public school teachers, as agents of the state, must remain neutral regarding religion. Obviously, faculty in private colleges and universities are under no constitutional obligation to be religiously neutral in the classroom. What about faculty in public universities?

The American Association of University Professors (AAUP) defined its doctrine of academic freedom in its 1915 *Declaration of Principles*, where it singled out scholars who work in philosophy and religion—the domains of "ultimate realities and values"—as particularly in need of the protections of academic freedom. The *Declaration* notes that in interpreting "the general meaning and ends of human existence and its relation to the universe, we are still far from a comprehension of the final truths, and from a universal agreement among all sincere and earnest men." Here, as elsewhere, "the first condition of progress is complete and unlimited freedom to pursue inquiry and publish its results." Of course, "it is scarcely open to question that freedom of utterance is as important to the teacher as it is to the investigator." Indeed, the confidence of one's students "will be impaired if there is suspicion on the part of the student that the teacher is not expressing himself fully or frankly, or that college and university teachers in general are a repressed and intimidated class."[24]

No doubt the authors of the *Declaration* were especially concerned to protect science and secular scholarship from religious dogmatism but, arguably, the principle of academic freedom cuts both ways. Only an unprincipled freedom would allow teachers to take positions critical of, perhaps even hostile to, religion, but not religious positions.

The Supreme Court only began to address academic freedom in the 1950s, largely as a consequence of legislative efforts to exclude Communists from universities. The landmark case was *Keyishian v. Board of Regents* (1966), in which the Court anchored academic freedom in the First Amendment. Writing for the Court, Justice William Brennan held that "our nation is deeply committed to safeguarding academic freedom, which is of transcendent value to all of us and not merely to the teachers concerned. That freedom is therefore a special concern of the First Amendment, which does not tolerate laws that cast a pall of orthodoxy over the classroom."[25] Unfortunately, as legal scholar David Rabban has noted, "The Supreme Court's glorification of academic freedom as a 'special concern of the First Amendment' has produced hyperbolic rhetoric but only scant, and often ambiguous, analytic content. The Court has never explained systematically the theory behind its relatively recent incorporation of academic freedom into the first amendment."[26]

Nor has the Court ever addressed the academic freedom of scholars to take positions on religion. Arguably, however, because college and university faculty have academic freedom they cannot be considered as agents of the state (as is the case with public school teachers) and therefore they are not bound by the Establishment Clause, which applies only to government and its agents.[27] No doubt it would be unconstitutional for the university (or for a department of religious studies) to take sides, to endorse or promote either specific religious claims or religion generally. The university, as a state institution, must remain neutral. But it would be a striking limitation of academic freedom if individual faculty members did not have the freedom to argue for, or take positions on, some of the most important questions in our intellectual life.

Perhaps the greater problem comes from another direction. Academic freedom was never meant to protect incompetence. A historian who taught students that the Holocaust didn't happen would surely be incompetent. But who determines competence? One's disciplinary colleagues. As Mark Edwards has recently put it, a scholar "enjoys academic freedom vis-à-vis outside interests [trustees or the government] only if one is a member of the disciplinary profession, and the price of that membership is reasonable fidelity to the goods and standards of the profession."[28] This means, "regrettably but understandably," that professional (or disciplinary) orthodoxies may prohibit taking religious positions or making religious arguments, for to do so would be to exceed one's competence as it is defined in many or most disciplines. For example, Edwards suggests, modern scientific method would not allow a biologist who was a creation-scientist to claim competence and the protection of academic freedom. Of course, some disciplines are rather more open to religion than others. Many philosophers would disagree with a colleague who argued for the existence of God but they wouldn't necessarily call into question the competence of such a maverick colleague as a philosopher. No doubt it would be much harder to make a scholarly case for God's existence (or for intelligent design in nature) from within the sciences or the hard social sciences.

Certainly, to be hired and given tenure scholars must fully understand and engage the range of orthodox methods within their disciplines. The question is how much freedom they should *then* have to challenge or reject those orthodoxies. I am inclined to think that they should have rather more freedom than they typically do—this is itself an implication of the commitment to critical reasoning that underlies all the disciplines—but there is no clear place to draw the line. I do think that even if religious arguments and claims exceed the competence of scholars in some disciplines—such as biology or economics—it should be acceptable in teaching an introductory (rather than a more specialized, higher-level) course, to locate the subject within our intellectual life broadly, drawing on traditions and literature from outside the discipline (including, perhaps, religious literature) without the faculty member taking any position on it, simply as a matter of intellectual history and liberal education. (And, of course, if religious claims exceed one's disciplinary competence, so do antireligious claims.)

Still, when the disciplines define the range of voices that are to be taken seriously in the curriculum, and the disciplines are defined by secular epistemological commitments, the case for taking religion seriously in the curriculum may be in some jeopardy. The AAUP *Declaration* states that while dealing with controversial matters the university teacher is "under no obligation to hide his own opinion under a mountain of equivocal verbiage"; he should also "set forth justly, without suppression or innuendo, the divergent opinions of other investigators; he should cause his students to become familiar with the best published expressions of the great historic types of doctrine upon the questions at issue." The goal is to enable students "to think for themselves, and to provide them access to those materials which they need if they are to think intelligently."[29] Moreover, according to the AAUP's 1985 "Observations on Ideology," where "ways of finding out and assessing the truth are precisely what is under debate, good teaching requires exposing students to all major alternatives. A department ought to try to insure that different currently debated and important approaches to its subject are presented to its students fairly and objectively, so that students are able to make informed choices among them."[30] But who gets to define the range of divergent opinions or the major alternatives? If each discipline controls the voices within its courses, is there some complementary right on the part of the university to ensure that students encounter alternatives—specifically religious alternatives—that might not find favor within the established disciplines?

In addition to the individual academic freedom possessed by scholars, courts and commentators have also argued for an institutional version of academic freedom, which gives the university the freedom to shape its curriculum. The relationship of individual and institutional academic freedom is a knotty one, but arguably, institutional academic freedom gives the university room to act on it commitment to liberal education (as well as to moral education, civic fairness, and its obligation to conform to constitutional neutrality) by requiring the inclusion of religious voices in the curricular conversation, perhaps by way of a department of religious studies.

The Civic Argument for Taking Religion Seriously

We—the American people—disagree about morality, politics, and religion. Often these disagreements cut deep, so deep we sometimes call them culture wars. Happily, we do not disagree about everything, but when deep disagreements exist, public schools and universities have an obligation to treat contending parties (cultures, subcultures, traditions) with fairness and respect and to nurture the kind of mutual understanding that is a precondition for peaceable and civic discourse within a democracy. This civic concern helped spark the multicultural movement in American education that K. Anthony Appiah has argued is necessary to "reduce the misunderstandings across subcultures."

Multicultural education is "a way of making sure we care enough about people across ethnic divides to keep those ethnic divides from destroying us." Consequently, it must be "a central part of the function of our educational system to equip all of us to share the public space with people of multiple identities and distinct subcultures."[31]

Our politics also divide us. It is not, I hope, particularly controversial to claim that public schools and universities have a civic obligation to nurture an understanding of the major political parties as live options. While academic freedom gives individual faculty members the right to argue for their own particular positions on political issues (when it is germane to their subject and when they do so as scholars), they also have a civic obligation, as teachers in a public university, to help students understand the different parties and to resist the temptation to either demonize or ignore those with whom they disagree.

Consider another example. Until the last several decades university courses and curricula ignored women's and minority history and literature. The problem wasn't just that they were ignored, however, it was that distinctively male, white, and Western ways of thinking and acting, and patterns of culture, were taught uncritically as normative. We are now (almost) all sensitive to the fact that this was not a benign neglect, but a kind of educational disenfranchisement. There are, of course, good educational reasons for including women's voices and multicultural perspectives in the curriculum (we have a good deal to learn from them), but it is also the case that public education also has a peculiar civic obligation to nurture the kind of mutual respect and understanding that enables us to live together in a democratic society. This is not an argument for an uncritical cultural relativism nor for the equal worth of every ideology or culture. It is an argument for fairness, especially for fairness when it comes to traditionally oppressed voices.

Of course, Americans are as deeply divided about religion as they are about politics, gender, or culture. But while higher education has gone a long way toward addressing various multicultural issues, religion has been virtually ignored within the multicultural and cultural studies movements.[32] Yet, religious identities and traditions are often more important to people than their ethnic, racial, or gender identities and traditions.

I should perhaps add that this civic obligation to be fair and neutral has its limits; there is no civic obligation to take seriously fascism, religious terrorism, or Greek religion because we are not currently divided about them. But when we are deeply divided by various religious and secular commitments, public universities have a civic obligation to include religious voices in the curricular conversation.

What It Would Mean to Take Religion Seriously

Religious voices must be allowed into the curricular conversation. They must also be allowed to engage and contend with secular alternatives. The underlying problem is that of creating curricular conversations in the face of what Gerald Graff calls curricular separatism. Perhaps the ideal way of dealing with this problem would be a broad interdisciplinary core curriculum. An alternative (partial) solution would be for textbooks for introductory courses (in subjects such as economics or biology) to have substantive chapters that locate the discipline within the broad cultural and philosophical movements of the day, mapping tensions and conflicts with other disciplines and other ways of making sense of the world (including religious ways of making sense of the subject at hand). Such an approach would alert students to the fact that disciplinary perspectives are often controversial and that critical thinking about deep differences is part of the critical thinking that is a goal of liberal education. Needless to say, such references to religious ways of making sense of the world, while helpful, would inevitably fall short of providing students any substantive understanding of religion.

If religion is to be taken seriously, students must be required to study religion in sufficient depth to actually make sense of it. Such a requirement would parallel the typical distribution requirements for courses in the humanities, the arts, and the natural and social sciences. It would provide students with an alternative perspective for making sense of the world. In fact, I would require two courses in religion for all undergraduates, one that addresses a contemporary, live religious tradition, and a second that addresses an alternative religious tradition (perhaps historically).

It is not sufficient to study religion simply from the perspective of another discipline if the result is that religion is understood reductionistically. No doubt religion might be studied in a history, literature, or philosophy course where, by studying primary texts, students would acquire some idea of what it means to make religious sense of the world and live their lives religiously. But because religion is so complex, and because it is so important, it requires a field of study devoted to making sense of it. That is, universities must have departments of religious studies.

As a result of the increasing secularization and specialization of scholarship over the course of the nineteenth century, the study of religion and theology was gradually exiled from the undergraduate curriculum to seminaries and divinity schools so that by the end of that century it had largely disappeared from university curricula.[33] It was only after World War II that a movement developed for creating departments of religious studies, and it was only in the 1960s that they became fairly common, so that a substantial minority of public universities now have such departments or curricula.[34] This growth was in part due to the assurance provided by the Supreme Court's 1963 ruling in *Abington Township v Schempp*.

Most scholars in both public and private universities draw a fairly sharp distinction between the secular discipline of religious studies and theology—and exclude theology from religious studies. According to the American Academy of Religion's 1991 self-study (*Religious and Theological Studies in American Higher Education*) "religious studies" is the name of the "scholarly neutral and nonadvocative study of multiple religious traditions."[35] The dominant view is that the epistemological and methodological commitments of religious studies are those of secular scholarship. As William Scott Green once put it, "Religion is the subject we study, not the way we study it."[36] The purpose of the field is certainly not to proselytize or promote religion, but rather to employ secular methods drawn from the humanities and social sciences to understand religion.

There is a potential problem with this. Certainly much, probably most, coursework in religious studies allows students to hear religious voices—to encounter primary source texts drawn from various religious traditions—but religious ways of thinking and living may still not be taken seriously. In some courses, students will encounter religions only in historical contexts, rather than as live options (in their intellectually, morally, and spiritually most compelling forms for understanding the world here and now). Some scholars in religious studies aspire to scientific objectivity or use reductionist approaches drawn from other disciplines, and will be wary of the idea of taking religion seriously in the classroom insofar as this cuts against the grain of their secular methodological commitments. Other scholars see it as their task to problematize religion, to disabuse students of their religious naïvete, or perhaps even of their religious convictions; indeed, some may problematize *all* frameworks of thought—perhaps because they are committed to some variety of postmodernism. As a result, students often don't learn how to think in religious ways in courses in religious studies so much as they learn to think in secular ways about religion.[37]

Consider an analogy. Many political scientists assume that truth is to be found in the scientific method they employ rather than in the normative ideological, philosophical, and political beliefs and values of the politicians, voters, and writers they study. As a result, they don't teach students how to think politically so much as how to think scientifically about politics. But surely what is most important in studying politics, at least from the perspective of a liberal and a moral education, is sorting out whether Democrats or Republicans, capitalists or socialists, have the more reasonable position. What is justice? How should I live? Similarly, the primary value of religious studies as part of a liberal education is that it enables students to think in informed and critical ways about the moral, existential, and spiritual dimensions of the world and their lives—and provides them with critical perspective on the secular ways of thinking and living they will encounter pretty much everywhere else in their education. Happily, many scholars in religious studies *do* take religion seriously.[38]

Clarifications and Conclusions

First, each of the four arguments (educational, moral, constitutional, and civic) that I have put forward for taking religion seriously requires universities to be fair to religion, including live religious voices in the curricular conversation. Being fair is, of course, different from drawing conclusions. A judge must be fair, but must also render a verdict, and I have argued that academic freedom gives individual scholars the right to render verdicts regarding religion just as they render verdicts on many other issues (though maintaining neutrality may often be pedagogically the wiser course). What constitutional neutrality forbids is that public universities, as state institutions, render verdicts. Public universities as institutions must be fair *and* neutral with regard to religion (requiring some study of religion).

Second, I am not arguing that secular disciplines need to be countered at every turn by religious alternatives. The arguments I have made do not apply to graduate or upper-level undergraduate courses. They apply to those lower-level courses that constitute the core of liberal and moral education at the university.

Third, taking religion seriously requires something more than merely taking one particular religion seriously. All four of my arguments require taking various religions seriously. Needless to say, there are inevitable trade-offs between breadth and depth in this daunting task.

Fourth, I want to underscore the fact that each of my four arguments is fully secular. No doubt, religious arguments for taking religion seriously could be made, but I have not made them.

Fifth, and finally, I recognize how naively unrealistic my proposal may appear to most readers. I would only note that if one steps off campus and takes in the full scope of the intellectual and cultural controversies that exist around the world, modern public universities can seem jarringly parochial and illiberal in their refusal to engage living religions. As I see it, this is something of a scandal.

Warren A. Nord is a Lecturer in Philosophy and former Director of the Program in the Humanities and Human Values at the University of North Carolina at Chapel Hill. He is author of *Religion and American Education: Rethinking a National Dilemma*.

12

Religious Pluralism, the Study of Religion, and "Postsecular" Culture

Amanda Porterfield

A dozen years ago, a colleague told me that he required his students to check their religious beliefs at the door, instructing them that what went on inside the classroom should be divorced from their own religious opinions and personal feelings. I sympathized with my colleague's desire for objective, historical analysis of religion and his impatience with students who wanted to use class time to witness to their peers. But I laughed at the notion of telling students to check their beliefs at the door, as if religion was a hat or coat someone could simply take off and come back for later. That image may be more appropriate today, however, given the fact that in our new era of religious expression many people do display their beliefs on T-shirts or other articles of clothing. Religious iconography is now fashion.

Today's visible markers of belief seem simplified and less deeply ingrained than was the case in the past, and political operatives seem able to manipulate religious behavior with astonishing skill and success. Perhaps my colleague a dozen years ago was an astute judge of people's ability to step in and out of religious beliefs. The increased interplay between fashion and religious iconography makes it easier to think of religion as something one can take up or leave behind. And the efforts we have seen to equate support for religion with support for a political party may simply make religion's pliability, and susceptibility to the latest mode of interpretation, more obvious. In any case, inviting students to experience the classroom as an arena of fair-minded neutrality cannot be dismissed as simply an outmoded expression of secular objectivity. In fact, the increased fluidity and manipulability of religion may make stepping out of religion in order to analyze it easier than before. Given the increasing need to understand religious violence and hatred, it may also be more important than ever.

Let us assume for the moment that *postsecular* describes the ubiquity of religious feeling, belief, and practice in twenty-first-century America, including the current wash of religion in politics and material culture. This essay examines the role that religious pluralism as a prevalent concept in higher education has played in facilitating that saturation. In taking up the question of what "postsecularity" means in higher education, my contention is that it may function as a euphemism for retreat from critical inquiry and rational debate. In this sense, "postsecularity" does not move us forward into a world of greater religious diversity, freedom of expression, and justice for all, but rather undermines the clearheadedness that makes rational public discourse possible. To the extent that higher education participates in this retreat from rational public discourse concerning religion, American democracy itself—the coming together in politics and government to make sensible decisions about our common future—is diminished.

Understanding as the Goal of Academic Coursework in Religion

Before addressing the meaning and implications of religious pluralism in higher education, I need first to say a few words about what I understand the purpose of the academic study of religion to be, and what I think it takes to achieve this purpose in college and university coursework. As I believe is the case for many professors who teach courses in religion, my principal goal as a classroom instructor is to facilitate understanding of the nature and power of religion. As a specialist in American religion, I attempt to achieve this goal by acquainting students with various religious traditions in colonial America and the United States and with some of the religious aspects of American patriotism. As a historian concerned with how religion changes over time, I teach my students to understand religious events through analyses of historical change. By examining some of the ways Americans have constructed religious ideals in response to historical change and have embodied those ideals in practice, students learn how religion works in people's lives and in different cultures.

Aspirations to fair-mindedness follow from the primary objective of such understanding. In my experience, fair-mindedness in the study of religion is an art involving a balance of empathy, historical investigation, and critical analysis.

Empathy enables students to enter imaginatively into the religious lives of others. Entering imaginatively into other lives is not the same as living them, of course. It is important to keep this distinction in mind since it is all too easy to foist our own ideals and frustrations onto people whose religions we study and to confuse what we imagine to be their feelings with our own. Historical investigation operates as a corrective for this sort of emotional overreaching. Gathering evidence, evaluating sources, and examining the cultural contexts of religious beliefs and practices along with the unique historical events that shaped those beliefs and practices are investigative steps that guard against the tendency to project our own feelings onto the religions of others.

Numerous theories and modes of critical analysis are available to religion scholars that enable investigation of the social functions and dynamics of religious belief and practice. While overreliance on theory is as much to be avoided as sentimentally confusing our own feelings with those of others, social theories of religion are valuable resources that aid investigations into the many different ways that religious belief and practice operate in people's lives. An integrated balance of empathy, theory, and historical investigation helps to keep the pursuit of fair-minded understanding on an even keel. Empathy is an antidote for theoretical tendencies to treat religious people like ciphers in equations about social functions, while historical documentation and critical theory are antidotes for overidentification with the people whose religious beliefs and practices we try to understand.

Understanding religion in any of its particular manifestations is an open-ended process that thrives on multiple points of view and modes of reflection. In a classroom context, the more often students bring their own insights and perspectives to the task of understanding a particular expression of religious life, and the more often various insights and perspectives are heard, the richer the process of investigation will be. The dangers of cacophony, frustration, and complete confusion should not be overlooked. But recognizing the legitimacy of multiple points of view about a particular religious event, movement, or person, and relying on other points of view to improve and correct one's own, are important parts of the process of understanding.

As these remarks suggest, academic understanding is facilitated by keeping some distinction between academic discussion of religious topics and the religious opinions of the people in the classroom. While the line between academic discussion and religious opinion may be permeable, upholding that line contributes to the primary goal of academic coursework in religion, which is to understand religion and how it works in people's lives. Erasure of that line subverts understanding and invites religious defensiveness and proselytizing instead.

Students are free to evaluate their own beliefs in light of course materials, but when that subjective process replaces social and historical analysis in the classroom, it can derail the effort to understand religion. When instructors make religious self-development part of academic work, the pedagogical logistics and problems of religious authority can create intellectual confusion. In bending the purpose of academic study to personal, therapeutic ends, the instructor faces the problem of having to grade students on the basis of their religious performance and on their ability to explain their own religious beliefs and backgrounds. Fair-minded explanations about the meaning and historical importance of religion require supporting evidence that everyone can recognize and evaluate, and questioning and countering evidence are part of the process. The problems involved in attempting to subject the personal religious opinions and backgrounds of students to the same critical inquiry as the religious topics addressed in class seem to me to be insurmountable. And the promotion or defense of particular ways of being religious seem to me to be counterproductive with respect to the goal of understanding religion and how it works in people's lives.

Religious Pluralism as an Ideal

Religious pluralism is an idealistic way to think about religion and one that, for a variety of reasons, flourishes in American colleges and universities. Religious pluralism is often promoted in higher education as a democratic solution to social discord. But however well intentioned this promotion of religious pluralism in higher education, I believe it contributes to an excessively charitable interpretation of religion that substitutes religious appreciation for more neutral forms of understanding. Moreover, instructors who advocate religious pluralism can create a special kind of religious pluralism within a classroom environment that is too easily equated with the compatibility of religious traditions outside the classroom. This promotion of religious pluralism in the classroom participates in and contributes to larger cultural trends of religious fashion and religious saturation in American society.

Religious pluralism is more than the acknowledgment that religious diversity exists; it is an idealized view of how religions should coexist. This idealized view of compatibility among different religions thrives in higher education for a constellation of reasons. Most obviously, the college classroom is an ideal environment for exposing people to a variety of different religions and inviting them to explore different religions. Because students are expected to be open-minded learners respectful of others, the classroom is well suited for the willing suspension of one's own beliefs in order to explore the existence of other religions and their claims to meaning and truth. The academic practices of the classroom encourage students from different religious backgrounds to detach themselves, at least partially and temporarily, from their own religious beliefs, or skepticism about religion, in order to investigate different beliefs and practices.

This imaginative entrance into other worlds is, however, just that. Detached from the communities, practices, and authority structures of lived religions, students in a university class are more or less exempt from pressures to conform to and support the system of religious beliefs they are studying. Students in religious colleges and universities may feel pressure to conform to and support the religion associated with their school and, if they appear too critical, they are vulnerable to the question "Then why are you here?" But even in religious schools, students taking academic coursework in religion may examine the structures, dynamics, contradictions, and effects of various belief systems, often including their own, with an investigative spirit and sense of freedom that can be distinguished from the religious practices and confessions of belief that characterizes adherence to a particular religious tradition, group, or movement.[1]

Learning about religions other than one's own, and learning about the history of one's own religion, is not the same thing as praying. Understanding the course material and performing proficiently on exams or papers requires the skill of critical analysis and some ability to explain how religion works in people's lives. While academic understanding does not preclude religious conviction, it requires the assessment of religious convictions in a way that involves some distancing. Some religious students find this hard to do because they come to class eager to defend the truth claims of their own religion and to explain why beliefs other than their own are false or even wicked. Given that dynamic, students with less religious training are sometimes more willing to enter imaginatively into the religious beliefs and practices of others.

Thriving in academic settings where instructors lead students to slip imaginatively into different religious worlds and beliefs systems for purposes of comparative analysis encourages respect for multiple religious communities, multiple forms of religious practice and expression, and multiple systems of belief and truth. Such affirmations of religious pluralism highlight the aesthetic dimensions of religion—the colors, sounds, sights, and poetry of religious expression, and the role that religion has played throughout human history in bringing human thought and feeling to expression. The pluralistic approach to religion accentuates the positive aspects of religion and the contributions that different forms of religious life make to society, drawing attention to the ways that religion draws people together in community and facilitates networks of support, commitment, and activity.

As a model for thinking about religion and religious diversity, pluralism tends to lift up the best and most socially constructive aspects of religion as normative and to downplay or critique those aspects of particular religions that fall short or fail to harmonize with other religions.[2] From a pluralist perspective, Islamist fundamentalism is not true Islam, but rather a distortion of a noble religious tradition. Similarly, from a pluralist approach, the Ku Klux Klan is not a Christian movement, despite what its members say, but a misunderstanding of authentic Christianity. The ugly, violent, and antisocial aspects of religion are hard to ignore entirely, but they are much less easily accommodated by a pluralistic framework of thought than religion's beautiful, marvelous, and socially beneficial aspects.

Although the flow would be hard to measure, affirmations of religious pluralism in higher education may spill out of the classroom and affect how American university graduates relate to one another in business, politics, neighborhoods, and other places of social interaction. Whatever the degree of its impact on American culture, religious pluralism in higher education complements the religious mobility of American people and the exchange and fusion of religious ideas and practices prevalent in American society.

As a metareligion with its own moral values, practices, and pieties, religious pluralism requires respect for different religious traditions and encourages appreciative, empathetic investigation. Affirmations of religious pluralism also facilitate religious shopping, experimentation, and participation in the practices, celebrations, and social networks of a variety of different religious traditions. The religious pluralism students imbibe in college has much the same effect as social mobility and interchange among people from different backgrounds in general. It tends to loosen the commitments people feel toward particular religious communities, doctrines, and liturgies and in doing so it makes those commitments more flexible.[3]

Pluralism's Endorsement of Religion

Religious pluralism in higher education has tended to promote widespread commitment to religion in general. This general respect for religion has developed as an important element of national identity, and American leaders have long championed religion for its role in upholding moral values, optimism, and commitment to public life. In 1952, when the military and corporate industry demanded a mobile and well-integrated work force, President-elect Dwight D. Eisenhower endorsed religion as a deeply held but also generic phenomenon holding America together: "Our form of government has no sense unless it is founded in a deeply religious faith, and I don't care what it is." Eisenhower then went on to lift up a broad constellation of traditions that he specifically equated with democracy: "With us of course it is the Judeo-Christian concept but it must be a religion that all men are created equal."[4]

Eisenhower's remarks reflect a broad view of religion as a constituent element of American cultural identity and social stability that was prevalent in popular literature about religion in the post–World War II era.[5] Although rooted in nineteenth-century evangelical idealism about America as a Protestant nation, Eisenhower's affirmation of religion's importance for American government endorsed a wider group of traditions that were subsumed under the banner of Protestantism. The "Judeo-Christian" underpinnings of American democracy endorsed by Eisenhower promoted the strength and unity of American society while allowing for a spectrum of religious choice. The choices available corresponded to the classification of American military personnel in the World War II as Protestant, Catholic, or Jew.

The study of religion in higher education expanded rapidly in the post–World War II period in the context of this cultural affirmation of religion as a bulwark of democracy. As religion departments and programs increased in number and size across the country, practitioners of the academic study of religion brought this democratic approach to the study of Hinduism, Buddhism, and other religions beyond the orbit of "Judeo-Christianity." As the United States exercised its military and economic influence around the world during the Cold War, the study of religion in higher education expanded to introduce American students to the religions of the world. While often critical of "Judeo-Christian" misunderstanding and disdain for other religions, proponents of religion in higher education often presumed that democracy and religious pluralism went hand in hand and that democracy entailed appreciation for religion's contributions to society and pious regard for its diverse manifestations.

While affirmations of religious pluralism and religion in general require mental flexibility and at least partial or temporary detachment from the practices and modes of thought associated with adherence to one tradition, they often involve an element of reverence for religion as a conduit for esthetic expression, moral values, and communal bonding. Thus while religious pluralism requires a lack of absolute and exclusive commitment to one tradition, religious pluralism is not detached from commitment to religion as a generically good thing. Moreover, this appreciation of religion's positive benefits often coincides with notions of an overarching spiritual reality that encompasses different human perspectives and situations. Proponents of religious pluralism often see a common human quest for spiritual meaning manifest in different cultures and religious traditions and look to the religious beliefs and practices of different cultures as the media through which that universal quest is manifest. These proponents frequently express the sentiment that we all worship the same God.

Philosophical theology from Europe contributed to American ideas about religious pluralism as a kaleidoscopic array of different religions, all of which could be viewed as manifestations of the common light of human longing for experiences of spiritual consciousness. In the postwar period, the European-born scholars Mircea Eliade and Paul Tillich each promoted a variant of this romantic approach to religion, and their influence as writers and teachers in the United States carried considerable sway in academic studies of religion during its era of great expansion in the 1960s and 1970s.

The Romanian-born philosopher Mircea Eliade advanced a systematic view of all religions as organizational systems centered on manifestations of "the sacred," which he defined as spiritual power apprehended by man. He regarded primitive man as the authentic "religious man" and argued that linear, historical thinking made it difficult for modern Western people to re-capture "the sacred." The German-born Paul Tillich, who taught with Eliade for a short time at the University of Chicago in the 1960s after being a celebrity teacher first at Union Theological Seminary and then at Harvard Divinity School, defined religion as the "ultimate concern" at the root of every human life and manifest in every great work of human expression. Tillich linked awareness of this ultimate concern to the God underlying the gods of particular religious faiths. Along with Eliade, Tillich affirmed the reality of a universal, ultimately mystical realm of human consciousness as the background against which particular religions, and other forms of human art and expression, should be appreciated.

The teachings of Tillich and Eliade deeply influenced the academic study of religion at a critical juncture in its development, providing an idealist philo-sophical basis for conceptualizing religious pluralism and affirming religion as a subject for study in American higher education.[6] But their way of under-standing religion also included a distinctly pro-religion bias. Religious plural-ism and religion in general were, for them, good things, and many Americans—including many historians of American religion—seemed to agree.

Pluralism in the Grand Narrative of American Democracy

Coinciding with affirmations of religious pluralism in higher education and widespread popular support for religion as essential to American national culture, historians of American religious history began to present religious pluralism as a defining characteristic of the history of American democracy. In several studies, including some of my own, historians of American religion treated progress toward pluralism as a grand historical narrative encompassing major trends and important dynamics in American religious history. Calling attention to this interpretation is not to argue that religious pluralism is a bad thing. Nor is it to deny that religious freedom is essential to democracy. Acknowledging the pro-religion bias in the progress-toward-pluralism narrative of American religious history is simply a call to step back from the affirmation of religion and instead to examine the implications of this affirmation and to understand its historical roots and social functions.

Diana Eck's *A New Religious America: How a "Christian Country" Has Become the World's Most Religiously Diverse Nation* is the clearest example of an American religious history textbook designed to show that religious pluralism has transformed America from a nation dominated by Protestant Christians who looked down on other groups to a more religiously democratic nation in which religious groups coexist in friendly equality and neighborliness. While acknowledging that this transformation is far from complete, and that religious hate and fear of religious diversity exist in some corners, Eck regards religious hate and fear as out of step with history. American democracy is portrayed as progressively marching toward the ever-greater embrace of religious diversity, and that diversity itself is portrayed as a principal source of the nation's social harmony and strength.

Taking a cue from Horace Kallen's 1915 image of American cultural pluralism as "a symphony of civilization" created by a rich variety of cultures working in concert as different instruments, Eck proposes jazz as an even better image for the interplay of America's diverse religious traditions. Jazz "is not all written out" and "requires even more astute attention to the music of each instrument" than symphonic music. For Eck, "learning to hear the musical lines of our neighbors, their individual and magnificent interpretations of the themes of America's common covenants, is the test of cultural pluralism." Appreciation of pluralism is the test of American democracy as well. "Our challenge today is whether it will be jazz or simply noise, whether it will be a symphony or a cacophony, whether we can continue to play together through dissonant moments."[7]

Originally a scholar of Hinduism in modern India, Eck turned her attention to Hindu, Buddhist, and Islamic communities in the United States, and to the development of religious pluralism in the United States as a democratic way of thinking about religion that accommodated these new communities. A recipient of the National Medal of Freedom in 1999, Eck promotes religious pluralism as a requirement of democracy and a source of national peace and solidarity. The Pluralism Project she directs at Harvard University, and the CDs she has developed as aids to classroom teaching, showcase co-operative efforts among different religious communities in various American cities and towns. One of her classroom CDs includes a stirringly heartfelt and entirely unambiguous rendition of "America the Beautiful" as background for inspiring words about the importance of religion—in all its glorious diversity—as a source of America's beauty and strength.

Eck's triumphal endorsement of religious pluralism can also be inter-preted as an extension of an earlier national narrative: the nineteenth century evangelical effort to conceptualize America as a Protestant nation in which people from a variety of different denominations cooperated together in en-terprises aimed at redeeming the world. This evangelical notion of America as a Protestant nation was rooted, in turn, in the even older New England Puritan concept of America as a nation in covenant with God—America as a New Israel and "a city on a hill" destined to be, as long as its people were faithful, a model for all other nations to follow.[8] Eck has stretched this patriotic celebration of religion far beyond anything earlier American Protestants had in mind, but the underlying endorsement of religion remains basically the same: Religion is essential to American identity and strength.

William R. Hutchison's book *American Religious Pluralism: The History of a Contentious Ideal* offers a more tempered view of the history of religious plu-ralism that takes account of the long tradition of mockery aimed at religion as well as the history of efforts to get along. While Hutchison identified religious pluralism as a source of controversy around which a good deal of American religious history revolved, his book also supports the equation between American democracy and religious pluralism.[9]

As a historian of American religion, and Eck's colleague at Harvard until his death in 2005, Hutchison was thoroughly familiar with the history of American efforts to create a unified religious culture and with the history of conflict between that desire for national unity and acceptance of religious diversity. Hutchison showed that the ideal of religious pluralism had never been fully accepted as a means of solving the problem of national unity, despite considerable gains in generating respect for it over the course of American religious history. In presenting religious pluralism as a contentious ideal, he showed that efforts to appreciate religious difference as a source of cultural strength was fiercely opposed in the past and that even now, despite its greater acceptance, many Americans still worry about the threat to national unity that religious pluralism seems to pose. Although Hutchison did not celebrate

American ecumenism with the same fervor as Eck, he clearly believed that religious pluralism, however contentious, was an ideal worth defending.

In their utilizations of religious pluralism as the framework for understanding American religious history, both Eck and Hutchison combine advocacy for religious pluralism with the objective of historical understanding. Both scholars acknowledge the gap between ideal and reality, with Hutchison going further in explaining that many Americans have never embraced pluralism as an ideal. Both scholars' defense of the ideal coincides with their use of it as an organizing framework for interpreting American religious history. Both scholars also downplay alternative, less self-congratulatory scenarios of how national unity was achieved—through, for example, Indian removals and compromises on slavery and racial segregation—and what role religion played in those activities. Finally, both scholars seem unwilling to consider the possibility that democracy and religious pluralism might, at times, conflict. Interpretations that diverge from equating democracy with religious pluralism never get a hearing.

The commitment to religious liberty central to American democracy may indeed lead inevitably to religious diversity. Given freedom to practice the religion they choose and the absence of any established religious authority, individuals with different backgrounds, priorities, and perspectives believe and practice as they will, and differ from one another accordingly. But the commitment to individual conscience at the root of the Declaration of Independence, the Bill of Rights, and other founding documents of American democracy is not the same thing as the commitment to religious pluralism, although the two are obviously not mutually exclusive.

To draw an economic analogy, the affirmation of religious pluralism is something like extending individual rights to corporations, and then cherishing and protecting those corporations as if they were individuals. While democracy is essentially about individual rights, religion is essentially a collective phenomenon. As many sociological theories explain, one of the main functions of religion is to draw people together in groups, encouraging them to think and act together. Linking religious pluralism to democracy tends to confuse the meaning of democracy, shifting it away from its historical meaning as a political system based on the rights of individuals, including the right of religious freedom, to being a political system based on the rights of cultural groups, including the protection of the religious beliefs and practices that hold those groups together.

While many scholars of religion seem comfortable with and supportive of this redefinition of democracy, I would suggest that it is precisely these shifting linkages between democracy and religious pluralism that we need to study more carefully. Drawing attention to the narrative of pluralism's progress as an expanded evangelical story enables us to sees its broad historiographic influence, beginning with Robert Baird, who, in the nineteenth century, defined American religious identity in terms of cooperation among evangelical denominations.[10] To question this vision of American history is not to deny that religion has contributed significantly to American national identity. It is, instead, to call for greater inspection of the ways in which historiography has contributed to an assumption that religion and democracy are fully and easily compatible.

Secularity

This discussion of the pro-religion bias in affirmations of American religious pluralism brings us to the question of what secularity and "postsecularity" might mean to a national culture that is thoroughly saturated with religion. Although many religious conservatives have used the term *secularity* as a synonym for *antireligious*, in its historical usage secularity does not imply hostility to religion. Historically, the word *secular* has referred merely to ordinary life in this world (as opposed to heaven). *Secular* has meant the actual world with all its complexities and ambiguities, the place where most people act out their lives, whatever their aspirations for heaven.

A good place to begin to understand this older construal of secularity is with Augustine's early fifth-century book *The City of God*. This text, which profoundly influenced the historical development of Western Christian thought, posits that there are two cities, "one existing in actuality, in this world, the other existing in hope which rests on God." While pagans live entirely in the first world, Augustine believed, Christians inhabit both, living in the earthly city of mortal life with their hopes set on the Celestial City of Heaven where their spiritual journeys will end.[11] Among those whose hope rested in God, a second division exists: holy men and women living apart from society were distinguished from ordinary Christians by their greater asceticism and by their elevated and unstinting adherence to the lifestyle of the Celestial City.[12]

According to Augustine, the secular realm was the world of ordinary life, but this was hardly a realm free of religion. Quite the contrary, the secular realm was full of religious activity and was defined in terms of its relationship to God. By all accounts, ordinary Christians in medieval Europe believed in the existence of an overarching Celestial City and engaged in a wide variety of spiritual practices aimed at clearing obstacles from their path to Heaven.

Laypeople toiling in the world and living amid its tangled demands and op-portunities were often devoted to Christ, his saints, and the sacraments of the Church, hopeful of entering the Celestial City. The term *secularity* referred to this earthly realm where laypeople and their diocesan priests lived. Those who lived a more thoroughly spiritual existence in a cloister removed from the world might be closer to the Celestial City than were these ordinary Christians, but the secular realm was full of pilgrims hoping for Heaven and doing their best to get there.

Reform movements repeatedly sprung up to challenge the view that cloistered Christians were more spiritual than those who lived in the ordinary world. These movements stressed that Jesus himself had lived in the secular world ministering to the sick and the poor and they called laypeople to work in the secular world following his example.[13] In the Protestant movements of the sixteenth century that broke off from the Catholic Church, reformers explicitly rejected the notion that monastic rules were a precondition for holiness, ar-guing that ordinary family life was the proper context for Christian spirituality, and elevating "the priesthood of believers" above the official hierarchy of the Catholic Church. Martin Luther, John Calvin, and other reformers challenged the idea that holiness belonged to an upper echelon of priests and monastics. They believed that the Church of Rome had lost sight of Augustine's belief that Christians were all equally pilgrims in the world. For Protestant reformers, the secular world was the locus of Christian practice and the domain where they hoped to see the sovereign will of God become manifest.[14]

This Protestant commitment to the priesthood of all believers and to the secular world as the arena where Christian living was to be displayed led ultimately to the ideas of religious freedom, democracy, and separation of church and state.[15] While Luther and Calvin still believed that religious uni-formity should be imposed on people, a growing number of English Protes-tants beginning in the seventeenth century promoted toleration of religious difference as a better, more Christian approach. In the late eighteenth century, when the First Amendment to the Constitution of the United States estab-lished religious freedom as federal policy, supporters of religious freedom stressed its compatibility with Protestant Christianity and its contribution to the strengthening and expansion of the Christian religion.

James Madison, the principal author of the First Amendment, went so far as to argue that a robust Christianity required religious freedom and that at-tempts to enforce religion lead either to resentment and violence or to religious passivity and indifference.[16] Religious freedom not only required separation of church and state but also allowed for the growth of a variety of different religious groups. Minority religions would no longer be cast as "dissenters."

Without an established church, every religion had some equal footing, at least in terms of the language of the First Amendment. The nation's overwhelmingly Protestant heritage meant that Protestant institutions enjoyed a de facto establishment, but at the same time, the absence of a national church enabled a variety of different religious groups to thrive.

Many evangelicals embraced this religious freedom because of the activism it encouraged—the very activism they embodied in their efforts to bring new people into the evangelical fold. Other groups valued religious freedom simply because it guaranteed freedom for their own traditions. For Catholics and Jews and others, religious freedom meant having the legal right to practice their religion, to establish religious institutions, and to disseminate religious literature. Members of minority religions were sometimes the objects of discrimination, harassment, intimidation, and hatred, but the nation's legal commitment to religious freedom allowed them to succeed nonetheless as they developed their religious communities and extended their religious services to others.

Originally developed out of the history of Western Christian thought to describe the realm of worldly affairs inhabited by ordinary Christians, the concept of secularity thus came to have meaning for people with backgrounds in other religions. In essence, secularity became the context of religious freedom and separation of church and state that allowed any religion to exist or fail on it own merits, and, of course, secularity guaranteed the freedom to live one's life without reference to God or Heaven. In the United States, this kind of secularity has generally been a boon for religion, at least in terms of supporting a wide variety of successful religious groups and organizations. Since no single church is recognized by the federal government as providing special access to the Celestial City, an increasing variety of religious institution—churches, synagogues, temples, mosques, gurdwaras, kingdom halls, and so on—all offer their own ways to salvation and spiritual enlightenment.

This historical understanding of secularity is both messy and ultimately neutral about the purposes and influence of religion. The secular world is the stage on which we live out our lives, and religion exists on that stage alongside other ways of making meaning and getting on with life. In this secular world, religion sometimes plays positive roles in the lives of individuals and groups, and sometimes has a negative impact. Religion sometimes makes the world a better place, and sometimes not. And, at times, religion can produce genuine evil. Those of us who study religion have to take all that into account: the good, the bad, and the many merely neutral facets of religion.

This is where notions like religious pluralism and postsecularity can become problematic. To the degree that either of these terms blinds us to the negative potential of religion in the world and encourages us only to see the positive, they dangerously mislead us. To the degree that either of these ways of construing the world makes us underestimate the potential tensions that exist between and among religions, they leave us ill equipped to face the realities of religious difference. To the degree that either of these approaches to understanding religion gives rise to unexamined mystical fantasies of religious convergence, they leave us unable to critically assess the strengths and weaknesses as well as the insights and delusions of particular religions. And it is against precisely these problems that a historically understood sense of secularity protects us.

The secular approach neither condemns nor praises religion in advance. Instead it asks us to analyze religious activity in the world as thoroughly and objectively as we can. No one can do this completely—the cultures we inhabit and the assumptions that condition our thinking do lead us to see things in certain ways. But at the same time, we also have some ability to transcend the cultures that shape us and reflect on our own assumptions. It is precisely this capacity for critical thinking that the secular study of religion encourages.

Amanda Porterfield is the Robert A. Spivey Professor of Religion at Florida State University and past President of the American Society of Church History. She is coauthor of *Religion on Campus: What Religion Really Means to Today's Undergraduates.*

13

Professing Understanding and Professing Faith: The Midrashic Imperative

Lee S. Shulman

Is there a distinctly Jewish way of knowing? Are there forms of scholarship, whether scholarships of teaching or of learning, that reflect Jewish traditions of inquiry and interpretation, of warrant and truth? Though I can claim no special qualifications to answer these questions—I am neither ordained as a rabbi nor trained as a theologian—I shall address them as a scholar of teaching and learning who takes seriously the Jewish tradition as a lens through which one might make sense of the world. I also raise these questions as a means of exploring more broadly how religious traditions and practices might shape and influence the ways some teachers teach and some students learn.

Text, Commentary, and a Jewish Conception of Knowledge

I begin with one of my favorite stories. It is a story about a man who was profoundly inspired by the spiritual impact of the twenty-four-hour fast and the associated liturgy of Yom Kippur. He wished to express his newfound religious commitment on the very next holiday of the Jewish calendar, the festival of Sukkoth (or the Feast of Tabernacles), which follows Yom Kippur by only five days. He went to his rabbi and said, "I want to build my own *sukkah* (the temporary booth in which we observe the traditions of the Feast of Tabernacles).

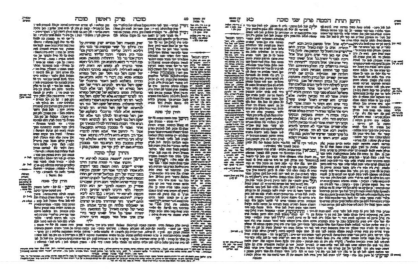

FIGURE 13.1. Typical Page of the Talmud

Please give me the building instructions. I will purchase the requisite materials, build a *sukkah* and so observe the commandments of the holiday." The rabbi said to him, "That's not the way we do things in our tradition. In our tradition you have to first study the laws before you are prepared to fulfill them. You are not ready to build the *sukkah* until you have immersed yourself in the entire volume of the Talmud that deals with the topic of *sukkah*. You must spend the next year studying this tractate. One year from now it will be time for you to build your *sukkah* and you will be able to build it following all of the instructions of the Talmud."

Lest you think that this assignment was like being told to study *Popular Mechanics* or *Architectural Digest* for a year, let me call your attention to one page (out of many dozen) of the Talmud volume *Sukkah* (see figure 13.1). This is a typical page of the Talmud. In the center is the text of the Mishnah or the Gemara (the two bodies of work that together make up the Talmud) appearing in either Hebrew or Aramaic. Wrapped around that text are commentaries in Hebrew comprising some 1,000 years of debate and argument concerning the meaning and application of the core texts.

Why is all this debate and commentary needed? Isn't the biblical commandment regarding the *sukkah* (Leviticus 23:39–43) simple and straightforward?

Remember that this seven-day festival to the LORD—the Festival of Sukkoth (huts)—begins on the fifteenth day of the appointed month, after you have harvested all the produce of the land. The first day and the eighth day of the festival will be days of complete rest. On the first day gather branches from magnificent trees—palm fronds, boughs from leafy trees, and willows that grow by the streams. Then celebrate with joy before the LORD your God for seven days. You must observe this festival to the LORD for seven days every year. This is a permanent law for you, and it must be observed in the appointed month from generation to generation. For seven days you must live outside in little huts. All native-born Israelites must live in huts. This will remind each new generation of Israelites that I made their ancestors live in huts when I rescued them from the land of Egypt. I am the LORD your God.

Then the commentary begins. In the selection reproduced here, the rabbis ask whether the commandment to dwell in the *sukkah* is fulfilled if an Israelite sleeps under a bed in the *sukkah* rather than under the frond-covered roof that is relatively open to the stars and to the elements. The biblical text says nothing about this matter, and the rabbis need to interpret and argue about it so the legal issue can be resolved. The earliest commentary, known as the Mishnah, which dates from Judea in the first century CE, is closest to the center of the page. Later texts, such as the Gemara, which ranges from the second century through the sixth, primarily in Babylonia, then fan out across the page. The most famous interpreter of these texts, Rashi, whose writings always occupy the inner margin of the Talmud page, wrote in France in the eleventh century. The commentators who followed him, beginning with his son-in-law, wrote in the eleventh to the fourteenth centuries. And on the edges of each page one can find even later interpreters and commentators. They engage in virtual dialogue and critique with one another, as if they had lived contemporaneously. And the reason so much commentary is needed is because of the subtle incompleteness and complexity of the text.

Let us return to the tale of the inspired *sukkah* builder. A year goes by, the man studies assiduously, and then he builds the *sukkah* as prescribed. The first day of the holiday he comes to the synagogue and approaches the rabbi looking very upset. "Rabbi, remember what you told me last year? I did as you instructed and then built my *sukkah*. Rabbi, it was a beautiful structure. We prepared a lovely meal and we sat in the *sukkah* for dinner last night. And the rabbi said, "What could be the problem?" He said, "Well, the first healthy gust of wind that came along blew the *sukkah* flat! Now how can that be? We followed precisely what the Talmud said we should do." The rabbi looked at him, smiled sweetly and said, "You know, Maimonides asked the same question."

What I love about this story is the way it represents the tension and ambivalence about the relationship of faith and learning, certainty and doubt, and belief and scholarship in my own religious tradition. On the one hand the Talmud is understood to be a holy book that many Jews believe was inspired by God. Indeed, some Jewish traditions assert that the "oral law" of the Talmud was transmitted to Moses on Sinai along with the written law. On the other hand, the published books of the Talmud exhibit a structure of layer upon layer of commentary, which indicates that this text that is so important is also inherently unclear, replete with internal contradictions and competing opinions from respected sages. It literally cries out for interpretation and explanation. As one becomes more familiar with the text, one slowly begins to sense that it is intended to be ambiguous. What appears to be simple turns out to be both subtle and complex. And that complexity and ambiguity demands people engage with it. As each generation reads and interprets the text, bringing its own questions to it, each generation adds its own insights and wisdom to the ever-growing concentric circles of interpretation and commentary that form the Jewish tradition.

There are in this story, and in the structure of the Talmud itself, the seeds, if you will, of a distinctive concept of knowledge and learning—a concept of knowledge and learning that may have broadly human appeal, but that is also deeply Jewish. Its relation to mainstream higher education is not entirely clear, but it raises questions about what counts as knowledge and about how learning happens. Scholarship is an intentional set of activities that individuals and their communities engage in to create, test, apply, and distribute knowledge, as well as to build knowledge structures in which past insights are combined with new ones. I am interested in examining the Jewish tradition for its views of learning, understanding, and teaching.

Knowledge as a Celebration of Possibility

We began with a story about building a *sukkah* and discovered that the rabbi was not surprised when his congregant's sense of the plain meaning of the Talmudic text regarding its construction produced a structure that could not withstand a strong wind. Indeed, the rabbi observed "Maimonides asked the same question," implying that it was no surprise that the text did not mean what it appeared to say. The Jewish scholar is admonished to approach a text in the spirit of "*d'rash.*"

The Hebrew root "DRSH," which is the core of the word *midrash*, itself has several meanings. The first sense of *drash* is the act of interpretation or a text that communicates an interpretation. Thus a *midrash* is a text that offers an interpretation of another text, either through analytical exegesis or through weaving a narrative that attempts to fill in the gaps or ambiguities in the original text. But the Hebrew word *drash* can also mean to request, demand, insist, or interrogate. Thus engaging in *drash* is to engage in an active interrogation of a text, demanding that the text give up its meaning in the face of the reader's hermeneutic powers. Not surprisingly, texts that require interrogation are neither simple accounts nor are they likely to offer up only one alternative interpretation. What characterizes the midrashic tradition in Jewish scholarship is the manner in which a single text inevitably yields multiple interpretations, and the competing interpretations become the center of attention as much as or more than the original text.

Let us now examine a page of biblical text as it is usually printed for scholarly study (see figure 13.2). This selection focuses on the first verse of the Ten Commandments as they are found in the twentieth chapter of Exodus. The biblical text on the two facing pages contains only eight words in Hebrew: "I am Yahweh your Lord who took you out of the land of Egypt, from the house . . ."

This "simple" text is surrounded by at least five layers of interpretation. We first find the translation of the Hebrew text into Aramaic by the Onkelos, who worked in the early second century CE. Next we again find the interpretations of Rashi, who wrote his commentary in France in the eleventh century. Accompanying Rashi we find the commentary of Abraham Ibn Ezra, who worked first in Spain and then traveled across Europe in the twelfth century. He often disagreed strongly with Rashi's interpretations. We also find Ramban

FIGURE 13.2. First Clause of Ten Commandments

(Nachmanides), a thirteenth-century Catalan scholar who regularly disagreed with both Rashi and Ibn Ezra and who also clashed repeatedly with Maimonides on matters of Jewish law. Finally, on these pages alone, we also find the commentaries of Sforno, who worked in Rome and Bologna in the sixteenth century. His interpretations acknowledge those that preceded his and often attempt to resolve some of their differences, though not with great success. Both Ibn Ezra and Ramban ended their lives in the Holy Land.

I find this page of the Hebrew Bible, replete with its layered, competing, complementary, and revered commentaries to be prototypical of a Jewish conception of knowing. Although the biblical text is the starting point for the exegetical and hermeneutic activity, the interpretations themselves rapidly assume center stage, nearly forcing the text into the background. Although always linked back to the original text, the object of study becomes not the text directly, but the logic and persuasiveness of the alternative interpretations. The *drash* is the central feature of the published texts. Moreover, the disagreements are among interpreters who rarely lived at the same time, much less directly exchanged their contrasting views. The interpretive clashes are thus presented as timeless, just as the original text is considered of eternal value.

What are the interpreters arguing about? Many things are puzzling. For example, why does God, in the first commandment, call himself Yahweh, and not one of the other names used to identify God in the Hebrew Bible? Why does he identify himself as he who liberated his people from Egypt? Why not he who created the heaven and the earth, or endowed Adam with language, or who brought the great flood, or who entered into the covenant with Abraham, or who brought the plagues onto Egypt, or who split the Red Sea, or who revealed himself to his people at Sinai? What is the significance of the exodus, that it should be the signature achievement of the Almighty? And if the Lord identifies himself so closely with the exodus, is he only the God of Israel, or is he the God of all the world? It is also unclear if this is, in fact, the first commandment, or just the core assertion presented as an introduction to the commandments that follow? The sacred text cries out for interpretation, but the resulting style of commentary does not drive toward a convergent, canonical consensus. Instead, it both displays and celebrates the complexities, contradictions, and disagreements of the commentators. The very design of the page exemplifies divergence, not consensus.

I recall sitting in the Hebrew Bible course of Professor Allen Cooper of the Jewish Theological Seminary of New York during our Carnegie Foundation studies of the education of clergy. This was a course that introduced the students to the particular compendium of interpretations, the "Mikraot Gedolot," one of whose pages is reproduced in figure 13.2. Cooper (who has recently become provost of the seminary) asked his rabbinical students to imagine themselves as the latest in an unbroken tradition of biblical commentators, to think of themselves as they studied these texts, to be writing around the edges, adding to the insights of their predecessors. He asked that they think of their own interpretations, what they would teach and preach to their future congregations, as adding their own additional layers to twenty centuries of *drash*. In my mind's eye, as I listened to Cooper and his rabbinical students, I imagined the huge trunk of a tree of knowledge, with each generation adding yet another ring of interpretation, yet all emerging from a common core, nourished by the same roots.

I find in this way of relating to a text both a theory of knowledge and a theory of pedagogy. From the very first encounter with a text, whether biblical or Talmudic, the reader is compelled to interrogate the text, to recognize immediately its nuances and complexities, its ambiguities and problematicity. The reader is immediately drawn into the process of interpretation and the negotiation of meaning. I would argue, though not without opposition, that in proceeding this way the Jewish tradition replaces the quest for certainty with a celebration of possibility. This emphasis—this conception of the ever-disputed nature and status of knowledge—calls naturally for a pedagogy of dialogue and debate rather than of exposition and inspiration. It is dialectic rather than didactic, and its paradigmatic embodiment is that of a "chevrutah" of two or more students studying or arguing together, rather than a rapt congregation listening devoutly to a teacher purveying unambiguous truths.

"It Is Not in Heaven": A Pedagogy for this World

Where and how does learning take place? In Jewish tradition it often occurs through *midrash*—through the interpretive narratives people create either to fill in the narrative gap left by an anomaly in the sacred text or to illustrate a moral or exegetical principle in a particularly forceful way. There are no shortcuts around this path. Learning comes through study and study involves conversation, dialogue, argument, and debate. Let me illustrate the deep and dramatic character of this midrashic way of knowing through two *midrashim*. The first is about revelation and idolatry, topics that are central to the Jewish religious vision and way of life; the second is about a much more mundane question involving the ritual purity of a stove.

The first *midrash* draws our attention to the drama of the revelation at Sinai and the lessons this drama holds for our understanding of knowledge and knowing. The biblical account begins with Moses ascending the mountain to receive the Torah from God. In this account, God actually carves the tablets from stone and with "his own hand" writes the commandments on the tablets. He teaches Moses everything the people of Israel need to know, both the written law and the oral law, and God instructs Moses to teach all of this to the people.

However, the people have grown restive in Moses' absence, and despairing after forty days that he will ever return, insist that Aaron fashion a golden calf for them to worship. They are dancing and carousing around the idol as Moses returns from his encounter with God on Sinai, and when he sees the sinfulness of the people, he becomes terribly angry and intentionally shatters the stones.

God is also angry, and proposes to eliminate the Israelites and offer his blessings to another people. But Moses intervenes and prevails. After negotiating with God to punish only the most sinful and to forgive most of the Israelites, Moses returns to the mountain once again, to receive the Torah from God. But this time, God instructs Moses to carve the tablets from stone himself, and he tells Moses to write the Law on the tablets with his own hand. Moses does as he is instructed, and returns to the repentant Israelites, who now accept the Torah as it has been given.

As you can imagine, this account has attracted hundreds of midrashic interpretations over the centuries. One of the loveliest of these was recently offered by Rabbi Shlomo Riskin:

> The first set of tablets, which Moses smashed after the sin of the golden calf, had been "inscribed with the finger of God" (Ex. 31:18), whereas the second tablets were carved by Moses and were created as a result of human involvement.
>
> Likewise, the oral law [the interpretive literature of the Talmud, the *midrash* and later rabbinic writings] not only accepts, but requires, the direct involvement of the people.... [T]he sages of each generation must actively interpret the Torah and often plumb from its depths great innovative concepts necessary for the needs of that generation.
>
> All of this suggests a Torah which is not divinely perfect, but is rather the result of a living partnership between God and his people. Apparently, the Almighty believed—after the tragic trauma of the golden calf—that only a Torah that involves the active participation of the Israelites could survive the seductive pitfalls of idolatry and immorality....
>
> Of course, opening up the process . . . is fraught with danger, but it is a chance that God must take if he wants his nation to be more

than marching robots. God didn't want us to receive a Torah on a
silver platter . . . because God realized that despite the inherent
risk that comes from involving the people, excluding them would be
a more likely prescription for disaster.[1]

This audacious *midrash* proposes that both Moses and God realized that
the text of the Torah written by God on tablets divinely carved was too perfect,
too complete, too unblemished for any people to embrace and commit themselves. They realized the deep pedagogical principle that real learning, learning that moves from understanding to commitment, must engage the learners
actively and interactively so they can own the lessons and be active partners in
the construction of the meanings. This is a powerful conception of knowledge
and learning. It eloquently addresses the midrashic imperative. It lays the responsibility for understanding and meaning-making on the rationality and
insight of the human interpreter of the text rather than on a process that attempts to divine the "real meaning" of the author.

This fundamental principle, that human interpretation must now take
precedence over divine revelation, is dramatically conveyed in this second
midrash, the case of the oven of Akhnai. It is one of the most famous narratives
in the entire Talmud. It tells of a debate between one of the seventy sages of the
Sanhedrin—the rabbinical assembly—and all the rest, regarding the purity of a
particular design for an oven.

> If a man made an oven out of separate coils [of clay, placing one upon
> another], then put sand between each of the coils, such an oven,
> R. Eliezer declared, is not susceptible to becoming impure, while the
> sages declared it susceptible.
>
> It is taught: On that day R. Eliezer brought forward every
> imaginable argument, but the Sages did not accept any of them.
> Finally he said to them: "If the Halakhah (religious law) is in ac-
> cordance with me, let this carob tree prove it!" Sure enough the carob
> tree immediately uprooted itself and moved one hundred cubits,
> and some say 400 cubits, from its place. "No proof can be brought
> from a carob tree," they retorted.
>
> And again he said to them: "If the Halakhah agrees with me, let
> the channel of water prove it!" Sure enough, the channel of water
> flowed backward. "No proof can be brought from a channel of water,"
> they rejoined.
>
> Again he urged, "If the Halakhah agrees with me, let the walls of
> the house of study prove it!" Sure enough, the walls tilted as if to
> fall. But R. Joshua rebuked the walls, saying, "When disciples of the

wise are engaged in a halakhic dispute, what right have you to interfere?" Hence in deference to R. Joshua they did not fall and in deference to R. Eliezer they did not resume their upright position; they are still standing aslant.

Again R. Eliezer then said to the Sages, "If the Halakhah agrees with me, let it be proved from heaven." Sure enough, a divine voice cried out, "Why do you dispute with R. Eliezer, with whom the Halakhah always agrees?" R. Joshua stood up and protested: "The Torah is not in heaven! (Deut. 30:12). We pay no attention to a divine voice because long ago at Mount Sinai You wrote in your Torah at Mount Sinai, 'After the majority must one incline' " (Ex. 23:2).

R. Nathan met [the prophet] Elijah [in heaven] and asked him, "What did the Holy One do at that moment?" Elijah: "He laughed [with joy], saying, 'My children have defeated Me, My children have defeated Me.' "[2]

What a remarkable account! When the voice of God speaks to the sages and asserts that Rabbi Eliezer's interpretation of the law is correct, he is immediately admonished by Rabbi Joshua, the head of the rabbinical court, who quotes from Deuteronomy, "The Torah is not in Heaven!" Once the revelation was completed and this imperfect, incomplete text was given to humankind, the process of interpretation, deliberation, and argument replaced revelation as the path to understanding and truth. The matter is no longer in the hands of God. And the moving coda to the story has God himself responding to this incident by laughing with joy and saying "My children have defeated me, my children have defeated me." This assertion that knowledge and its explanation is no longer in Heaven but is now the responsibility of human exegetes is a powerful statement of both epistemology and pedagogy in the Jewish tradition.

Weaving Webs of Knowledge and Meaning

The power of the Deuteronomic assertion that "it is not in Heaven" not only liberates, it also obligates. It liberates the interpreter to construct meanings through reason and intuition rather than searching for signs of divine purpose. It also places an obligation on the interpreter, an obligation that forbids an interpretation to be locked totally within the solipsistic universe of the texts themselves. This obligation forces the move from the hermeneutic to the homiletic as ways of knowing, learning, and teaching. In the Jewish tradition, this way of knowing is captured in the phrase used to describe the full act of biblical interpretation, the homiletic that moves from text to context and back again.

The classic rabbinical homiletic, the *d'var* Torah (literally, a word or a piece of Torah) always begins with a piece of sacred text, explores various interpretations of that text and the ambiguities inherent in it, and then asks what are the lessons of that text and its interpretations for making sense of, or finding meaning in, the world around us. In *Educating Clergy*, a book that describes and critiques the preparation of ministers, priests, and rabbis in seminaries, the authors use the term *pastoral imagination* to describe the processes by which clergy move from textual exegesis to its many meanings—for example, social criticism, congregational leadership, marital counseling, or consolation of the bereaved—and then back to the texts in theologically meaningful ways.[3] In this sense, the question of what a text means is not answerable solely from internal linguistic or historical evidence alone. The meaning of a text is in large measure a function of how it can be used to make sense of new situations that challenge humankind in a variety of ways. Once again, it is not solely in heaven.

What form might such knowledge take? How can we imagine the structure of knowledge or scholarship constituted of chains or networks of interpretation, along with their interconnections and their applications to new settings or problems? Let me offer a metaphor from the work of an anthropologist who has had the most profound impact on my work, even though I never met him personally, the late Clifford Geertz. In his classic work from 1973, *The Interpretation of Cultures*, he offers many definitions of culture. I have always found one of those definitions particularly powerful: "Man is an animal suspended in webs of meaning he himself has spun. I take culture to be those webs."[4] I consider human understanding with its fragile integration of reason and intuition, discovery and faith, and experience and values, along with all the other complex elements that taken together account for human formation as such a concatenation of webs. Individually and collectively, we live suspended in webs of meaning we ourselves have spun.

There is a powerful ambiguity in the word *suspended*. Webs are what spiders spin, and for spiders webs serve as a means of locomotion and mobility, allowing them to move from place to place and to make connections among otherwise disparate corners and boundaries. For the insects caught in them, however, the web is a trap, imprisoning the being that is suspended, limiting its mobility and ultimately ending its capacity for growth and even survival. And yet these are webs we ourselves have spun. So it is with all forms of human knowledge and meaning. We are not in heaven, but are suspended in webs of our own making. University scholars, and by extension those students who learn from and with them, weave webs of meaning, understanding, and interpretation. These can be taught and learned in ways that either entrap through dogma and diktat, or they can liberate, nurturing future growth, understanding, and formation.

The beauty of Geertz's image is the reminder that webs of meaning are needed both for locomotion and for stability, both for the unexamined and unexaminable premises that ultimately anchor all webs, and for the remarkable flexibility with which they offer access to the most remote and difficult corners of thinking and learning. The webs we weave must play both roles, equipping those who teach and learn to cope with the inherent uncertainty of interpretation even as they also connect us with the world in ways that allow us to repair and understand it, even if we must necessarily undertake that work without certainty.

In this regard, I am reminded of two experiences I had at Messiah College in Grantham, Pennsylvania (the institutional home of the Jacobsens, who have edited this volume). The first time I visited this quite religious and very Christian campus, I arrived on a flight that originated in Jerusalem many hours earlier and landed in Philadelphia at 3 A.M. My host and driver was a young man who had graduated the year before with a major in theology. As we drove west across Pennsylvania during those hours when the dead of night yields its power to the early light of dawn, I asked the young driver about his future plans. He explained that he had been admitted to the Yale Divinity School and would begin as a graduate student the coming September.

My silence must have been particularly expressive. He asked whether I found that plan surprising. I admitted that I wondered whether the style of textual analysis and criticism I associated with Yale might be somewhat alien to him. He smiled indulgently and explained that he, like most Messiah students, arrived at the school as a freshman believing that there was only one way to read the Bible, and that was devotionally. At Messiah, he asserted, he had learned that one could read sacred texts both devotionally and analytically, without losing the capacity to do either. I was both impressed and moved. Here was a student who had developed, through the teaching of the scholars at his college, a suite of webs of meaning that he himself had spun, which he could use to achieve both a deep faith and a capacity and disposition for analysis and interpretation, no holds barred.

When I subsequently visited classes at Messiah, I observed a pedagogy of homiletic in which classroom learning, whether biblical interpretation or theoretical physics, was regularly connected to the world. At the end of most classes, I listened as instructors asked their students how they could use what they had learned in class that day to make a difference in the world tomorrow.

This was a pedagogy I understood empathically. It was the *d'var* Torah, a homiletic move that disposes students to think actively about the connections between textual interpretation and making a difference in the world that we call *tikkun olam* in the Jewish tradition, the repair of the world.

Balancing Skeptical Inquiry and Commitment
(While Standing on One Leg)

The deepest levels of understanding require both teachers and learners to strike a balance between the complexities, nuances, and constant skepticism that modern science and postmodern humanistic scholarship value, and the simplifications that are necessary for making distinctions of significance and particularly for applying scholarly knowledge to policy and practice. Many leading scientists have pointed out that scientific progress is achieved through a beautiful dance between empirical findings that inevitably make the world more messy and complex, and periodic leaps of scholarly imagination that provide theoretical formulations offering simplicity and elegance where cacophony had previously reigned. Neither process can flourish without the other. Similarly, policy makers must learn to set aside their appreciation for the subtleties of imprecision and interaction that will paralyze them if taken too seriously. They must self-consciously simplify in order to act in the world. As we learned in our study of seminaries, great preaching requires both subtle hermeneutic and inspiring homiletic that combine in creating connections that link the timeless to the timely in powerful and inspiring ways.

The truly educated person must learn to profess her understanding and analytic prowess under some circumstances, and to profess her love, faith, and commitment under others. When we read Shakespeare's *King Lear* or *Othello*, we encounter unforgettable characters whose tragedy is a function of getting that very balance out of whack. Neither the king nor the general can profess his faith in the love of his wife or his daughter without reservation. Othello falls prey to Iago's putative evidence of Desdemona's infidelity and Lear obsessively insists on Cordelia's public attestation of devotion when neither is necessary. They have tragically not learned when to be skeptical and when to have faith.

I began this chapter with the promise to offer a Jewish conception of knowledge and scholarship that would in turn connect with approaches to learning and teaching appropriate to the college and university. Are these ideas, emanating from and consistent with the Jewish tradition, "postsecular"? Indeed, I have long marveled at the consistency I find between these particular Jewish perspectives and many of the habits of mind I associate with modern secular institutions of higher learning. Perhaps none of these labels—postsecular, secular, or even religious—is in the end all that helpful. I have thus offered in this essay a conception of knowledge that is inherently and necessarily uncertain and ambiguous at its core, and I have offered examples from biblical *midrash* and Talmudic *aggadah* to support my claim that there is something fundamentally Jewish about this conception.

Nevertheless, rest assured that I could readily cite many other Jewish scholars who would disagree energetically with my claims. And they would offer very persuasive arguments in support of their assertions and refutations. Remember, I am part of a tradition in which jousting interpretations occupy far more of the airtime of the religious sources than do consensual mandates. The conception of scholarship and of teaching that I see emanating from this religious tradition is one of debate and dialogue, of ceaseless questioning and a quest for ever more inventive interpretations, commentaries, simplifications, and complications. It lends itself to pedagogies of engagement and inquiry, the celebration of doubt and deep skepticism about intellectual convergence. And yet, it seeks to engage Jews in the obligation to repair the world. It also insists on their participation in the rituals, liturgies, and practices of the Jewish tradition, however interpreted. Thus, there was no doubt that the inquisitive congregant was obligated to build and sit in a *sukkah* five days after Yom Kippur. What was in doubt was how to interpret the obligation.

I close with one of the most famous vignettes in the Jewish tradition, told about the great Rabbi Hillel who lived 2,000 years ago. He was once asked by a skeptic to summarize the Torah in the time someone could remain balanced on a single foot. Hillel's response, with its three separate clauses, has been, I believe, widely repeated and almost universally misinterpreted. He said:

> That which is despicable to you, do not do onto your neighbor.
> That is the essence; the rest is commentary.
> Now go and learn.

Our inclination is to place the greatest emphasis on Hillel's version of the Golden Rule. We explain Hillel as saying: "Treat every human being as you would wish to be treated yourself. That's the huge, universal, big idea. The rest of the Torah is merely commentary. Once you understand that big idea, you can go study the rest, which is presumably less essential."

I believe the vignette is to be understood in quite the opposite manner. Hillel's response says to me: "I can give you one big idea, but you had best understand that all these big ideas from sacred texts are inherently uncertain, ambiguous and—upon careful analysis—impossible to apply as they stand. Those statements are merely the essence. What really counts is the commentary, for that is the route you must take from the vagueness and incom-pletcncss of the principles to a level of understanding that permits one to live intelligently and virtuously in the world. Therefore, you must live your life through constant study, interrogating the texts, investigating the challenges of life, and connecting them relentlessly."

That is the lesson of Hillel, and I believe it is also the essence of a Jewish conception of teaching and of learning. But it's merely the central principle. How it applies to higher education in general is ambiguous. How it translates into the practices of any specific classroom is unclear. What new webs of understanding and knowledge it might produce is yet undetermined. It is not complete. It cries for commentary. So go and learn.

Lee S. Shulman is President of the Carnegie Foundation for the Advancement of Teaching and past President of the American Educational Research Association, and the National Academy of Education.

PART III

A Framework for Academic Conversation

14

Talking about Religion

Douglas Jacobsen and Rhonda Hustedt Jacobsen

To warn that "the slovenliness of our language makes it easier for us to have foolish thoughts"[1] seems especially fitting when the topic is as potentially divisive and as ultimately consequential as religion. Words are the tools of the academic task, and educators are expected to use them with care and deftness. Perhaps it is time for the academy to clarify its vocabulary regarding matters religious. There will always be some slippage between what we intend to say and what actually gets communicated, and individual words themselves often contain their own ambiguities, but that does not absolve us of the need to use words with as much honesty and precision as possible.

Religion evokes universal questions as well as deeply personal ones, so it is no surprise that conversations about the place of religion in higher education have been varied and wide-ranging. Some of those discussions have focused on spirituality; others have centered on questions of meaning and purpose, on the practice of contemplation, on theology and its relationship to academic inquiry, on values and civic engagement, and on ways of both celebrating and coping with religious diversity on campus. All of those topics, along with many others, deserve attention, but is there a meaningful way to tie them all together, to consider them as a whole?

One possibility would be to develop a working definition of religion that articulates its one true essence or underlying dynamic. That would make it easier to sort out the truly religious from the religiously ephemeral, but such an option is unfeasible. Academicians would never agree to be boxed in by a single definition. More to the point, it is not the job of higher education to sort the really religious from the hardly religious at all. That is a role for saints or theologians. So, instead of a *definition*, we offer merely a *description* of religion, focusing on the different ways religion has been embodied in human life and history. Our goal is to provide a modest, simplified map of the religious domain that lays out the terrain and contours of its geography.

Spatial metaphors like map, terrain, and geography are appropriate here because, like space itself, religion operates in three dimensions, each with its own logic and affectivity: the historic, the personal, and the public. While these three dimensions of religion can be separated conceptually for the sake of clarity, it is important to remember that these three dimensions of religion are typically intertwined in human experience. One particular dimension may be dominant, but the other two will usually be present to some degree in less visible or even hidden form.

Historic Religion

The early twentieth-century philosopher George Santayana once observed that it is as impossible to be religious in general as it is to speak language in general. Religion, he said, is always particular; a person belongs to one religious tradition or another.[2] What Santayana described is historic religion. Historic religion is observable, it is organized, and it is embodied in communities that define themselves largely in terms of the normative beliefs and practices they affirm in common.

Historic religion includes the various large religious groups discussed in any introduction to religion textbook (e.g., Buddhism, Christianity, Hinduism, Islam, and Judaism), and it also includes the many smaller subtraditions within these large groups that exist as independent historic religions in their own right (such as Lutheran Christianity, Orthodox Judaism, Sunni Islam, or Zen Buddhism). A huge percentage of the world's population is affiliated with one or another of these organized religious groups, and many of these people take their faith very seriously. Religion shapes their daily, weekly, and yearly schedules; religion provides guidance for how to behave in family, business, and social relations; and religion helps them understand the world intellectually.

Historic religion is historic because it is *traditional*, a term derived from the Latin word *traditio*, which means to hand down or to hand over. Historic religions hand down wisdom from generation to generation. They hand down beliefs and religious practices. They even hand down affective orientations toward the world. They pass on this religious heritage both because adherents think it encapsulates truth and because they believe religion can never be a merely individual invention. Historic religion exists before the individual, and it is bigger than the individual. That is part of its appeal: historic religion gives people a point of reference that transcends the limits of their own short lives. Historic religions are not changeless; they all have developed and altered over time, but many of the world's historic religions have existed in recognizable form for hundreds or even thousands of years.

To join or be reared in a traditional religious community is to be nurtured into a very specific way of seeing, feeling, and behaving in the world, a way of life that a whole community shares. Different historic religions tell different stories, affirm different beliefs, follow different moral codes, and value different emotional states of being. Followers of Islam believe Muhammad was God's last and best prophet; Hindus tell stories of the playful god Krishna; Christians claim that Jesus was uniquely God incarnate; Buddhists venerate many bodhisattvas. While these different religions may overlap with regard to some beliefs and practices, and while all religions may agree that there is truth beyond the merely human, the overall configuration of each religion is unique. They do not converge. Because of that, pluralism is a genuine and irreducible fact of life within the domain of historic religion.

It is true that some religious communities have, in recent years, become more porous than in the past and the depth of attachment to religious tradition has become thinner, but in other cases the boundaries of faith have been clarified and the power of tradition has grown stronger. There is ongoing waxing and waning of historic religion in all cultures, and individuals experience more or less intense attachment to historic religion at different points in life. Yet even weak ties to historic religion can have indelible effects. The religious particularity that is woven into one's soul through childhood participation in a historic religious tradition is difficult or impossible to ever fully wash out. Even those who self-consciously abandon the religion of their youth often retain a spiritual accent reflective of their community of origin.

Personal Religion

Personal religion refers to the many ways individual human beings experience their lives as imbued with sacred meaning, purpose, and significance. While historic religion is defined by organizational structures, rituals, and beliefs that can be handed down from generation to generation, personal religion is about meaning and experience in the present, about an existential sense of being centered, and about knowing what one is called to do and why one's life matters. Personal religion has to do with the "inner life" of the individual as much as it has to do with the outer life everyone else can observe, and typically the ability to put that inner experience into words is not the central concern. Life itself is what counts, not the way it is explained.

The term *spirituality* is often used as a synonym for personal religion. When linked to the domain of historic religion, spirituality refers to the lived experience of faith and is often associated with "spiritual disciplines" like meditation, prayer, fasting or other ascetic practices, and acts of charity. Sometimes, however, the word *spirituality* is used in contrast to "religion," as if the two had little if anything to do with each other. Thus it is not uncommon today to hear people describe themselves as "spiritual, but not religious," indicating an uneasiness about submitting to the strictures of any organized, historic religious tradition.

There was a time when most believers thought of themselves as *dwelling* in a religious tradition where the meaning and purpose of life was clearly defined. Contemporary Americans, confronted with a culture that emphasizes freedom and that provides a dizzying array of personal and religious choices, are more likely to think of themselves as spiritual *seekers*.[3] Seekers assume that all the answers of life have not yet been found by them or by anyone else. Even if they are relatively satisfied with their present spiritual state, seekers are always on the lookout for something deeper or more compelling. Whereas personal religion used to emphasize "faithfulness"—continuing commitment to a firm set of convictions—it is now more likely to be associated with growth, development, and openness to the new.

With this shift, the notion of faith itself has undergone a change. In times past, faith was often used as a synonym for belief. To ask "What is your faith?" was to ask about one's religious affiliation and the content of one's religious view of the world. But faith today is often defined in terms of the individual's search for meaning and purpose in life, and personal religion is rarely confined within the boundaries of any one set of doctrines, practices, or rules of behavior. Faith described in this way may contain historic religious overtones, yet lack traditional religious form. Questions about God and ultimate values naturally blend into questions about the meaning of human life in general. Religions—at least most of them—acknowledge that fact. They know that hints and flashes of the sacred can be present in even the most mundane facets of life: The divine and the human overlap. In the Roman Catholic tradition this is described in terms of the confluence of nature and grace. Other traditions have developed different ways of acknowledging the presence of the holy in the most ordinary. Within the domain of personal religion, our humanity and religiosity intermingle, and many people neither need nor desire to draw a sharp line between the two.

Public Religion

Religious experience is never merely personal; religion always has a public or social dimension. Public religion focuses on the world in its entirety and on understanding one's proper role or roles in that world. Public religion is like a social compass, supplying a sense of location and direction in life and pointing the way forward to a better world. Public religion focuses neither on personal meaning and salvation nor on doctrine and religious ritual. Rather, its concern is the shape and structure of our common life in the here and now and our shared work toward a better tomorrow.

Public religion is sometimes political. Public religion is political when *shari'a* law defines the jurisprudence of a country or when abortion is legally restricted on specifically religious grounds. Those who pursue such goals assume that the implementation of their religious ethics will make the world a better place for everyone, even if some people must be coerced into behavior change. From the perspective of those who hold different moral and social values, of course, coercion de facto makes the world a worse and not a better place. Political religion can lead to social strife as well as to progress. It has motivated countless conservative as well as progressive causes in the United States, ranging from nineteenth-century abolitionism to twenty-first-century immigration activism. Progressive or conservative or something in-between, there is no question that religion can promote powerful, even cataclysmic, social change.

Yet public religion need not be political and, in fact, it usually is not. Much more often public religion is a matter of cultural orientation. Cultural orientation is simply a way of seeing the world that gives individuals and groups a sense of their special responsibilities within society. For example, Americans were transfixed by the cultural orientation of the Amish community in Lancaster County, Pennsylvania that allowed them to move toward forgiveness of the man who had senselessly murdered five schoolgirls from their community. The actions of the Amish reflected their long-standing cultural orientation, steeped in awareness of being a people set apart from the larger society and commanded to be peaceable even in the face of evil. The public religion of the Amish was newsworthy in part because of its stark contrast with the cultural orientation of other Christians in America.[4]

Public religion is often connected to a particular historic religion, but at other times it is not. In Latin America, for example, the public religion of liberation theology is deeply and explicitly rooted in biblical teaching and Catholic tradition. In the United States, American "civil religion" is a curious blend of patriotism, veneration of the ideals of freedom and democracy, commitment to economic capitalism, and belief that the nation is the last, best hope for humankind.[5] This civil religion, the essentially religious devotion that many Americans feel toward the United States, has been a significant shaper of public policy and a powerful motivator of public service. While American civil religion borrows much of its imagery from the Bible, its basics tenets can be affirmed without reliance on any specific historic religion.

Public religion is not only a matter of ideas and ideals. It is also a matter of social practices and the common good created in and through those practices. In recent years, discussions about the common good have often been informed by the notion of "social capital." Social capital refers to the resources created by the connections people have with one another. Those resources help individuals to weather the downturns of life, such as sickness, marital problems, loss of a job, or personal injury, or to take on the positive risks involved in trying to enhance life, such as raising a family, furthering one's education, starting a new business, or organizing a community service project. All of these activities require not only dollars, but also the moral and psychological support of others. Studies of social capital show that "faith communities in which people worship together are arguably the single most important repository of social capital in America."[6] Religiously rooted social capital is a powerful expression of public religion in action.

Public religion is not an unmitigated good. It has inspired a variety of efforts intended to help make the world a kinder, gentler, and more livable place, but it has also at times precipitated violence and promoted social rules and structures that diminish rather than enhance the human spirit. It is a complex phenomenon that has to be studied in context. Public religion, like historic religion and personal religion, cannot be simply rejected as evil or embraced as good.

Religion as the Subject of Discussion

Understanding the role and significance of religion in any context requires careful analysis and assessment. There is no way to reduce its complexity to just a few safe concerns, and there is no way to simply declare certain permutations out of bounds. When religion is the subject of discussion, the whole mix—this whole messy reality of religion in all its historic, personal, and public forms—is what colleges and universities must confront.

While the complexity of religion can be daunting, it is that very complexity that distinguishes higher education's current postsecular engagement with religion from the way that college and university campuses dealt with religion before the academy was secularized. In the presecular world of American higher education, religion—in particular, Protestant Christianity—typically claimed hegemony. Religious folks wanted to be in charge; sometimes they insisted on being in charge. The secularization of the academy has so dismantled the hegemonic power of religion that at this point it would be virtually impossible to reconstruct. No longer able to presume its own right to proclaim truth to the academy, religion is now only one dialogue partner sitting at the table. Furthermore, it isn't just a singular religion that is to be engaged, but rather a plurality of religions, each with its own historic, personal, and political dimensions.

In the culture at large, many religions see themselves, at least to some degree, as competitors, seeking loyal followers and devotees. In the academy, however, the rules are different. In the academy, understanding is the goal, not conversion, and the voices of religion are expected to follow the rules of academic discourse. Most people who favor taking religion more seriously in higher education would strongly affirm that there is a distinction between making space for religious perspectives and opening the door to proselytism. The editors of a new translation of The Analects of Confucius exemplify this stance when they express hope that readers will find "much in this text that speaks not only to East Asians, but perhaps to everyone; not only to scholars of the past, but perhaps to all those who wish to help shape a more decent and humane future today."[7] Their goal is not to convert readers to Confucianism, but rather to present Confucian insights that have the potential to enrich the human conversation about values, ethics, and the purposes of life.

Religion no longer dictates to the academy, but it can still speak—and if we listen to what religion in all its many guises is saying to us, we can learn. Learning does not mean accepting what is said uncritically. It may, in fact, mean rejecting what is said. But religious voices can help us ask and answer questions that the academy might otherwise ignore. That is what the new postsecular conversation about religion and higher education promises. The goal is not to help religion regain its lost power, but rather to foster new ways of understanding, evaluating, exploring, and enriching the teaching and learning process. In order for this to happen, however, faculty may need to rethink their own roles inside and outside the classroom as Mark Edwards and Eugene Rice discuss in their essays in this volume.

Colleges and universities will likely benefit by clarifying which of the three different dimensions of religion is predominant in any particular campus conversation. For example, Stephen Prothero's best-selling book *Religious Literacy* is primarily about historic religion. His proposal is that colleges and universities ought to help students become sufficiently informed about religion so that they can "participate fully in social, political, and economic life in a nation and a world in which religion counts." And about what are they to be informed? Prothero's answer is straightforward: "the seven great religious traditions of the world—Hinduism, Buddhism, Confucianism, Taoism, Judaism, Christianity, and Islam," though he adds that local circumstances might make it desirable to include a few other religions as well, such as Native American religions, Sikhism, or Santería.[8] Conversations about religious literacy are conversations about historic religion, and they are likely to result in energetic debates about general education that will vary significantly from campus to campus. The essays in this volume by Warren Nord and Amanda Porterfield illustrate this with their markedly divergent assumptions and recommendations concerning the place of religious studies in the curriculum.

Very different conversations occur when campuses address issues like those raised by the educator Sharon Parks in her book *Big Questions, Worthy Dreams*.[9] She argues that universities have the responsibility to raise the big questions for students: Who am I? What gifts do I possess? How can I help make the world a better place? Those kinds of questions move into the realm of personal religion. Some faculty members may prefer to point students with such questions toward the career center or some other cocurricular office, but those questions also are part and parcel of many of the best teaching and learning experiences. In this volume, Robert Nash and DeMethra Bradley point out that spiritual questions—questions related to personal religion—are ubiquitous among contemporary students, but come in a wide variety of guises, and Elizabeth Tisdell describes how those questions can be meaningfully and appropriately included in class assignments and conversations.

Campus discussions related to public religion occur both inside and outside the classroom. Often public religion operates only "under the radar" in conversations about civic engagement, community service, and individual responsibility, but at times religious dimensions may become explicit. This is the case, for example, when students participate in community projects that are directed or sponsored by faith-based organizations, something described by John DiIulio in this volume. But public religion is not only local, it also pertains to national and international affairs. Almost every current hotspot of violence around the world involves religious faith in one way or another. What can colleges and universities do to help students understand those dynamics? Charles Kimball, author of *When Religion Becomes Evil*,[10] believes that we all need to be educated about when and how to keep religion in check. Scott

Appleby, director of the Kroc Institute for International Peace Studies at the University of Notre Dame, suggests that we also need to be aware of the many ways in which religious traditions are committed to and can assist in the building of a more just and peaceful future for everyone.[11] The place of religion in the public sphere is, of course, highly debatable, but perhaps such debate is something that a healthy university (or a healthy democracy) will not only endure but promote.

Religion and Academic Conversational Manners

There is no doubt that conversing about religion—whether the topic under discussion is historic, personal, or public—carries risks. Religion is explosive stuff. Because of that the advice of Mark Schwehn, professor of humanities at Valparaiso University, is worth heeding. He has noted that constructive academic conversation requires both critical acumen on the part of those involved and attention to "the manner in which [we] respect and listen to each other."[12] Good academic conversational manners can be difficult to maintain in many circumstances, but perhaps no more so than when the topic is religion.[13]

In matters of religion, we all necessarily speak out of our own particularity. Our life histories have shaped us in different ways, predisposing us to be more or less inclined toward religion in general or to embrace or reject one religion in particular. Thus it is no surprise when John DiIulio ends his essay in this volume with a very Christian "amen" or when Lee Shulman concludes with a story about the famous rabbi Hillel. The differences are not a matter of vocabulary alone, since our life histories have also shaped the underlying categories through which we view the world, the ways we process information, and the emotional associations we bring to our perceptions of reality and our relationships with others.

Yet our biographies do not determine everything. We are capable of conscious growth and change, and we can, at least when dealing with certain subjects, step outside ourselves to some degree. In order to do that, however, we must first be aware of who we are—and the more the subject under discussion approaches our own core dispositions toward the world, the more effort it takes to remain aware of how much our own personalities, values, and ways of thinking may predispose us toward some responses and away from others.

When talking about religion, then, neutrality is not necessarily the goal. In fact, trying to be fully neutral may make it harder to see our own prejudices—and we all do have prejudices in this area. We have biases; we have gut-level positive and negative reactions to particular religious ideas and practices; we understand some things intuitively—sensing the inner subjective structure of selected religious experiences—and we are totally tone deaf in other situations. Some people find particular forms of religious life attractive and others repulsive, and some people find it incomprehensible that religion has any power whatsoever either to attract or to repulse. Because every one of us has these kinds of "natural" reactions to religion, it is important to remember that what feels natural (or some would say self-evident) to one person is not necessarily natural (or self-evident) to anyone else.

Intelligent discussion of religion therefore requires self-conscious honesty about who we are and awareness of how our own predispositions can undermine the conversation or skew it in one direction or another. Good intentions in this regard are not enough. Self-conscious conversational honesty is not a matter of desire, but of skill. In fact, it is appropriately considered a virtue, and like all virtues it can be acquired only through discipline and practice.

Talking about religion with critical acumen and respect for others also requires facility with two very different kinds of speech: the language of religion itself in addition to the more abstract and scholarly language about religion that prevails in the academy. On some occasions, the language of religion itself will need to be part of the conversation that takes place in the academy. Religious particularity can be authentically included in academic conversation only if people are sometimes allowed to speak with their own distinctive religious voices. Listeners will benefit as well, since the ability to hear and understand religious language "in the raw" is a valuable skill in our religiously pluralistic world. Also, there may be times when academic conversations that begin with purely rational language find it helpful to incorporate concepts drawn from religion. For example, the study of persons in the psychological sciences might at times require the inclusion of essentially religious concepts such as ultimate meaning and the search for transcendence.

In higher education, however, the primary mode of speech is not religious, but rational. Accordingly, individuals must develop the ability to translate religious speech into rational discourse, as much as that is possible and whenever that is necessary, so that the academic conversation about religion and about other topics that might potentially be affected by religious perspectives can proceed. For example, it is one thing to say that the Ten Commandments declare lying to be wrong; it is another thing to explore how lying and truth-telling are perceived in different social and cultural settings. Similarly, to declare that Jesus taught the Golden Rule (i.e., to act toward others as you would want them to act toward you) might be the beginning, but it will not be the end of any academic discussion of the origin, nature, and possible limits of the practice of altruism in human societies.

Helping students develop this dual facility with language—the ability to hear and to talk about religion and religious concerns in two different ways—is not an easy task. Yet this capacity will be increasingly necessary if constructive and effective dialogue is to take place between people from different religious traditions and between people who are religious and those who are not. This is not only a matter of neighbors relating to neighbors, it is also a prerequisite for effective civic and political life.[14]

The distinguished American educator Ernest L. Boyer once said: "Good communication means not just cleverness, not just clarity; it means integrity as well. This, in my judgment, is the key to building community on campus."[15] Conversations about religion on college and university campuses require that kind of good communication. These are not discussions where clever repartees are the best way forward, and the goal is not to win an argument. Clarity is essential, but clarity by itself is not sufficient. The aim is genuine dialogue, authentic encounters between people where the hopes and fears of religious faith can be discussed alongside hopes and fears about religion's influence in the world.

To include religion in the educational programs and policies of a college or university creates the potential for discord. When religion promotes anti-intellectualism, it is antithetical to critical thinking and rational discourse, legitimating the concerns of those who worry about the resurgence of religion in the world generally and in higher education specifically. But religion in its various historic, personal, and public incarnations also has the potential to deepen and enrich the learning that takes place on college and university campuses. Orchestrating honest conversations about religion in the context of higher education will never be easy. Fostering those conversations is, however, one of the most important challenges facing the American university in our now postsecular age.

Notes

CHAPTER 1

1. For Voltaire's view of Anabaptism, see *Candide*, chapter 3. For his views of Chinese religion, see the entry on "fanaticism" in his *Philosophical Dictionary*. The relevant passages from both works can be found in *Candide and Other Writings by Voltaire*, ed. Haskell M. Block (New York: Modern Library, 1956), 115, 407.

2. A recent book that provides both a history and an example of secularist thinking is Susan Jacoby, *The Freethinkers: A History of American Secularism* (New York: Metropolitan, 2004).

3. On Euhemerus, see Truesdell S. Brown, "Euhemerus and the Historians," *Harvard Theological Review* 39, no. 4 (October 1946): 259–74. On Lucretius, see Lucretius, *On the Nature of Things*, trans. Anthony M. Esolen (Baltimore: Johns Hopkins University Press, 1995).

4. See Andrew Dickson White, *A History of the Warfare of Science with Theology in Christendom* (New York: Appleton, 1896).

5. While large numbers of books and articles describe the secularization of the academy, the following works are among the best. They all argue that the secularization of higher education was a relatively slow process that to some degree was an unintended consequence of various other educational developments and reforms. See George M. Marsden, *The Soul of the American University: From Protestant Establishment to Established Nonbelief* (New York: Oxford University Press, 1994); Julie A. Reuben, *The Making of the Modern University: Intellectual Transformation and the Marginalization of Morality* (Chicago: University of Chicago Press, 1996); and Jon H. Roberts and James Turner, *The Sacred and the Secular University* (Princeton, N.J.: Princeton University Press, 2000). A different interpretation is set forth in

The Secular Revolution: Power, Interests, and Conflict in the Secularization of American Public Life, ed. Christian Smith (Berkeley and Los Angeles: University of California Press, 2003), which argues that the secularization of the academy was the result of a deliberate attempt by secularists to alter the practices of higher education in the United States.

6. William F. Buckley Jr., *God and Man at Yale* (Chicago: Regnery, 1951).

7. For a discussion of Buckley's book and Yale's response, see Marsden, *The Soul of the American University*, 10–15.

8. A sizable amount of sociological literature has been produced in the last few years about secularization and its continuing viability as a paradigm for understanding global and regional developments. Peter Berger, Rodney Stark, and Grace Davie have been at the forefront of those seeking to overthrow classical secularization theory; Steve Bruce is, by contrast, one of the staunchest defenders of the theory. The writings of people like David Martin and Talal Asad have tended to complexify the notion of secularization and, by doing so, they too have helped open a space for new ways of understanding religion's continuing influence in the world. See Talal Asad, *Formations of the Secular: Christianity, Islam, Modernity* (Stanford, Calif.: Stanford University Press, 2003); Peter L. Berger, ed., *The Desecularization of the World: Resurgent Religion and World Politics* (Grand Rapids, Mich.: Eerdmans, 1999); Steve Bruce, *God Is Dead: Secularization in the West* (Oxford: Blackwell, 2002); Grace Davie, *Europe: The Exceptional Case* (London: Darton, Longman, and Todd, 2002); Grace Davie, Paul Heelas, and Linda Woodhead, eds., *Predicting Religion: Christian, Secular and Alternative Futures* (Burlington, Vt.: Ashgate, 2003); David Martin, *On Secularization: Towards a Revised General Theory* (Burlington, Vt.: Ashgate, 2005); Pippa Norris and Ronald Inglehart, *Sacred and Secular: Religion and Politics Worldwide* (Cambridge: Cambridge University Press, 2004); and Rodney Stark and Roger Finke, *Acts of Faith: Explaining the Human Side of Religion* (Berkeley and Los Angeles: University of California Press, 2000).

9. See Richard Dawkins, *The God Delusion* (Boston: Houghton Mifflin, 2006); Daniel C Dennett, *Breaking the Spell: Religion as a Natural Phenomenon* (New York: Viking, 2006); Sam Harris, *The End of Faith: Religion, Terror, and the Future of Reason* (New York: Norton, 2005); and Sam Harris, *Letter to a Christian Nation* (New York: Knopf, 2006).

10. Samuel P. Huntington, *The Clash of Civilizations and the Remaking of the World Order* (New York: Touchstone, 1996).

11. Madeleine Albright, *The Mighty and the Almighty: Reflections on America, God, and World Affairs* (New York: HarperCollins, 2006), 9–11.

12. Andrew M. Greeley, *Religion in Europe at the End of the Second Millennium: A Sociological Profile* (New Brunswick, N.J.: Transaction, 2003), 120. The general statistics for the resurgence of religion in Russia appear in chapter 6, "Russia: The Biggest Revival Ever?"

13. See Thomas J. Altizer, *Towards a New Christianity: Readings in the Death of God Theology* (New York: Harcourt, Brace, and World, 1967); and Harvey Cox, *The Secular City* (New York: Macmillan, 1966).

14. See the essays in this volume by Neil Gross and Solon Simmons, "The Religious Convictions of College and University Professors" and Larry A. Braskamp, "The Religious and Spiritual Journeys of College Students."

15. "Report of the Task Force on General Education" (Cambridge, Mass.: Harvard University, Faculty of Arts and Sciences, 2007), 11–12.

CHAPTER 2

1. Christopher Jencks and David Riesman, *The Academic Revolution* (Garden City, N.J.: Doubleday, 1968).

2. David Hollinger, *Science, Jews, and Secular Culture: Studies in Mid-Twentieth-Century American Intellectual History* (Princeton, N.J.: Princeton University Press, 1996).

3. George Marsden, *The Soul of the University: From Protestant Establishment to Established Nonbelief* (New York: Oxford University Press, 1994), 430. Marsden himself offers a more complex version of this narrative.

4. The survey also included professors teaching in Canadian colleges and universities. See Stanley Rothman, S. Robert Lichter, and Neil Nevitte, "Politics and Professional Advancement among College Faculty," *The Forum* 3, no. 2 (2005).

5. See http://nces.ed.gov/das/library/tables_listings/show_nedrc.asp?rt=p&tableID=2988.

6. The study was funded by the Richard Lounsbery Foundation. The views expressed in this essay are the authors' own and not necessarily those of the Foundation.

7. Karin Knorr Cetina, *Epistemic Cultures: How the Sciences Make Knowledge* (Cambridge, Mass.: Harvard University Press, 1999).

CHAPTER 3

1. An article by Megan Rooney mentions that only 41 percent of freshmen currently include developing a meaningful philosophy of life as an important value, down substantially from comparable figures in the 1960s; although the question does not pertain directly to religion, it casts doubt on claims that college students are suddenly searching for spiritual answers in higher proportions than in the past. See Megan Rooney, "Freshmen Show Rising Political Awareness and Changing Social Views," *Chronicle of Higher Education* 49 (Apr. 25, 2003).

2. George M. Marsden, *The Soul of the American University: From Protestant Establishment to Established Nonbelief* (New York: Oxford University Press, 1994); James T. Burtchaell, *The Dying of the Light: The Disengagement of Colleges and Universities from Their Christian Churches* (Grand Rapids, Mich.: Eerdmans, 1998); Conrad Cherry, Amanda Porterfield, and Betty A. DeBerg, *Religion on Campus* (Chapel Hill: University of North Carolina Press, 2001); Richard T. Hughes and William B. Adrian, eds., *Models for Christian Higher Education: Strategies for Success in the Twenty-first Century* (Grand Rapids, Mich.: Eerdmans, 1997); John Schmalzbauer, *People of Faith: Religious*

Conviction in American Journalism and Higher Education (Ithaca, N.Y.: Cornell University Press, 2003).

3. The arguments I present here are indebted much more deeply than I can acknowledge in specific references to participating with forty other scholars in a four-year seminar organized by James Turner and Nicholas Wolterstorff and sponsored by the Lilly Endowment; many of the contributions to that seminar have been collected in Andrea Sterk, ed., *Religion, Scholarship, and Higher Education: Perspectives, Models, and Future Prospects* (Notre Dame, Ind.: University of Notre Dame Press, 2002).

4. Diane Winston, "From Sideshow to Center Stage: Mainstreaming the Study of Religion at Major Research Universities" (annual meeting of the American Academy of Religion, Atlanta, November 22, 2003).

5. Marsden, *The Soul of the American University*; Christian Smith, ed., *The Secular Revolution: Power, Interests, and Conflict in the Secularization of American Public Life* (Berkeley and Los Angeles: University of California Press, 2003).

6. Will Herberg, *Protestant-Catholic-Jew: An Essay in American Religious Sociology* (New York: Doubleday, 1955).

7. I have discussed these and other changes involving higher education in *The Restructuring of American Religion: Society and Faith Since World War II* (Princeton, N.J.: Princeton University Press, 1988).

8. Among the many possible sources, see Stanley Fish, *The Trouble with Principle: Essays on Law, Liberalism and Religion* (Cambridge, Mass.: Harvard University Press, 1999).

9. Robert Wuthnow, *The Struggle for America's Soul* (Grand Rapids, Mich.: Eerdmans, 1989).

10. Robert Wuthnow, *Religion and Diversity Survey* (machine-readable datafile and codebook) (Princeton, N.J.: Princeton University, Department of Sociology, 2003).

11. These three options roughly parallel those identified by Marsha G. Witten, *All Is Forgiven: The Secular Message in American Protestantism* (Princeton, N.J.: Princeton University Press, 1993).

12. Derek Alan Woodard-Lehman, "Concluding Theological Postscript on *Scholarship Reconsidered*: An Apocalyptic Identity and Scholarship of Possibility for the Ancient-Future," *Christian Scholar's Review* 30 (Summer 2001).

13. Richard T. Hughes, *How Christian Faith Can Sustain the Life of the Mind* (Grand Rapids, Mich.: Eerdmans, 2001).

CHAPTER 4

1. William F. Buckley Jr., *God and Man at Yale: The Superstitions of "Academic Freedom"* (Chicago: Regnery, 2001).

2. Jerry Weinberger, *Benjamin Franklin Unmasked: On the Unity of His Moral, Religious, and Political Thought* (Lawrence: University Press of Kansas, 2003).

3. Peter A. Lillback, *George Washington's Sacred Fire* (West Conshohocken, Pa.: Providence Forum, 2006).

4. Garrett Ward Sheldon, *The Political Philosophy of James Madison* (Baltimore: Johns Hopkins University Press, 2001); Jeffrey H. Morrison, *John Witherspoon and the Founding of the American Republic* (Notre Dame, Ind.: University of Notre Dame Press, 2005).

5. Franklin, as quoted in Walter Isaacson, *Benjamin Franklin: An American Life* (Simon and Schuster, 2003), 87–88.

6. Ibid., 468.

7. Jennifer Reiss, "The Schemes of Public Parties: Provost Smith, Dr. Franklin, and the Struggle for Control of the University of Pennsylvania," *Penn History Review: Journal of Undergraduate Historians* 13, no. 2 (Spring 2006): 36–54. My entire discussion of this eighteenth-century Penn history, not just the direct quotations cited below, is adapted from this superb article. As of this writing, the author is in the early stages of doing a senior thesis on the same subject. I am very grateful to her for discussing the history with me and for bringing her outstanding insights to my attention.

8. Ibid., 43.

9. Ibid., 43–44.

10. Ibid., 48.

11. Ibid.

12. For example, see Joseph P. Tierney, *The Catholic Puzzle Revisited: A Preliminary Profile of Catholic Community-Serving Institutions in Philadelphia*, PRRUCS Report 2006–2 (University of Pennsylvania, April 2005).

13. Letter to Reverend Ezra Stiles, Mar. 9, 1790, in *Benjamin Franklin: Autobiography and Selected Writings* (Holt, Rinehart, and Winston, 1959), 274.

14. Buckley, *God and Man at Yale*, 3–4. Emphasis added.

15. Ibid., 4–5.

16. McGeorge Bundy, "The Attack on Yale," *The Atlantic Monthly* (Nov. 15, 1951): 50.

17. Ibid.

18. Coffin as quoted in Buckley, *God and Man at Yale*, xxxv.

19. Buckley, ibid., 157.

20. Ibid., 139.

21. Ibid., 23.

22. Ibid., 33.

23. John I. Jenkins and Thomas Burish, "Reason and Faith at Harvard," *The Washington Post*, Oct. 21, 2006, A21.

24. Ibid.

25. Ibid.

26. Institute of Politics, *Spring Student Survey*, "Religion, Morality Playing Key Roles in College Politics," Harvard University (June 2006): 9–10.

27. Conrad Cherry, Betty A. DeBerg, and Amanda Porterfield, *Religion on Campus* (Chapel Hill: University of North Carolina Press, 2001), 295.

28. Francis Collins, *The Language of God* (New York: Free, 2006).

29. Jeff Levin and Harold Koening, eds., *Faith, Medicine, and Science* (Binghamton, N.Y.: Haworth Pastoral, 2005).

30. John J. DiIulio Jr., *Godly Republic* (Berkeley and Los Angeles: University of California Press, 2007), chapter 5.

31. Anne Morrison Piehl, *Faith-Based Prisoner Reentry* (a report to the National Academy of Sciences, Committee on Law and Justice, July 2006), 18.

32. Robert George, *The Clash of Orthodoxies: Law, Religion, and Morality in Crisis* (Wilmington, Del.: Intercollegiate Studies Institute, 2001).

33. Franklin, Letter to Stiles, *Autobiography*, 274.

CHAPTER 5

1. U.S. Department of Education. *Digest of Education Statistics: 2005.* National Center for Education Statistics 2006–030, June 2006. "Table 175: Total fall enrollment in degree-granting institutions, by level of enrollment, sex, attendance status, and type and control of institution: 2004."

2. Ibid., "Table 178: Fall enrollment and number of degree-granting institutions, by control and affiliation of institution: Selected years, 1980 through 2003."

3. U.S. Department of Education, National Center for Education Statistics, Institute of Education Sciences, College Opportunities Online Locator (COOL). Data in COOL is compiled from the Integrated Postsecondary Education Data System (IPEDS) (accessed Mar. 26, 2007).

4. Diana L. Eck, *A New Religious America: How a "Christian Country" Has Become the World's Most Religiously Diverse Nation* (San Francisco: HarperSanFrancisco, 2001).

5. Based on IPEDS data from the U.S. Deptartment of Education, COOL (accessed Mar. 26, 2007).

6. Naomi Schaefer Riley, *God on the Quad: How Religious Colleges and the Missionary Generation Are Changing America* (New York: St. Martin's, 2005), 5.

7. David Wheaton, *University of Destruction: Your Game Plan for Spiritual Victory on Campus* (Minneapolis: Bethany House, 2005), 89. The cover blurb written by Sean Hannity, cohost of the *Hannity and Colmes* television show, describes the publication as "the perfect book to help students stay in the center of their Christian faith during college."

8. Sam Harris, *The End of Faith: Religion, Terror, and the Future of Reason* (New York: Norton, 2004), 13.

9. This wording is taken from the "statement of Mission and Vision" on the Patrick Henry College Web site.

10. John Henry Newman, *The Idea of a University*, ed. Frank M. Turner (New Haven, Conn.: Yale University Press, 1996), 227–28, 230.

11. Ibid., 43.

12. John Henry Cardinal Newman, *An Essay on the Development of Christian Doctrine* (Westminster, Md.: Christian Classics, 1968), 40.

13. John R. Thelin, *A History of American Higher Education* (Baltimore: Johns Hopkins University Press, 2004), 4–5.

14. Ibid., 72.

15. See Mark R. Schwehn, *Exiles from Eden: Religion and the Academic Vocation in America* (New York: Oxford University Press, 1993) for a thoughtful analysis of this history.

16. Our description of events largely follows the Protestant pattern. Similar tensions were also present in the Roman Catholic tradition but they played themselves out differently. For two alternative readings of those Catholic developments, see Philip Gleason, *Contending with Modernity: Catholic Higher Education in the Twentieth Century* (New York: Oxford University Press, 1995); and David J. O'Brien, *From the Heart of the American Catholic Church: Catholic Higher Education and American Culture* (Maryknoll, N.Y.: Orbis, 1994).

17. Based on IPEDS data from the U.S. Deptartment of Education, COOL (accessed Mar. 26, 2007).

18. Richard A. McCormick, "What Is a Great Catholic University?" in *The Challenge and Promise of a Catholic University*, ed. Theodore M. Hesburgh (Notre Dame, Ind.: University of Notre Dame Press, 1994), 167–68.

19. For an interesting discussion of what this kind of religiously neutral approach can look like, see Scotty McLennan's *Finding Your Religion: When the Faith You Grew Up with Has Lost Its Meaning* (San Francisco: HarperSanFrancisco, 1999).

20. Robert Orsi, *Between Heaven and Earth: The Religious Worlds People Make and the Scholars Who Study Them* (Princeton, N.J.: Princeton University Press, 2005), 183.

21. Dale T. Irvin, *Christian Histories, Christian Traditioning: Rendering Accounts* (Maryknoll, N.Y.: Orbis, 1998), 41.

22. Ibid., 29.

23. On the variety of Christian traditions and their implications for teaching and scholarship, see Douglas Jacobsen and Rhonda Hustedt Jacobsen, *Scholarship and Christian Faith: Enlarging the Conversation* (New York: Oxford University Press, 2004), especially chapter 3. See also Richard T. Hughes and William B. Adrian, eds., *Models for Christian Higher Education: Models for Success in the Twenty-First Century* (Grand Rapids, Mich.: Eerdmans, 1997).

24. On the ways in which church-related colleges and universities foster holistic learning on their campuses, see Larry A. Braskamp, Lois Calian Trauvetter, and Kelly Ward, *Putting Students First: How Colleges Develop Students Purposefully* (Boston: Anker, 2006).

CHAPTER 6

1. This essay is drawn largely from my recent book *Religion on Our Campuses: A Professor's Guide to Communities, Conflicts, and Promising Conversations* (New York: Palgrave Macmillan, 2006).

2. On this point, see Mark R. Schwehn, *Exiles from Eden: Religion and the Academic Vocation in America* (New York: Oxford University Press, 1993).

3. Dan Oren points to a single Jewish professor in all of Yale College in 1950 and only a scattering of Jews within the professional schools. Dan A. Oren, *Joining the Club: A History of Jews and Yale* (New Haven, Conn.: Yale University Press, 1986). On

discrimination against Jews in American higher education, see also David A. Hollinger, *Science, Jews, and Secular Culture: Studies in Mid-Twentieth-Century American Intellectual History* (Princeton, N.J.: Princeton University Press, 1996); David A. Hollinger, "Why Is There So Much Christianity in the United States? A Reply to Sommerville," *Church History* 71, no. 4 (2002); and Jerome Karabel, *The Chosen: The Hidden History of Admission and Exclusion at Harvard, Yale, and Princeton* (New York: Houghton Mifflin, 2005).

4. See, for example, Paul Blanshard, *American Freedom and Catholic Power* (Boston: Beacon, 1949); J. T. McGreevy, "Thinking on One's Own: Catholicism in the American Intellectual Imagination, 1928–1960," *The Journal of American History* (1997): 97–131; Philip Gleason, "American Catholic Higher Education, 1940–1990," in *The Secularization of the Academy*, ed. George M. Marsden and Bradley J. Longfield (Oxford: Oxford University Press, 1992); Mark S. Massa, *Anti-Catholicism in America: The Last Acceptable Prejudice* (New York: Crossroad, 2003); and David J. O'Brien, *From the Heart of the American Church: Catholic Higher Education and American Culture* (Maryknoll, N.Y.: Orbis, 1994).

5. For a more detailed discussion of academic freedom and religion, see Edwards, *Religion on Our Campuses*, 111–34.

6. My argument here is drawn largely from Jon H. Roberts and James Turner, *The Sacred and the Secular University* (Princeton, N.J.: Princeton University Press, 2001).

7. My argument here is drawn largely from Julie A. Reuben, *The Making of the Modern University: Intellectual Transformation and the Marginalization of Morality* (Chicago: University of Chicago Press, 1996).

8. Cited in ibid., 20.

9. For a survey of the issues and an introduction to the vast literature spawned by the "culture wars" and the "battle over the canon," see http://chronicle.com/indepth/culture/canon.htm (accessed December 9, 2006). For useful background, see also W. B. Carnochan, *The Battleground of the Curriculum: Liberal Education and American Experience* (Stanford, Calif.: Stanford University Press, 1993); Bruce A. Kimball, *Orators and Philosophers: A History of the Idea of Liberal Education* (New York: Teachers College Press, 1986); and Roberts and Turner, *The Sacred and Secular University*.

10. See Burton J. Bledstein, *The Culture of Professionalism: The Middle Class and the Development of Higher Education in America* (New York: Norton, 1976); Thomas L. Haskell, *The Emergence of Professional Social Science: The American Social Science Association and the Nineteenth-Century Crisis of Authority* (1977; repr., Johns Hopkins University Press, 2000); and Bruce A. Kimball, *The "True Profession Ideal" in America: A History* (London: Rowman and Littlefield, 1995).

11. These learning stages are suggested by Hubert L. Dreyfus, *On the Internet* (New York: Routledge, 2001), 33–49.

12. Richard Dawkins, *A Devil's Chaplain: Reflections on Hope, Lies, Science, and Love* (London: Weidenfeld & Nicolson, 2003); and Alvin Plantinga, *Warranted Christian Belief* (New York: Oxford University Press, 2000).

13. My thinking on these issues has been deeply influenced by three authors: Mary Midgley, Hilary Putnam, and Charles Taylor. See, for example, Mary Midgley, *Science and Poetry* (London: Routledge, 2001); Mary Midgley, *Wisdom, Information and*

Wonder: What Is Knowledge For? (New York: Routledge, 1989); Hilary Putnam, *The Collapse of the Fact/Value Dichotomy and Other Essays* (Cambridge, Mass.: Harvard University Press, 2002); Hilary Putnam, *Pragmatism* (Oxford: Blackwell, 1995); Charles Taylor, *Philosophy and the Human Sciences* (Cambridge: Cambridge University Press, 1985); and Charles Taylor, *Sources of the Self: The Making of the Modern Identity* (Cambridge, Mass.: Harvard University Press, 1989).

14. See Michele M. Moody-Adams, *Fieldwork in Familiar Places: Morality, Culture, and Philosophy* (Cambridge, Mass.: Harvard University Press, 1997).

15. *The Encyclopedia of Philosophy* (New York: Macmillan, 1967), 5:448.

16. Warren A. Nord, *Religion and American Education: Rethinking a National Dilemma* (Chapel Hill: University of North Carolina Press, 1995), 210.

17. See Diana L. Eck, *A New Religious America: How a "Christian Country" Has Now Become the World's Most Religiously Diverse Nation* (San Francisco: HarperSan-Francisco, 2001).

18. See Alasdair MacIntyre, *After Virtue: A Study in Moral Theory*, 2nd ed. (South Bend, Ind.: University of Notre Dame Press, 1984).

CHAPTER 7

1. Richard Rorty, *Philosophy and Social Hope* (London: Penguin, 1999), 168.

2. William G. Perry Jr., *Forms of Intellectual and Ethical Development in the College Years: A Scheme* (New York: Holt, Rinehart, and Winston, 1970).

3. Alexander W. Astin, Helen S. Astin, Jennifer A. Lindolm, Alyssa N. Bryant, Shannon Calderon, and Katalin Szelényi, *The Spiritual Life of College Students: A National Study of College Students' Search for Meaning and Purpose* (Los Angeles: Higher Education Research Institute, 2005), 6–7.

4. Alexander W. Astin, Helen S. Astin, Jennifer A. Lindolm, *Spirituality and the Professoriate: A National Study of Faculty Beliefs, Attitudes, and Behaviors* (Los Angeles: Higher Education Research Institute, 2005), 3, 9.

5. "Religion and Public Life: Engaging Higher Education," (Johnson Foundation Wingspread Conference, sponsored by Society for Values in Higher Education, Summer 2005).

6. Max Weber, "Science as a Vocation" in *From Max Weber: Essays in Sociology*, trans. and ed. H. H. Gerth and C. W. Mills (New York: Oxford University Press, 1946), 129–56.

7. Robert Wuthnow, *The Restructuring of American Religion: Society and Faith Since World War II* (Princeton, N.J.: Princeton University Press, 1988).

8. Christopher Jenks and David Riesman, *The Academic Revolution* (New York: Doubleday, 1968).

9. Max Weber, *The Protestant Ethic and The Spirit of Capitalism* (New York: Scribner, 1958), 182.

10. Richard Madsen, William Sullivan, Ann Swidler, and Steven Tipton, eds., *Meaning and Modernity: Religion, Polity, and Self.* (Berkeley and Los Angeles: University of California Press, 2002), 258.

11. Wallace Stevens in Robert Bellah, *Beyond Belief: Essays on Religion in a Post-Traditional World* (New York: Harper and Row, 1970), 203.

12. Bellah, ibid., 257.

13. Jack H. Schuster and Martin J. Finkelstein, *The American Faculty: The Restructuring of Academic Work and Careers* (Baltimore: Johns Hopkins University Press, 2006), 191.

14. R. Eugene Rice, "From Athens and Berlin to L.A.: Faculty Work and a Changing Academy," *Liberal Education* 92, no. 4 (Fall 2006): 6–13.

15. Martha C. Nussbaum, *Cultivating Humanity: A Classical Defense of Reform in Liberal Education* (Cambridge, Mass.: Harvard University Press, 1997), 15.

16. Parker Palmer, "Community, Conflict, and Ways of Knowing: Ways to Deepen Our Educational Agenda," *Change* 26, no. 3 (May–June 1994): 41–42.

17. Sharon Daloz Parks, *Big Questions, Worthy Dreams: Mentoring Young Adults in the Search for Meaning, Purpose, and Faith* (San Francisco: Jossey-Bass, 2000), 163.

18. Ibid., 159, 161, 166.

19. Wayne C. Booth, *The Vocation of the Teacher* (Chicago: University of Chicago Press, 1988).

20. Jane Tompkins, *A Life in School: What the Teacher Learned* (Reading, Mass.: Perseus, 1996), 119.

21. Parker J. Palmer, *The Courage to Teach* (San Francisco: Jossey-Bass, 1998).

22. Lee Shulman, *Making Teaching Public* (San Francisco: Jossey-Bass, 2005).

23. R. Eugene Rice, M. D. Sorcinelli, and Anne E. Austin, *Heeding New Voices*, New Pathway Working Paper Series, American Association for Higher Education (Washington, D.C.: Stylus, 2000).

24. "Young Ph.D.'s Say Collegiality Matters More Than Salary," *Chronicle of Higher Education* 53, no. 6 (Sept. 29, 2006): 1.

25. John B. Bennett, *Academic Life: Hospitality, Ethics, and Spirituality* (Bolton, Mass.: Anker, 2003).

26. Ibid., 37.

27. Robert Bellah, "Courageous or Indifferent Individualism," *Ethnical Perspectives* 5, no. 2 (1998): 92–102.

28. Henri Nouwen, *Reaching Out: Three Movements of the Spiritual Life* (Garden City, N.Y.: Doubleday, 1975), 67.

29. Dan A. Oren, *Joining the Club: A History of Jews and Yale* (New Haven, Conn.: Yale University Press, 1986).

30. Na'ilah Suad Nasir and Jasiyah Al-Amin, "Creating Identity-Safe Spaces on College Campuses for Muslim Students," *Change* 38, no. 2 (March–April 2006): 22–27.

CHAPTER 8

1. Most researchers now agree that religious beliefs and religious practices are intrinsically connected. The definition of religion provided by Rebecca S. Chopp, in her presentation "Hidden Wholeness: Student's Search for Meaning and Purpose in College" (Institute on College Student Values Conference, Tallahassee, Fla., Feb. 3,

2006), captures this wholeness, defining religion as "narratives and institutions of communities that provide meaning and purpose in the context of some vision of wholeness."

2. The results of the NSYR are published in Christian Smith and Melinda Lundquist Denton, *Soul Searching: The Religious and Spiritual Lives of American Teenagers* (New York: Oxford University Press, 2005).

3. Ibid., 260.

4. Ibid., 262.

5. Ibid., 263.

6. Mark D. Regnerus, "Religion and Positive Adolescent Outcomes: A Review of Research and Theory," *Review of Religious Research* 44 (2003): 409.

7. Smith and Denton, *Soul Searching*, 264.

8. See Paul I. Hettich and Camile Helkowski, *Connect Career to College: A Student's Guide to Work and Life Transitions* (Belmont, Calif.: Wadsworth, 2005); W. Robert Connor, "The Right Time and Place for Big Questions," *The Chronicle of Higher Education* (June 9, 2005): B8–B9; and Sharon Daloz Parks, *Big Questions, Worthy Dreams: Mentoring Young Adults in Their Search for Meaning, Purpose, and Faith* (San Francisco: Jossey-Bass, 2000). Parks, in particular, refers to this time as a period of "shipwreck" to highlight the severity of the ordeal facing college students.

9. See Arthur Levine and Jeanette S. Cureton, *When Hope and Fear Collide* (San Francisco: Jossey-Bass, 1998), 15. In the 1990s Levine and Cureton visited twenty-eight campuses, interviewing nearly 2,000 campus leaders, student newspaper editors, and campus leaders, and twice surveyed a representative sample of 270 student affairs officers.

10. Ibid., 9.

11. Peter J. Gomes, *The Good Life: Truths That Last in Times of Need* (San Francisco: HarperSanFrancisco, 2002), 4–5.

12. Neal Howe and William Strauss, *Millennials Go to College* (New York: Life-Course, 2003), 5.

13. Larry A. Braskamp, Lois Calian Trautwetter, and Kelly Ward, "How College Fosters Faith Development in Students," *Spirituality in Higher Education Newsletter* 2 (July 2005): 1–6.

14. Diana Denton, "Fostering Spiritual Depth in a Trans-Traditional Context: Communicating across Differences," *Religion and Education* 31 (Spring 2004): 20–45; and L. Sue Hulett, "Being Religious at Knox College: Attitudes toward Religion, Christian Expression, and Conservative Values on Campus," *Religion and Education* 31 (Fall 2004): 41–61. Both works use the term *postmodern* to describe college students.

15. Mark L. Taylor, "Generation NeXt Comes to College: 2006 Updates and Emerging Issues, in a Collection of Papers on Self-Study and Institutional Improvement, 2006," *The Higher Learning Commission* 2 (Chicago: The Higher Learning Commission, 2006): 48–55.

16. See Rebekah Nathan, *My Freshman Year: What a Professor Learned by Becoming a Student* (Ithaca, N.Y.: Cornell University Press, 2005). Nathan is a professor of anthropology who dropped out of her faculty role for a year to become a freshman

student, attending classes and living in a residence hall with other students at a regional state university. She found that students were disengaged from the college community and the current structure of the curriculum.

17. Naomi Shaefer Riley, *God on the Quad: How Religious Colleges and the Missionary Generation Are Changing America* (New York: St. Martin's, 2005). This study focuses largely on the 1.3 million students enrolled in the several hundred church-affiliated colleges in America. Special attention is given to the approximately 100 colleges that are members of the Coalition of Christian Colleges and Universities (CCCU).

18. Alyssa N. Bryant, "Evangelicals on Campus: An Exploration of Culture, Faith, and College Life" (presentation at Institute on College Student Values, Tallahassee, Fla., February 2005).

19. See Conrad Cherry, Betty A. DeBerg, and Amanda Porterfield, *Religion on Campus* (Chapel Hill: University of North Carolina Press, 2001).

20. See James M. Penning and Corwin Smidt, *Evangelicalism: The NEXT Generation* (Grand Rapids, Mich.: Baker Academics, 2002), 177. This extensive and well-designed study examines the theological, social, and political attitudes and behavior of students attending the same church-related colleges as those studied two decades earlier by James D. Hunter in *Evangelicalism: The Coming Generation* (Chicago: University of Chicago Press, 1987).

21. Thomas K. Hearn Jr., "Magic Carpet Ride," *Wake Forest* 52, no. 3 (March 2005): 64.

22. Harold V. Hartley III, "How College Affects Students' Religious Faith and Practice: A Review of Research," *The College Student Affairs Journal* 23 (2004): 111–29.

23. Alexander W. Astin, Helen S. Astin, Jennifer A. Lindolm, Alyssa N. Bryant, Shannon Calderon, and Katalin Szelényi, *The Spiritual Life of College Students: A National Survey of College Students' Search for Meaning and Purpose* (Los Angeles: Higher Education Research Institute, 2005).

24. Ibid., 22.

25. Alyssa N. Bryant, Jeung Yun Choi, and Maiko Yasuno, "Understanding the Religious and Spiritual Dimensions of Students' Lives in Their First Year of College," *Journal of College Student Development* 44 (2003): 723–45.

26. Sharon Parks, *Big Questions, Worthy Dreams*; Marcia Baxter Magolda, "Helping Students Make Their Way to Adulthood: Good Company for the Journey," *About Campus* 1 (2002): 2–9.

27. Astin, Astin, Lindolm, Bryant, Calderon, and Szelényi, *The Spiritual Life of College Students*.

28. Harvard Institute of Politics, *Spring Student Survey*, "Religion, Morality Playing Key Roles in College Politics," Harvard University (June 2006): 9–10.

29. Cherry, DeBerg, and Porterfield, *Religion on Campus*, 294.

30. This basic "4 C framework" is developed in more depth in Larry A. Braskamp, Lois Calian Trautvetter, and Kelly Ward, *Putting Students First: How Colleges Develop Students Purposefully* (Boston: Anker, 2006).

31. National Survey of Student Engagement, *Student Engagement: Pathways to Collegiate Success* (Bloomington: Indiana Center for Postsecondary Research, 2004), 16.

32. James Day, "Comparative Alumni Research: What Matters in College after College" (presented at Lutheran Education Conference of North America, Chicago, October 26, 2000).

33. Jenny J. Lee, "Religion and College Attendance: Change among Students," *Review of Higher Education* 25 (2002): 369–84; Jenny J. Lee, "Changing Worlds, Changing Selves: The Experience of the Religious Self among Catholic Collegians," *Journal of College Student Development* 43 (2002): 341–56.

34. Ernest T. Pascarella and Patrick T. Terenzini, *How College Affects Students* (San Francisco: Jossey-Bass, 1991).

35. Harold V. Hartley, "Influencers of Religious Engagement in the First Year of College" (presented at the Association for Institutional Research Annual Forum, Chicago, May 2006).

36. See Bryant, Choi, and Yasuno, "Understanding the Religious and Spiritual Dimensions"; Lee, "Changing Worlds, Changing Selves"; Cherry, DeBerg, and Porterfield, *Religion on Campus*.

37. Cherry, DeBerg, and Porterfield, ibid., 288.

38. Astin, Astin, Lindolm, Bryant, Calderon, & Szelényi, *The Spiritual Life of College Students*.

39. Hartley, "Influencers of Religious Engagement," 14.

40. Lee, "Religion and College Attendance"; Bryant, Choi, and Yasuno, "Understanding the Religious and Spiritual Dimensions"; George D. Kuh and P. D. Umbach, "College and Character: Insights from the National Survey of Student Engagement," in *Assessing Character Outcomes in College*, ed. Jon C. Dalton, Terry Russell, and Sally Kline (San Francisco: Jossey-Bass, 2006).

41. Lee, "Religion and College Attendance"; Pascarella and Terenzini, *How College Affects Students*.

42. National Survey of Student Engagement, *Student Engagement*, 22.

43. George D. Kuh and Robert M. Gonyea, "Spirituality, Liberal Learning, and College Student Engagement," *Liberal Education* 92 (2006): 46.

44. Pascarella and Terenzini, *How College Affects Students*; Pascarella and Terenzini, *How College Affects Students: A Third Decade of Research*, vol. 2 (San Francisco: Jossey-Bass, 2005).

45. Braskamp, Trautvetter, and Ward, *Putting Students First*.

46. Darnell Cole and Shafiqa Ahmadi, "Perspectives and Experiences of Muslim Women Who Veil on College Campuses," *Journal of College Student Development* 44 (2003): 47–66.

47. Michael K. Herndon, "Expressions of Spirituality among African American College Males," *The Journal of Men's Studies* 12 (2003): 75–84.

48. Lilly Endowment Inc. has given millions of dollars to eighty-eight colleges to pursue the "Theological Exploration of Vocation." See www.ptev.org.

49. Scotty McLennan, "The Importance of Educating College Students for Religious Literacy and Spirituality in a Global Society: An Interview with Scotty McLennan," *Journal of College and Character* 6 (November 2005): 2.

CHAPTER 9

1. See Conrad Cherry, Betty A. DeBerg, and Amanda Porterfield, *Religion on Campus* (Chapel Hill: University of North Carolina Press, 2001); Diana L. Eck, *A New Religious America: How a "Christian Country" Has Become the World's Most Religiously Diverse Nation* (New York: Harper Collins, 2001); Wade Clark Roof, *Spiritual Marketplace: Baby Boomers and the Remaking of American Religion* (Princeton, N.J.: Princeton University Press, 1999); Christian Smith, *Soul Searching: The Religious and Spiritual Lives of American Teenagers* (New York: Oxford University Press, 2005); Alan Wolfe, *The Transformation of American Religion: How We Actually Live Our Faith* (Chicago: University of Chicago Press, 2003); and Robert Wuthnow, *America and the Challenges of Religious Diversity* (Princeton, N.J.: Princeton University Press, 2005).

2. For two different takes on spirituality, see Wade Clark Roof, *A Generation of Seekers: The Spiritual Journeys of the Baby Boom Generation* (San Francisco: HarperSanFrancisco, 1993); and Robert C. Solomon, *Spirituality for the Skeptic: The Thoughtful Love of Life* (New York: Oxford University Press, 2002). For spirituality as it relates to higher education, in particular, see Arthur W. Chickering, Jon C. Dalton, and Liesa Stamm, *Encouraging Authenticity and Spirituality in Higher Education* (San Francisco: Jossey-Bass, 2006).

3. This spiritual typology is based on various previous publications by the authors. See, for example, Robert J. Nash, *Religious Pluralism in the Academy: Opening the Dialogue* (New York: Peter Lang, 2001); Robert J. Nash, *Spirituality, Ethics, Religion, and Teaching: A Professor's Journey* (New York: Peter Lang, 2002); and Robert J. Nash and DeMethra LaSha Bradley, "A Theoretical Framework for Talking about Spirituality on College Campuses," in *Searching for Spirituality in Higher Education*, ed. Sherry L. Hoppe and Bruce W. Speck (New York: Peter Lang, 2007). For an applied discussion see Robert J. Nash, "How September 11, 2001 Transformed My Course on Religious Pluralism, Spirituality, and Education," *Religion and Education* 29 (Spring 2002): 1–22.

4. The authors describe this work of "moral conversation" more fully in Robert J. Nash, "Fostering Moral Conversations in the College Classroom," *Journal on Excellence in College Teaching* 7, no. 1 (1996): 83–106; and in Robert J. Nash, DeMethra LaSha Bradley, and Arthur W. Chickering, *Rekindling the Fire of Conversation: How to Talk about Hot Topics across College Campuses without Getting Burned* (San Francisco: Jossey-Bass, forthcoming).

5. Diana Eck, *Encountering God: A Spiritual Journey from Bozeman to Banaras* (Boston: Beacon, 1993), 197–98.

6. Rainer M. Rilke, *Letters to a Young Poet*, trans. M. D. Herter (1934; New York: Norton, 1954), 34–35.

CHAPTER 10

1. Parker Palmer, *The Promise of Paradox* (Notre Dame, Ind.: Ave Maria, 1980).

2. Thomas Merton, *The Sign of Jonas* (New York: Harcourt, Brace, 1953), 11.

3. Much of the material in this essay appears in Elizabeth J. Tisdell, "Diversity and Spirituality in Secular Higher Education: The Teaching Paradox," *Journal of Religion and Education* 33, no. 1 (2006): 49–68.

4. Douglas Robertson, "Generative Paradox in Learner-Centered College Teaching," *Innovative Higher Education* 29, no. 3 (2005): 181–94.

5. Ibid., 182.

6. Cynthia B. Dillard, Daa'lyah Abdur-Rashid, and Cynthia Tyson, "My Soul Is a Witness: Affirming Pedagogies of the Spirit," *International Journal of Qualitative Studies in Education* 13, no. 5 (2000): 447–62.

7. Ibid., 448.

8. See, for example, Alexander W. Astin, "Why Spirituality Deserves a Central Place in Liberal Education," *Liberal Education* 90, no. 2 (2004): 34–41; John B. Bennett, *Academic Life: Hospitality, Ethics, and Spirituality* (Boston: Anker, 2003); Steven Glazer, ed., *The Heart of Learning: Spirituality in Education* (New York: Putnam, 1999); Margaret A. Jablonski, ed., *The Implications of Students' Spirituality for Student Affairs Practice* (San Francisco: Jossey-Bass, 2001); Victor H. Kazanjian and Peter L. Laurence, eds., *Education as Transformation: Religious Pluralism, Spirituality, and a New Vision for Higher Education* (New York: Peter Lang, 2000); Martin E. Marty, *Education, Religion, and the Common Good* (San Francisco: Jossey-Bass, 2000); and Sharon Daloz Parks, *Big Questions, Worthy Dreams* (San Francisco: Jossey-Bass, 2000).

9. See, for example, Will Ashton and Diana Denton, eds., *Spirituality, Ethnography, and Teaching: Stories from Within* (New York: Peter Lang, 2006); Arthur W. Chickering, Jon C. Dalton, and Lieasa Stamm, *Encouraging Authenticity and Spirituality in Higher Education* (San Francisco: Jossey-Bass, 2005); Diana Denton, "Fostering Spiritual Depth in a Trans-Traditional Context: Communicating across Differences," *Religion and Education* 31, no. 1 (2004): 20–45; Douglas Jacobsen and Rhonda Hustedt Jacobsen, *Scholarship and Christian Faith: Enlarging the Conversation* (New York: Oxford University Press, 2004); Robert J. Nash, *Spirituality, Ethics, Religion, and Teaching: A Professor's Journey* (New York: Peter Lang, 2002); Parker Palmer, *The Courage to Teach* (San Francisco: Jossey-Bass, 1998); and Laura I. Rendón, "Recasting Agreements That Govern Teaching and Learning: An Intellectual and Spiritual Framework for Transformation," *Religion and Education* 32, no. 1 (2005): 79–108.

10. See, for example, Cynthia B. Dillard, *On Spiritual Strivings: Transforming an African American Woman's Academic Life* (Albany: State University of New York Press, 2006); and bell hooks, *Teaching Community* (New York: Routledge, 2003).

11. My own writings in this area include Elizabeth J. Tisdell, *Exploring Spirituality and Culture in Adult and Higher Education* (San Francisco: Jossey-Bass, 2003); Elizabeth J. Tisdell, "Spirituality, Cultural Identity, and Epistemology in Culturally Responsive Teaching in Higher Education," *Multicultural Perspectives* 8, no. 3 (2006): 19–25;

Elizabeth J. Tisdell, "Diversity and Spirituality in Secular Higher Education: The Teaching Paradox," *Religion and Education* 33, no. 1 (2006): 49–68; and Elizabeth J. Tisdell and Derise E. Tolliver, "Claiming a Sacred Face: The Role of Spirituality and Cultural Identity in Transformative Adult Higher Education," *Journal of Transformative Education* 1, no. 4 (2003): 368–92.

12. Diana L. Eck, *A New Religious America* (San Francisco: HarperSanFrancisco, 2001), 2–3.

13. James W. Fowler, *Stages of Faith: The Psychology of Human Development and the Quest for Meaning* (San Francisco: Harper and Row, 1981).

14. Martin E. Marty, *Education, Religion, and the Common Good* (San Francisco: Jossey-Bass, 2000).

15. Fowler, *Stages of Faith*; and Parks, *Big Questions, Worthy Dreams*.

16. David T. Abalos, *La Communidad Latina in the United States* (Westport, Conn.: Praeger, 1998).

17. On this point see Martha C. Nussbaum, *Cultivating Humanity: A Classical Defense of Reform in Liberal Education* (Cambridge, Mass.: Harvard University Press, 1997).

18. See note 1.

19. Beverly Daniel Tatum, *"Why Are All the Black Kids Sitting Together in the Cafeteria?" and Other Conversations about Race* (New York: Basic, 1997).

20. See bell hooks, *Teaching Community*; and Parker Palmer, *The Courage to Teach: Exploring the Inner Landscape of a Teacher's Life* (San Francisco: Jossey-Bass, 1998).

21. Diana Denton, "Fostering Spiritual Depth in a Trans-Traditional Context."

22. Laura I. Rendón, "Academics of the Heart: Reconnecting the Scientific Mind with the Spirit's Artistry," *Review of Higher Education* 24, no. 1 (2000): 1.

23. Parker Palmer, *The Promise of Paradox*.

24. Douglas Robertson, "Generative Paradox in Learner-Centered College Teaching."

CHAPTER 11

1. Conrad Cherry, Betty A. DeBerg, and Amanda Porterfield end their fine book *Religion on Campus* (New York: University of North Carolina Press, 2001) with the following assessment: "We found both the practice and the study of religion to be vital aspects of the slices of American higher education that we observed. . . . It is possible that young people in American culture have never been more enthusiastically engaged in religious practice or with religious ideas" (pp. 294–95). But we cannot extrapolate from their in-depth study of four universities to public universities generally. Only one of the four universities they studied was a public university, and unlike the majority of public universities it had a department of religious studies. Nor do they pay adequate attention, in this concluding generalization, to the elective nature of religion courses.

2. Here is how I arrive at 10 percent. Fewer than 40 percent of American public universities have departments of, or curricula in, religious studies. In public universities, coursework in religious studies is almost always elective. I will estimate that

half of the students at these universities will take an elective course in religious studies. This would mean that fewer than 20 percent of *all* undergraduates at public universities will take a single course in religious studies. Some of these courses will be highly specialized, some will address religion in narrowly historical contexts (not as live options for students), and some will employ reductionistic approaches. Where does this leave us? Eliminating those courses from the mix, I would guess that about 10 percent of undergraduates in public universities ever take a course in religious studies in which religion is taken seriously. If we add in the smattering of courses in other disciplines that address religion seriously, the percentage might go up a little, but not much because most of those courses will be either highly specialized, narrowly historical, or reductionistic.

3. Peter Berger is the most famous convert from the secularization to a desecularization thesis. See his introduction to *The Desecularization of the World* (Grand Rapids, Mich.: Eerdmans, 1999) and the interview with Berger in *The Hedgehog Review* 8, no. 1-2 (Spring/Summer 2006), 152–61. That issue of the *Review*, which is devoted to the theme "After Secularization," includes reassessments of the secularization thesis by many of its most prominent defenders and critics.

4. George Marsden has argued that if scholars are going to operate on the postmodern assumption that all judgments are "relative to communities" then we should "follow the implications of that premise as consistently as we can and not absolutize one or perhaps a few sets of opinions and exclude all others." Universities should foster a broad pluralism that allows "all sorts of Christian and other religiously based intellectual traditions back into the discussion." See Marsden, "Soul of the American University: An Historical Overview," in *The Secularization of the Academy*, ed. George M. Marsden and Bradley J. Longfield (New York: Oxford University Press, 1992), 39. Also see Marsden, *The Outrageous Idea of Christian Scholarship* (New York: Oxford, 1997), especially chapter 3.

5. There is a truly immense literature in this new field of science/religion studies. The best introduction to it is Ian Barbour's *Religion and Science: Historical and Contemporary Issues* (San Francisco: HarperSanFrancisco, 1997).

6. See chapter two in this volume, Neil Gross and Solon Simmons, "The Religious Convictions of College and University Professors." According to a 2004-5 UCLA study of more than 40,000 faculty members at 421 colleges and universities, 64 percent consider themselves to be religious (29 percent to some extent, 35 percent to a great extent) and 81 percent consider themselves spiritual. See *Spirituality and the Professoriate: A National Study of Faculty Beliefs, Attitudes, and Behaviors* (Los Angeles: Higher Education Research Institute at UCLA, 2004-5).

7. George Marsden, *The Outrageous Idea of Christian Scholarship*, 4.

8. It is interesting, for example, that, according to a 1996 survey in *American Men and Women of Science* of 1,000 randomly selected scientists, 40 percent believe that God guided evolution. (Reported in Larry Witham, *Where Darwin Meets the Bible* [Oxford: Oxford University Press, 2002], 271–76.) One wonders how these scientists reconcile their religious views with neo-Darwinism, which excludes the idea of purpose from evolution.

9. Virtually all the world's religious traditions address justice and the moral dimensions of social and economic life in some way. Within the last hundred years, especially, a vast body of religious literature dealing with justice and economics has been produced. Central to this literature is the claim that to understand the world of economics we must include moral and religious categories. Most religious traditions teach that people are by nature social beings, born into webs of obligation to other people and to God. Even if human beings are sinful and often fail to live up to their moral ideals, most religions teach that people should try to rise above self-interest. Religious traditions have also emphasized cooperation over competition, and are deeply wary of the corrupting influence of wealth, materialism, and consumer culture. Virtually all religious traditions pay special attention to the needs of the poor—the widow, the orphan, the alien. Needless to say, economics textbooks say nothing about most of these religious concerns. Instead they demoralize and secularize the economic realm.

10. While public education is overwhelmingly secular, most people continue to be religious; they continue to hold religious beliefs and attend religious services. Still, education is quite successful at nurturing a secular mentality in this sense: It convinces most students that religion is a private matter and thus tends to marginalize religion from our public lives and our work.

11. To indoctrinate students is to uncritically initiate them into one way of thinking, systematically ignoring other alternatives, marginalizing them, or making them seem irrational. Many would agree that students exposed only to fundamentalist Christian interpretations of history, biology, and sexuality in a Christian college would be indoctrinated. What, in turn, should we think when students are exposed only to secular interpretations of history, biology, and sexuality in public schools and universities? I say that this borders on indoctrination because public education often (though certainly not always) gives students some opportunity to learn about religion. But those opportunities are often severely limited, and in public universities they are virtually never required.

12. Ninian Smart, *Religion and the Modern Mind* (New York: McMillan, 1987), 20.

13. Gerald Graff, *Beyond the Culture Wars* (New York: Norton, 1992), 13.

14. Ibid., 12.

15. Bruce A. Kimball, *Orators and Philosophers: A History of the Idea of Liberal Education* (New York: Teachers College Press, 1986).

16. I have addressed the role of religion in moral education more fully in my essay "Liberal Education, Moral Education, and Religion," in *Moral Formation and the University*, ed. Douglas Henry and Michael Beatty (Waco, Tex.: Baylor University Press, forthcoming).

17. *Abington Township v. Schempp*, 374 U.S. 203, 225 (1963).

18. *Everson v. Board of Education*, 330 U.S. 1, 16 (1947).

19. *Abington Township v. Schempp*, 374 U.S. 203, 225 (1963).

20. *Abington Township v. Schempp*, 374 U.S. 203, 306 (1963).

21. Douglas Laycock, "Formal, Substantive, and Disaggregated Neutrality toward Religion," *DePaul Law Review* 39 (1990): 1001–2.

22. Douglas Laycock, "Religious Liberty as Liberty," *Journal of Contemporary Legal Issues* 7 (Fall 1996): 348.

23. *Abington Township v. Schempp*, 374 U.S. 203, 225, 306 (1963). I discuss the constitutional argument for including religion in the curriculum at greater length in *Religion and American Education* (Chapel Hill: University of North Carolina Press, 1995), 241–49.

24. American Association of University Professors, *Declaration of Principles* (1915), reprinted in *Academic Freedom and Tenure: A Handbook of the American Association of University Professors* (Madison: University of Wisconsin Press, 1967), 164.

25. *Keyishian v. Board of Regents*, 385 U.S. 589, 603 (1966).

26. David Rabban, "A Functional Analysis of 'Individual' and 'Institutional' Academic Freedom under the First Amendment," *Law and Contemporary Problems* 53 (Summer 1990): 230.

27. While the Supreme Court has never weighed academic freedom against the Establishment Clause, an appallingly bad ruling by the Eleventh Circuit Court does cut against the grain of my position. See *Bishop v. Aronov*, 926 F.2d 1066 (11th Cir. 1991). I discuss the details of this decision in *Religion and American Education*, 269–74.

28. Mark U. Edwards Jr., *Religion on Our Campus* (New York: Palgrave Macmillan, 2006), 118.

29. American Association of University Professors, *Declaration of Principles*, 169.

30. American Association of University Professors, "Some Observations on Ideology, Competence, and Faculty Selection," *Academe* 72 (January–February 1986): 2a.

31. K. Anthony Appiah, "Culture, Subculture, Multiculturalism: Educational Options" in *Public Education in a Multicultural Society: Policy, Theory, Critique*, ed. Robert K. Fullinwider (New York: Cambridge University Press, 1996), 84.

32. I discuss the relationship of religion to the multicultural movement and the "justice" argument for including religion in the curriculum at much greater length in "Religion and Multiculturalism," in *The Politics of Multiculturalism and Bilingual Education*, ed. Carlos Ovando and Peter McLaren (New York: McGraw-Hill, 1999), 63–81.

33. No doubt religious organizations, religious rhetoric and symbols, and chapel services survived around the periphery of some public universities well into the twentieth century, but religion had long since disappeared from the curriculum. For the story of the secularization of higher education, see George Marsden, *The Soul of the American University* (New York: Oxford University Press, 1994); Jon H. Roberts and James Turner, *The Sacred and the Secular University* (Princeton, N.J.: Princeton University Press, 2000); and Julie Ruben, *The Making of the Modern University* (Chicago: University of Chicago Press, 1996).

34. See note 2.

35. Ray S. Hart, "Religious and Theological Studies in American Higher Education," *Journal of the American Academy of Religion* 59 (Winter 1991): 716.

36. William Scott Green, "Something Strange, Yet Nothing New: Religion in the Secular Curriculum," *Soundings* 71 (Summer–Fall 1988): 274.

37. I have developed my position on the field of religious studies most fully in my essay "Liberal Education and Religious Studies," in *Religion, Education, and the*

American Experience, ed. Edith Blumhofer (Tuscaloosa: University of Alabama Press, 2002), 9–40. Also see *Religion and American Education*, chapter 10.

38. John Dixon once put it this way: Because "religious studies" makes *studies* rather than religion its primary focus, students learn that "truth is in the systems of study" rather than in the religion that is studied—though he acknowledges that the "actual effect is far more muddled than that, simply because so much of the material we study is more powerful than the prejudices of the methods we apply to them, and many teachers are exceedingly respectful of the integrity of their subject." See John W. Dixon Jr., "What Should Religion Departments Teach?" *Theology Today* 46 (January 1990): 369–70.

CHAPTER 12

1. See, for example, the discussion of religion classes at a prominent Catholic school in Conrad Cherry, Betty A. DeBerg, and Amanda Porterfield, *Religion on Campus* (Chapel Hill: University of North Carolina Press, 2001), 195–214.

2. I take some of my own previous work as an example, especially *The Power of Religion: A Comparative Introduction* (New York: Oxford, 1997). The most extreme example of pluralistic enthusiasm for religion would be Huston Smith, *Religions of Man* (New York: Harper, 1958; rev. ed. published as *The World's Religions: Our Great Wisdom Traditions* [San Francisco: HarperSanFrancisco, 1991]). But even in the most well-grounded historical studies, pluralistic and appreciative tendencies often go hand in hand. See, for example, *World Religions Today*, ed. John L. Esposito, Darrell J. Fasching, and Todd Lewis (New York: Oxford University Press, 2001).

3. See Catherine L. Albanese, "Exchanging Selves, Exchanging Souls: Contact, Combination, and American Religious History," in *Retelling U.S. Religious History*, ed. Thomas A. Tweed (Berkeley and Los Angeles: University of California Press, 1997), 200–226.

4. Quoted in Mark Silk, "Notes on the Judeo-Christian Tradition in America," *American Quarterly* 36, no. 1 (Spring 1984): 65.

5. Erin A. Smith, "Liberal Religion, Therapeutic Culture, and the World: Reading 'America's Preacher' at Home and Abroad"; and Matthew S. Hedstrom, "The Construction of 'Judeo-Christian' Spirituality in Postwar America," papers presented at the annual meeting of the American Studies Association, Oakland, Calif., Oct 12, 2006.

6. Amanda Porterfield, "The Pragmatic Role of Religious Studies," in *The Transformation of American Religion: The Story of a Late Twentieth-Century Awakening* (New York: Oxford University Press, 2001), 202–26.

7. Diana L. Eck, *A New Religious America: How a "Christian Country" Has Become the World's Most Religiously Diverse Nation* (San Francisco: HarperSanFrancisco, 2001), 58–59.

8. See John Winthrop, "Model of Christian Charity" (1630); and *Old South Leaflets*, no. 207, reprinted in *The Puritans in America: A Narrative Anthology*, ed. Alan Heimert and Andrew Delbanco (Cambridge, Mass.: Harvard University Press, 1985), 91.

9. William R. Hutchison, *Religious Pluralism in America: The Contentious History of a Founding Ideal* (New Haven, Conn.: Yale University Press, 2003).

10. Robert Baird, *Religion in America*, ed. Henry W. Bowden (1844; New York: Harper and Row, 1970).

11. Augustine, *Concerning the City of God against the Pagans*, ed. David Knowles, trans. Henry Bettenson (Baltimore: Penguin, 1972), 635.

12. See C. H. Lawrence, *Medieval Monasticism* (1984; London: Pearson, 2001); Ramsay MacMullen, *Christianity and Paganism in the Fourth to Eighth Centuries* (New Haven, Conn.: Yale University Press, 1997); Peter Brown, *Society and the Holy in Late Antiquity* (Berkeley and Los Angeles: University of California Press, 1982); and Henry Chadwick, *The Early Church* (1967; New York: Dorset, 1986), 174–83.

13. See Steven Ozment, *The Age of Reform, 1250–1550: An Intellectual and Religious History of Late Medieval and Reformation Europe* (New Haven, Conn.: Yale University Press, 1980); and Herbert Grundmann, *Religious Movements in the Middle Ages: The Historical Links between Heresy, the Mendicant Orders, and the Women's Religious Movement in the Twelfth and Thirteenth Century, with the Historical Foundations of German Mysticism*, trans. Steven Rowan (German edition originally published 1935; South Bend, Ind.: University of Notre Dame Press, 1955).

14. See Euan Cameron, *The European Reformation* (New York: Oxford University Press, 1991); Martin Marty, *Martin Luther* (New York: Viking Penguin, 2004); and Jan Rohls, *Reformed Confessions: Theology from Zurich to Barmen* (Louisville: Westminster John Knox, 1988).

15. See Carlos M. N. Eire, *War against the Idols: The Reformation of Worship from Erasmus to Calvin* (Cambridge: Cambridge University Press, 1986).

16. See *James Madison on Religious Liberty*, ed. Robert S. Alley (Buffalo: Prometheus, 1985).

CHAPTER 13

1. Shlomo Riskin, "God Wants Partners," *Jewish News of Greater Phoenix* 50, no. 38 (June 19, 1998), http://www.jewishaz.com/jewishnews/980619/torah.shtml (accessed April 2, 2007).

2. Babylonian Talmud, Baba Metzia 59b, http://www.jhom.com/topics/voice/bat-kol-bab.htm (accessed April 2, 2007).

3. Charles M. Foster, ed., *Educating Clergy: Teaching Practices and the Pastoral Imagination* (San Francisco: Jossey-Bass, 2006).

4. Clifford Geertz, *The Interpretation of Cultures* (New York: Basic, 1973), 5. In this passage I have changed the original phrase "webs of significance" to "webs of meaning," I do this on the basis of Geertz's own recollection of what he said or intended. In 2000 he wrote: "They [recent developments in linguistics, hermenutics, and cognitive science] provided the ambience, and, again, the speculative instruments, to make the existence of someone who saw human beings as, quoting myself paraphrasing Max Weber, 'suspended in webs of meaning they themselves had spun' a good deal easier."

Clifford Geertz, *Available Light: Anthropological Reflections on Philosophical Topics* (Princeton, N.J.: Princeton University Press, 2000), 17.

CHAPTER 14

1. George Orwell, "Politics and the English Language," in *Modern British Writing*, ed. Denys Val Baker (New York: Vanguard, 1947), 190.

2. George Santayana, *Reason in Religion* (New York: Scribner, 1905), 5.

3. On religious seekers, see Wade Clark Roof, *A Generation of Seekers: The Spiritual Journeys of the Baby Boom Generation* (San Francisco: HarperSanFrancisco, 1993); and Wade Clark Roof, *Spiritual Marketplace: Baby Boomers and the Remaking of American Religion* (Princeton, N.J.: Princeton University Press, 1999). On the notion of "dwelling," see Robert Wuthnow, *After Heaven: Spirituality in America Since the 1950s* (Berkeley and Los Angeles: University of California Press, 1998).

4. See Donald B. Kraybill, Steven M. Nolt, and David L. Weaver-Zercher, *Amish Grace: How Forgiveness Transcended Tragedy* (San Francisco: Jossey-Bass, 2007).

5. The term *civil religion* was first coined by Robert Bellah in his essay entitled "Civil Religion in America," *Daedalus* 96, no. 1 (Winter 1967): 1–21.

6. Robert D. Putnam, *Bowling Alone: The Collapse and Revival of American Community* (New York: Simon and Schuster, 2000), 66.

7. *The Analects of Confucius: A Philosophical Translation*, trans. Roger T. Ames and Henry Rosemont Jr. (New York: Ballantine, 1998), 19.

8. Stephen Prothero, *Religious Literacy: What Every American Needs to Know—and Doesn't* (San Francisco: HarperSanFrancisco, 2007), 15, 136. Jacques Berlinerblau, *The Secular Bible: Why Nonbelievers Must Take Religion Seriously* (New York: Cambridge University Press, 2005) argues that it is particularly important for self-conscious secularists to know more about the Bible and about religion in general.

9. Sharon Daloz Parks, *Big Questions, Worthy Dreams: Mentoring Young Adults in Their Search for Meaning, Purpose, and Faith* (San Francisco: Jossey-Bass, 2000).

10. Charles Kimball, *When Religion Becomes Evil* (San Francisco: HarperSanFrancisco, 2002).

11. R. Scott Appleby, *The Ambivalence of the Sacred: Religion, Violence, and Reconciliation* (New York: Rowman and Littlefield, 2000).

12. Mark R. Schwehn, *Exiles from Eden: Religion and the Academic Vocation in America* (New York: Oxford University Press, 1993), 34.

13. See Douglas Jacobsen and Rhonda Hustedt Jacobsen, *Scholarship and Christian Faith: Enlarging the Conversation* (New York: Oxford University Press, 2004), especially chapter 4, "Scholarship Defined and Embodied."

14. For two different views concerning the role of religious discourse in politics, see Robert Audi, *Religious Commitment and Secular Reason* (Cambridge: Cambridge University Press, 2000); and Christopher J. Eberle, *Religious Convictions in Liberal Politics* (Cambridge: Cambridge University Press, 2002).

15. Ernest L. Boyer, *Selected Speeches 1979–1995* (Princeton, N.J.: Carnegie Foundation for the Advancement of Teaching, 1997), 67.

Index